RAIL ATLAS
Great Britain & Ireland

S. K. Baker

9th Edition

OPC

Oxford Publishing Co

Glossary of Abbreviations

ABP	Associated British Ports	Jn or Junc.	Junction
ARC	Amey Roadstone Co	LIFT	London International Freight Terminal
ASW	Allied Steel & Wire	L.L.	Low Level
BnM	Bord na Mona (Peat Board)	LUL	London Underground Ltd
BSL	Bord Solathair an Leactreachais	MDHC	Mersey Docks & Harbour Co
BP	British Petroleum	MoD	Ministry of Defence
C. & W.	Carriage & Wagon	MSC	Manchester Ship Canal
Cal-Mac	Caledonian MacBrayne	OLE	Overhead Line Equipment
C.C.	County Council	P.S.	Power Station
CE	Civil Engineer	PTE	Passenger Transport Executive
C.S.	Carriage Sidings	P.W.	Permanent Way
D.C.	District Council	RJB	R. J. Budge Mining
Dist	Distribution	RPS	Railway Preservation Society
D.P.	Disposal Point (Opencast Coal)	RPSI	Railway Preservation Society of Ireland
ECC	Imerys (formerly English China Clays International)	RTK	Railtrack
		S. & T.	Signal & Telegraph
EMU	Electric Multiple Unit	SAI	Scottish Agricultural Industries
FLT	Freightliner Terminal	T. or Term.	Terminal
H.L.	High Level	Tun.	Tunnel
IE	Iarnrod Eireann (Irish Rail)		

Publisher's Note

Although situations are constantly changing on the railways of Britain, every effort has been made by the author to ensure complete accuracy of the maps in the book at the time of going to press.

First published 1977
2nd Edition 1978
3rd Edition 1980
4th Edition 1984
Reprinted 1985
5th Edition 1988
Reprinted 1988 and 1989
6th Edition 1990
7th Edition 1992
Reprinted 1995
8th Edition 1996
Reprinted 1998
9th Edition 2001

ISBN 0 86093 553 1

Published by Oxford Publishing Co

an imprint of Ian Allan Publishing Ltd, Hersham, Surrey KT12 4RG.
Printed by Ian Allan Printing Ltd, Hersham, Surrey KT12 4RG.

Code: 0105/H

Cartography by Map Creation Ltd, Maidenhead, Berks

Cover illustration:
The 15.40 Belfast-Whitehead leaves Whitehead Tunnel and nears its destination on 9 May 1995, formed of railcar No 69. The line at this point has been affected by problems with this single track tunnel and by coastal erosion on the other track which runs alongside the sea wall. *Stuart Baker*

Contents

Preface to First Edition

The inspiration for this atlas was two-fold; firstly a feeling of total bewilderment by 'Llans' and 'Abers' on first visiting South Wales four years ago, and secondly a wall railway map drawn by a friend, Martin Bristow. Since then, at university, there has been steady progress in drawing the rail network throughout Great Britain. The author feels sure that this atlas as it has finally evolved will be useful to all with an interest in railways, whether professional or enthusiast. The emphasis is on the current network since it is felt that this information is not published elsewhere.

Throughout, the main aim has been to show clearly, using expanded sheets as necessary, the railways of this country, including the whole of London Transport and the light railways. Passenger lines are distinguished by colour according to the operating company and all freight-only lines are depicted in red. The criterion for a British Rail passenger line has been taken as at least one advertised train per day in each direction. On passenger routes, to assist the traveller, single and multiple track sections with crossing loops on single lines have been shown. Symbols are used to identify both major centres of rail freight, such as collieries and power stations and railway installations such as locomotive depots and works. Secondary information, for example junction names and tunnels over 100 yards long, with lengths if over one mile, have been shown.

The author would like to express his thanks to members of the Oxford University Railway Society and to Nigel Bird, Chris Hammond and Richard Warson in particular for help in compiling and correcting the maps. His cousin, Dr Tony McCann deserves special thanks for removing much of the tedium by computer sorting the index, as do Oxford City Libraries for providing excellent reference facilities.

June 1977

Preface to Ninth Edition

This ninth edition of the *Rail Atlas* is a full revision and has been completely redrawn, bringing significantly improved clarity, having been transferred from traditional artwork to digital format.

There is a significantly faster rate of change in both the main and light rail networks of the country. It is very pleasing to note the considerable expansion of the railway which has both taken place recently and to record many of the future development plans. In particular, the light rail system has grown, with many lines now fully operational and several more exciting schemes underway. The Channel Tunnel Rail Link is now well advanced and two new inserts have been provided to clarify the route this will take. More stations, freight terminals and even new routes and line reopenings are being examined to enable the network to tap and handle substantial growth in both the passenger and freight markets.

This edition is the first under the prestigious 'Ian Allan' ownership and the author is very pleased that the company has invested substantially in the time and effort to give the Atlas a fresh start using new technology. This will enable future revisions to be undertaken far more easily, but has meant that every entry in this edition has had to be drawn and checked from scratch. However, it is a great delight to have colour proofs to check and no longer to have to simultaneously hold four black and white photocopies up to the light for checking!

The author would like to thank the many people who have contacted him to supply material for this new edition. Thanks are also due to his family for their patience and support.

Stuart K. Baker
York
April 2001

KEY TO ATLAS

		Surface	Tunnel	Tube
Passenger Rail Network *(With gauge where other than standard gauge: i.e. 4' 8½" Britain/5' 3" Ireland)*	Multiple Track			
	Single Track			
Municipal/Urban Railways or Irish Peat Railways *(London Underground Ltd lines indicated by code, Irish Peat lines are 3' gauge unless shown)*	Multiple Track	C	C	C
	Single Track	C	C	C
Preserved & Minor Passenger Railways *(With name, and gauge where other than standard gauge)*	Multiple Track			
	Single Track			
Freight only lines	No Single/ Multiple Distinction			

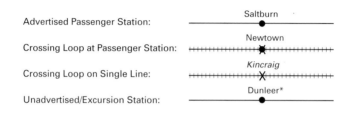

Advertised Passenger Station: Saltburn

Crossing Loop at Passenger Station: Newtown

Crossing Loop on Single Line: *Kincraig*

Unadvertised/Excursion Station: Dunleer*

Major Power Signal Boxes	PRESTON	Line Ownership Boundaries	RTK ǀ LUL
Carriage Sidings	C.S.	Colliery (incl. Washery & Opencast site)	▲
Freight Marshalling Yard		Power Station	△
Freightliner Terminal	FLT	Oil Refinery	●
Locomtive Depot/Stabling Point	■ BS	Oil Terminal	○
Railway Works	▨	Cement Works or Terminal	■
Junction Names	*Haughley Junc.*	Quarry	▫
Country Border		Other Freight Terminal	ǀ
County Boundary *(PTE Areas, London & Ireland only)*		Proposed Railway	=========
Shipping Service			

DIAGRAM OF MAPS

INSETS
MAIN SHEETS
OVERLAP

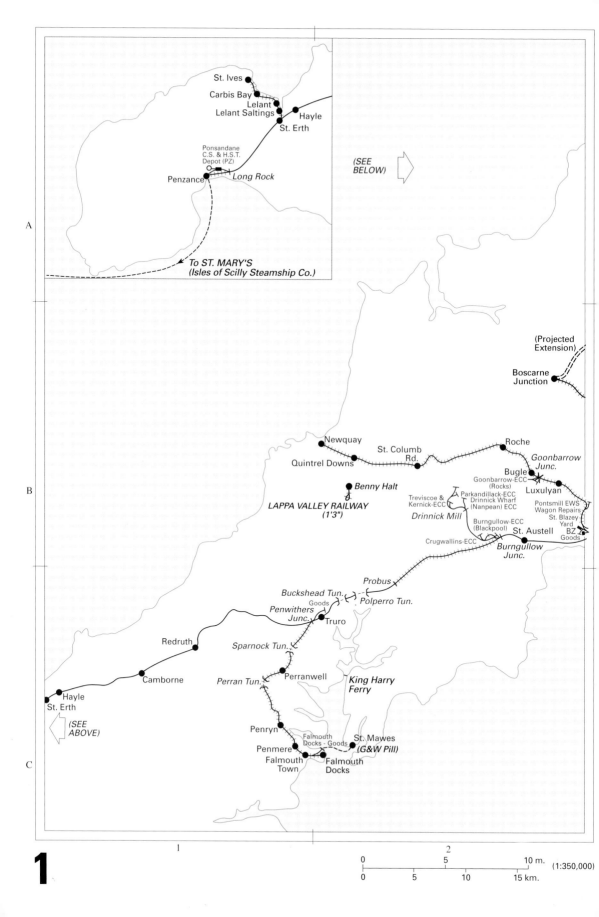

St. Ives

Carbis Bay

Lelant
Lelant Saltings

Hayle

St. Erth

Ponsandane
C.S. & H.S.T.
Depot (PZ)

Penzance — Long Rock

(SEE BELOW)

To ST. MARY'S
(Isles of Scilly Steamship Co.)

A

(Projected Extension)

Boscarne
Junction

Newquay

Quintrel Downs

St. Columb
Rd.

Roche

Goonbarrow Junc.

Bugle

Goonbarrow-ECC
(Rocks)

Luxulyan

Benny Halt

LAPPA VALLEY RAILWAY (1'3")

Treviscoe &
Kernick-ECC

Parkandillack-ECC
Drinnick Wharf
(Nanpean) ECC

Drinnick Mill

Pontsmill EWS
Wagon Repairs

St. Blazey
Yard

BZ
Goods

Burngullow-ECC
(Blackpool)

St. Austell

Crugwallins-ECC

Burngullow Junc.

B

Probus

Buckshead Tun.

Goods

Penwithers Junc.

Polperro Tun.

Truro

Redruth

Sparnock Tun.

Camborne

Perran Tun.

Perranwell

King Harry Ferry

Hayle
St. Erth

(SEE ABOVE)

Penryn

Penmere

Falmouth
Docks - Goods

St. Mawes
(G&W Pill)

Falmouth
Town

Falmouth
Docks

C

1

2

0   5   10 m.

0   5   10   15 km.

(1:350,000)

1

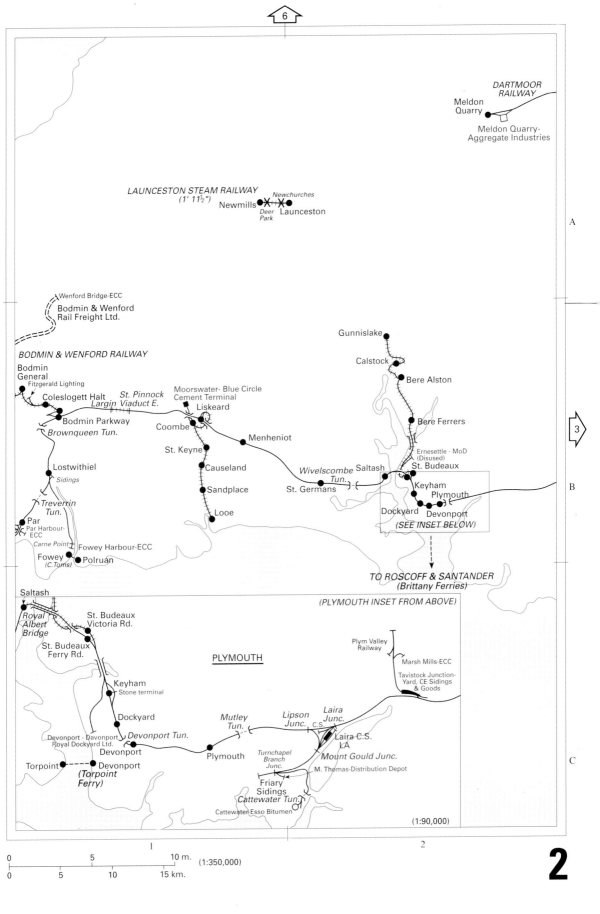

DARTMOOR RAILWAY

Meldon Quarry

Meldon Quarry-
Aggregate Industries

A

LAUNCESTON STEAM RAILWAY
(1' 11½")
Newmills   Newchurches
          Deer
          Park   Launceston

Wenford Bridge-ECC
Bodmin & Wenford
Rail Freight Ltd.

BODMIN & WENFORD RAILWAY

Gunnislake

Calstock

Bere Alston

Bodmin
General
Fitzgerald Lighting
Coleslogett Halt   St. Pinnock
          Largin Viaduct E.   Moorswater- Blue Circle
Bodmin Parkway   Cement Terminal
Brownqueen Tun.   Liskeard
          Coombe

Bere Ferrers

St. Keyne

Lostwithiel
Sidings

Causeland

Menheniot

Ernesettle - MoD
(Disused)

Wivelscombe   Saltash
Tun.   St. Budeaux

Treverrin
Tun.
Par
Par Harbour-
ECC
Carne Point
Fowey   Polruan
(C.Toms)

Sandplace

Looe

St. Germans

Keyham
Plymouth

Dockyard   Devonport
(SEE INSET BELOW)

B

3

Fowey Harbour-ECC

TO ROSCOFF & SANTANDER
(Brittany Ferries)

Saltash

Royal
Albert
Bridge

St. Budeaux
Victoria Rd.

(PLYMOUTH INSET FROM ABOVE)

Plym Valley
Railway   Marsh Mills-ECC

St. Budeaux
Ferry Rd.

PLYMOUTH

Tavistock Junction-
Yard, CE Sidings
& Goods

Keyham
Stone terminal

Dockyard

Devonport - Davenport
Royal Dockyard Ltd.   Devonport Tun.

Devonport

Mutley
Tun.

Lipson
Junc.
C.S.

Laira
Junc.

Laira C.S.
LA

Plymouth

Torpoint   Devonport
(Torpoint
Ferry)

Turnchapel
Branch
Junc.

Mount Gould Junc.

M. Thomas-Distribution Depot

Friary
Sidings
Cattewater Tun.

Cattewater-Esso Bitumen

(1:90,000)

C

0   5   10 m.   (1:350,000)
0   5   10   15 km.

2

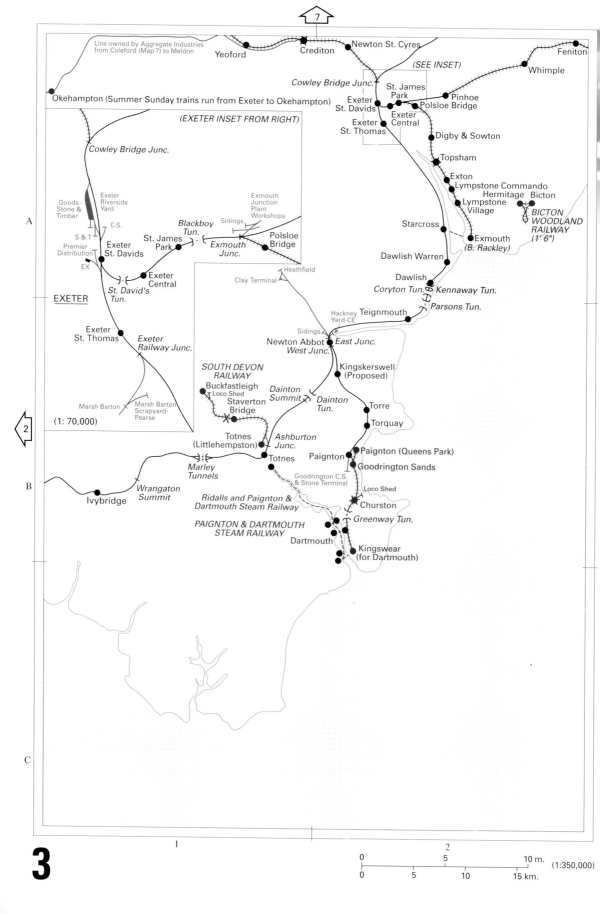

Line owned by Aggregate Industries
from Coleford (Map 7) to Meldon

Yeoford

Crediton

Newton St. Cyres

Feniton

Whimple

(SEE INSET)

Cowley Bridge Junc.

St. James
Park

Pinhoe

Exeter
St. Davids

Polsloe Bridge

Okehampton (Summer Sunday trains run from Exeter to Okehampton)

Exeter
Central

Exeter
St. Thomas

Digby & Sowton

(EXETER INSET FROM RIGHT)

Topsham

Cowley Bridge Junc.

Exton
Lympstone Commando
Hermitage Bicton

Goods -
Stone &
Timber

Exeter
Riverside
Yard

Exmouth
Junction
Plant
Workshops

Lympstone
Village

BICTON
WOODLAND
RAILWAY
(1' 6")

C.S.

*Blackboy
Tun.*

Sidings

Starcross

S & T

St. James
Park

*Exmouth
Junc.*

Polsloe
Bridge

Exmouth
(B. Rackley)

Premier
Distribution

Exeter
St. Davids

Dawlish Warren

EX

Exeter
Central

Heathfield

Dawlish

EXETER

*St. David's
Tun.*

Clay Terminal

Coryton Tun. *Kennaway Tun.*

Parsons Tun.

Exeter
St. Thomas

*Exeter
Railway Junc.*

Hackney
Yard-CE

Teignmouth

Sidings

Newton Abbot *East Junc.*

Marsh Barton

Marsh Barton
Scrapyard-
Pearse

SOUTH DEVON
RAILWAY

West Junc.

Kingskerswell
(Proposed)

(1: 70,000)

Buckfastleigh

*Dainton
Summit*

*Dainton
Tun.*

Torre

Loco Shed
Staverton
Bridge

Torquay

Totnes
(Littlehempston)

*Ashburton
Junc.*

Paignton (Queens Park)

Paignton

Goodrington Sands

*Marley
Tunnels*

Totnes

Goodrington C.S.
& Stone Terminal

Loco Shed

Ivybridge

*Wrangaton
Summit*

Ridalls and Paignton &
Dartmouth Steam Railway

Churston

Greenway Tun.

PAIGNTON & DARTMOUTH
STEAM RAILWAY

Dartmouth

Kingswear
(for Dartmouth)

3

0   2
   5   10 m. (1:350,000)
0   5   10
   5   15 km.

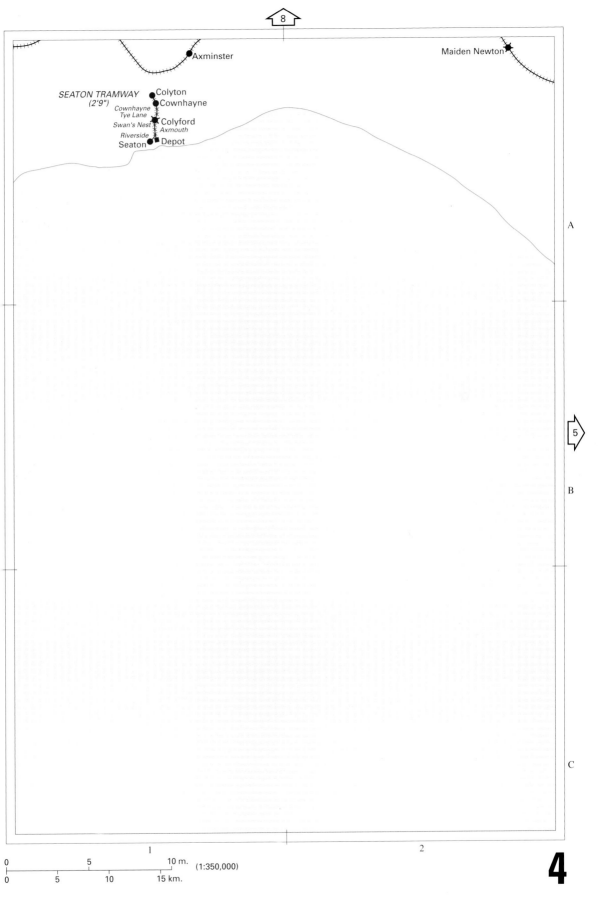

Axminster

Maiden Newton

SEATON TRAMWAY
(2'9")
Colyton
Cownhayne
Cownhayne
Tye Lane
Swan's Nest
Colyford
Axmouth
Riverside
Seaton
Depot

8

5

A

B

C

1

2

0   5   10 m.
                        (1:350,000)
0   5   10   15 km.

4

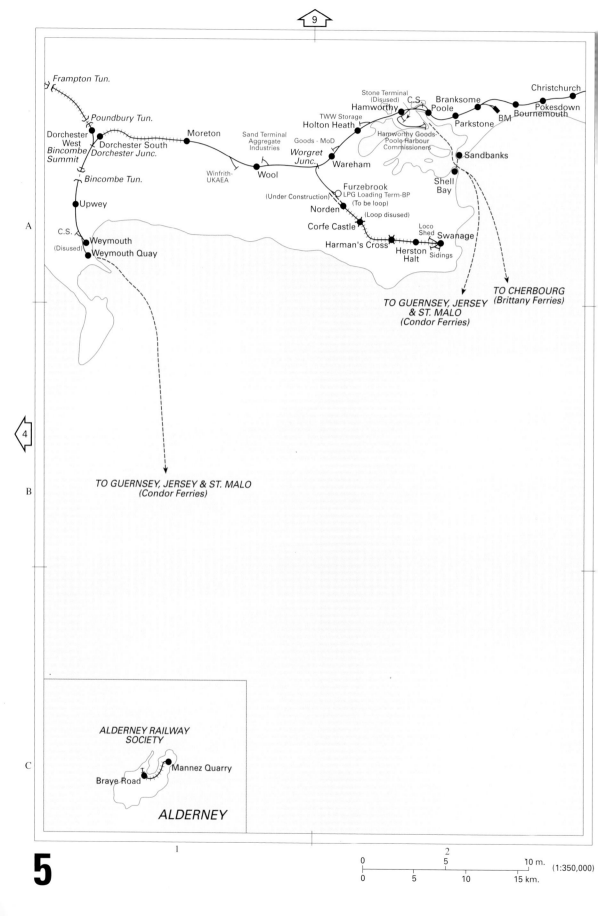

Frampton Tun.

Poundbury Tun.

Dorchester
West
Bincombe
Summit

Dorchester South
Dorchester Junc.

Moreton

Sand Terminal
Aggregate
Industries

Goods - MoD

Worgret
Junc.

Wareham

Winfrith-
UKAEA

Wool

Bincombe Tun.

Upwey

C.S.
(Disused)

Weymouth
Weymouth Quay

Furzebrook
(Under Construction) LPG Loading Term-BP
(To be loop)

Norden

(Loop disused)

Corfe Castle

Harman's Cross

Loco
Shed   Swanage

Herston
Halt   Sidings

Stone Terminal
(Disused)   C.S.

Hamworthy   Branksome
Poole

TWW Storage
Holton Heath   Parkstone   Bournemouth

Hamworthy Goods
Poole Harbour
Commissioners

Christchurch

Pokesdown
BM

Sandbanks

Shell
Bay

TO GUERNSEY, JERSEY
& ST. MALO
(Condor Ferries)

TO CHERBOURG
(Brittany Ferries)

A

B

4

TO GUERNSEY, JERSEY & ST. MALO
(Condor Ferries)

C

ALDERNEY RAILWAY
SOCIETY

Mannez Quarry

Braye Road

ALDERNEY

5

1

0   2
0   5
5   10 m.
10   15 km.   (1:350,000)

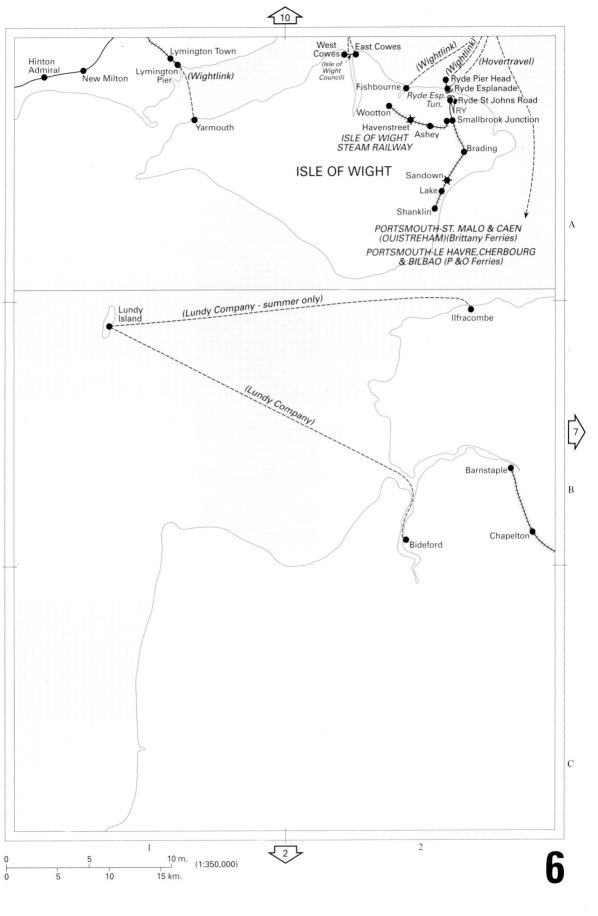

Hinton
Admiral

New Milton

Lymington Town

Lymington
Pier *(Wightlink)*

Yarmouth

West
Cowes
(Isle of
Wight
Council)

East Cowes

(Wightlink)

(Wightlink)

(Hovertravel)

Fishbourne

Ryde Pier Head

Ryde Esplanade

*Ryde Esp.
Tun.*

Ryde St Johns Road

Wootton

IRY

Smallbrook Junction

Havenstreet

Ashey

*ISLE OF WIGHT
STEAM RAILWAY*

Brading

ISLE OF WIGHT

Sandown

Lake

Shanklin

*PORTSMOUTH-ST. MALO & CAEN
(OUISTREHAM)(Brittany Ferries)*

*PORTSMOUTH-LE HAVRE,CHERBOURG
& BILBAO (P &O Ferries)*

A

Lundy
Island

(Lundy Company - summer only)

Ilfracombe

(Lundy Company)

Barnstaple

Bideford

Chapelton

7

B

C

0   5   10 m.   (1:350,000)

0   5   10   15 km.

2

6

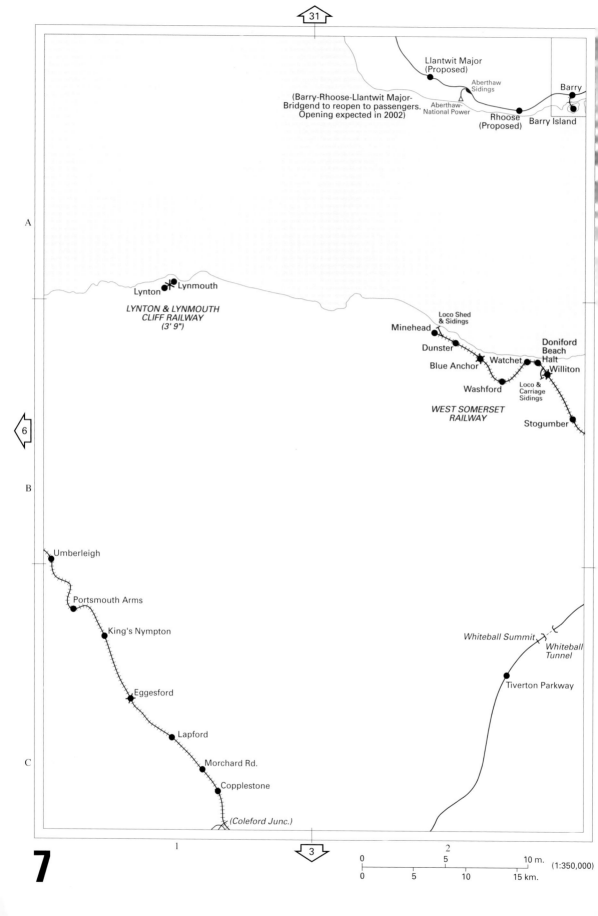

Llantwit Major
(Proposed)

Aberthaw
Sidings

Barry

(Barry-Rhoose-Llantwit Major-
Bridgend to reopen to passengers.
Opening expected in 2002)

Aberthaw-
National Power

Rhoose
(Proposed)

Barry Island

A

Lynton ● ✠ Lynmouth

LYNTON & LYNMOUTH
CLIFF RAILWAY
(3' 9")

Loco Shed
& Sidings

Minehead

Dunster

Blue Anchor

Washford

Doniford
Beach
Halt

Watchet

Williton

Loco &
Carriage
Sidings

WEST SOMERSET
RAILWAY

Stogumber

6

B

Umberleigh

Portsmouth Arms

King's Nympton

Whiteball Summit

Whiteball
Tunnel

Eggesford

Tiverton Parkway

Lapford

Morchard Rd.

C

Copplestone

(Coleford Junc.)

7

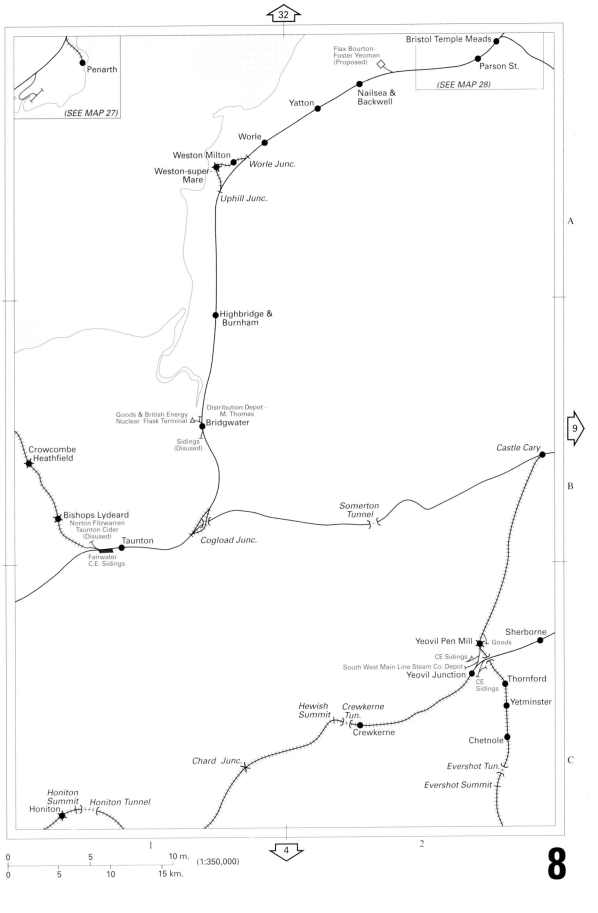

Penarth

(SEE MAP 27)

Flax Bourton-
Foster Yeoman
(Proposed)

Bristol Temple Meads

Parson St.

Nailsea &
Backwell

(SEE MAP 28)

Yatton

Worle

Weston Milton

Worle Junc.

Weston-super-
Mare

Uphill Junc.

A

Highbridge &
Burnham

Distribution Depot -
M. Thomas

Goods & British Energy
Nuclear Flask Terminal

Bridgwater

Sidings
(Disused)

Castle Cary

9

Crowcombe
Heathfield

B

*Somerton
Tunnel*

Bishops Lydeard
Norton Fitzwarren
Taunton Cider
(Disused)

Taunton

Cogload Junc.

Fairwater
C.E. Sidings

Sherborne

Yeovil Pen Mill   Goods

CE Sidings

South West Main Line Steam Co. Depot

Yeovil Junction

CE
Sidings

Thornford

Yetminster

*Hewish
Summit*

*Crewkerne
Tun.*

Crewkerne

Chetnole

Chard Junc.

Evershot Tun.

C

Evershot Summit

*Honiton
Summit*

Honiton Tunnel

Honiton

1

2

0   5   10 m.   (1:350,000)

0   5   10   15 km.

8

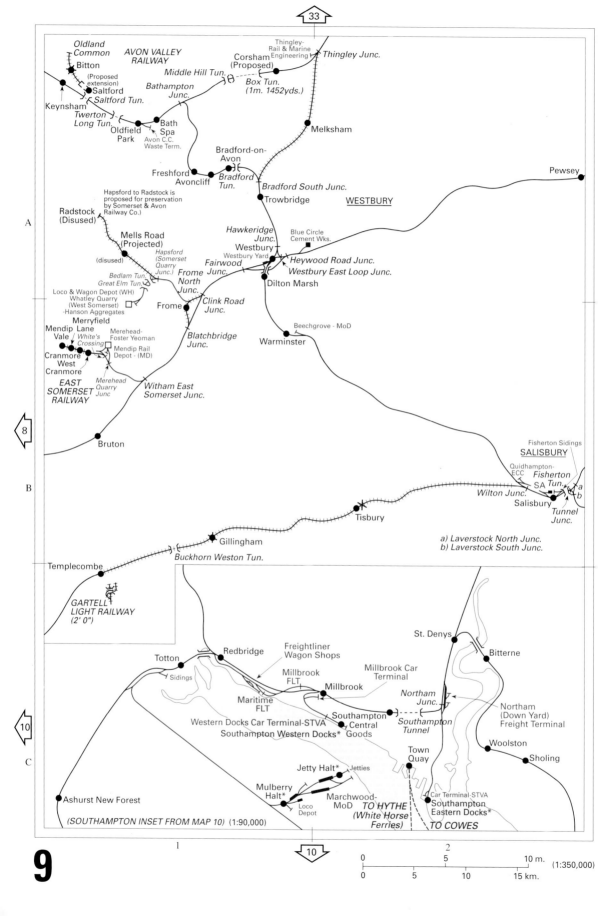

Oldland Common

Bitton

AVON VALLEY
RAILWAY

(Proposed
extension)

Saltford

Keynsham

Saltford Tun.

Middle Hill Tun.

Bathampton
Junc.

Corsham
(Proposed)

Thingley-
Rail & Marine
Engineering

Thingley Junc.

Box Tun.
(1m. 1452yds.)

Twerton
Long Tun.

Oldfield
Park

Bath
Spa

Avon C.C.
Waste Term.

Melksham

Freshford

Avoncliff

Bradford
Tun.

Bradford-on-
Avon

Trowbridge

Bradford South Junc.

WESTBURY

Pewsey

Radstock
(Disused)

Mells Road
(Projected)

(disused)

Hapsford to Radstock is
proposed for preservation
by Somerset & Avon
Railway Co.)

Hapsford
(Somerset
Quarry
Junc.)

Hawkeridge
Junc.

Blue Circle
Cement Wks.

Westbury

Westbury Yard

Fairwood
Junc.

Heywood Road Junc.

Westbury East Loop Junc.

Dilton Marsh

Bedlam Tun.
Great Elm Tun.

Frome
North
Junc.

Loco & Wagon Depot (WH)
Whatley Quarry
(West Somerset)
-Hanson Aggregates

Frome

Clink Road
Junc.

Merryfield

Mendip
Lane

White's
Crossing

Vale

Merehead-
Foster Yeoman

Mendip Rail
Depot - (MD)

Blatchbridge
Junc.

Beechgrove - MoD

Warminster

Cranmore

West
Cranmore

Merehead
Quarry
Junc

EAST
SOMERSET
RAILWAY

Witham East
Somerset Junc.

Bruton

Fisherton Sidings

SALISBURY

Quidhampton-
ECC

Fisherton
Tun.

SA

a
b

Wilton Junc.

Salisbury

Tunnel
Junc.

Tisbury

a) Laverstock North Junc.
b) Laverstock South Junc.

Templecombe

Gillingham

Buckhorn Weston Tun.

GARTELL
LIGHT RAILWAY
(2' 0")

St. Denys

Bitterne

Totton

Redbridge

Freightliner
Wagon Shops

Millbrook Car
Terminal

Sidings

Millbrook
FLT

Millbrook

Northam
Junc.

Northam
(Down Yard)
Freight Terminal

Maritime
FLT

Western Docks Car Terminal-STVA
Southampton Western Docks*

Southampton
Central

Goods

Southampton
Tunnel

Woolston

Sholing

Ashurst New Forest

Jetty Halt*

Jetties

Town
Quay

Car Terminal-STVA

Mulberry
Halt*

Marchwood-
MoD

Loco
Depot

TO HYTHE
(White Horse
Ferries)

Southampton
Eastern Docks*

TO COWES

(SOUTHAMPTON INSET FROM MAP 10) (1:90,000)

9

0   2
0   5   10 m.

0   5   10   15 km.

(1:350,000)

A

8

B

10

C

1

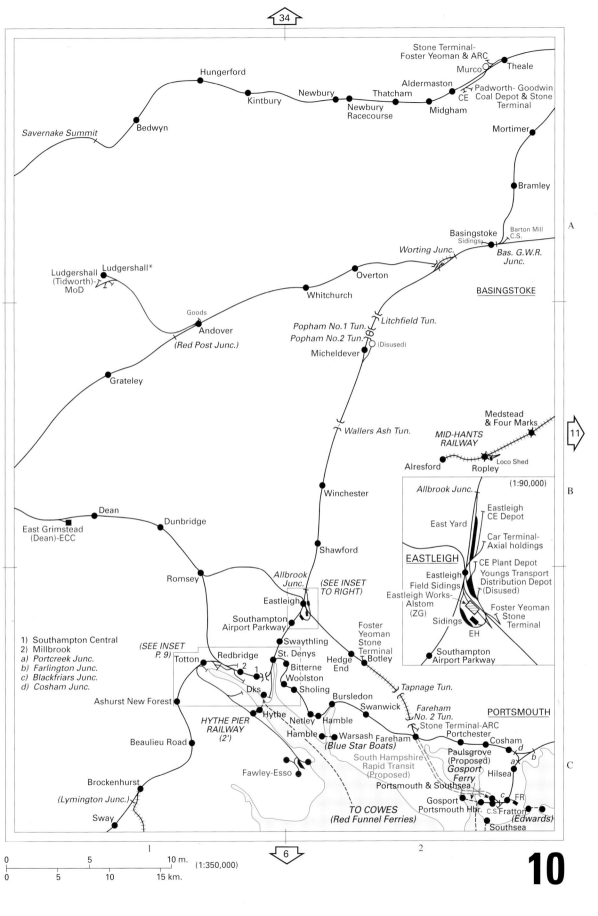

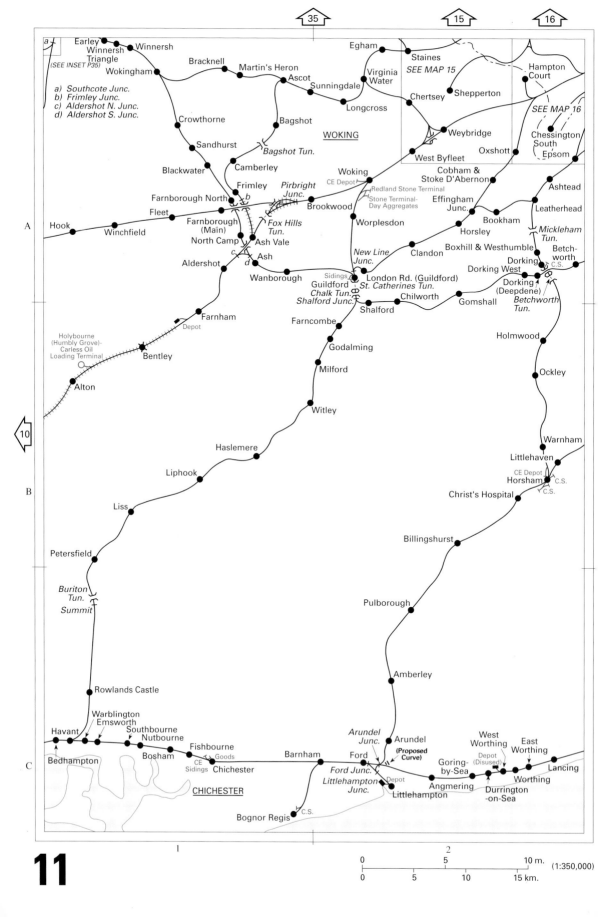

Earley
Winnersh
Triangle
Winnersh
Wokingham
(SEE INSET P35)

a) *Southcote Junc.*
b) *Frimley Junc.*
c) *Aldershot N. Junc.*
d) *Aldershot S. Junc.*

Bracknell
Martin's Heron
Ascot
Sunningdale
Crowthorne
Sandhurst
Bagshot
Bagshot Tun.
Blackwater
Camberley
Frimley
Farnborough North
Pirbright Junc.
Fleet
Farnborough (Main)
Hook
Winchfield
North Camp
Fox Hills Tun.
Ash Vale
Aldershot
Ash
Wanborough

Egham
Staines
Virginia Water
SEE MAP 15
Hampton Court
Chertsey
Shepperton
Longcross
SEE MAP 16
WOKING
Weybridge
West Byfleet
Oxshott
Chessington South
Epsom
Woking
CE Depot
Redland Stone Terminal
Stone Terminal-
Day Aggregates
Cobham & Stoke D'Abernon
Ashtead
Brookwood
Effingham Junc.
Leatherhead
Worplesdon
Bookham
Horsley
Horsley
Mickleham Tun.
New Line Junc.
Boxhill & Westhumble
Betchworth C.S.
Clandon
Dorking
Dorking West
Sidings
London Rd. (Guildford)
Dorking (Deepdene)
Guildford
St. Catherines Tun.
Chalk Tun.
Shalford Junc.
Chilworth
Betchworth Tun.
Shalford
Gomshall
Farncombe

Farnham
Depot
Holybourne
(Humbly Grove)-
Carless Oil
Loading Terminal
Godalming
Holmwood
Bentley
Milford
Ockley
Alton
Witley
Warnham
Haslemere
Littlehaven
Liphook
Horsham CE Depot C.S.
C.S.
Liss
Christ's Hospital
Petersfield
Billingshurst
Buriton Tun.
Summit
Pulborough
Rowlands Castle
Amberley
Warblington
Emsworth
Southbourne
Nutbourne
Havant
Arundel Junc.
Arundel
West Worthing
East Worthing
Bedhampton
Bosham
Fishbourne
Goods
Barnham
Ford
(Proposed Curve)
Depot (Disused)
Lancing
CE Sidings
Chichester
Ford Junc.
Littlehampton Junc.
Goring-by-Sea
Worthing
Durrington-on-Sea
CHICHESTER
Depot
Littlehampton
Angmering
Bognor Regis C.S.

11

A

B

C

10

0   1   2   5   10 m.

0   5   10   15 km.

(1:350,000)

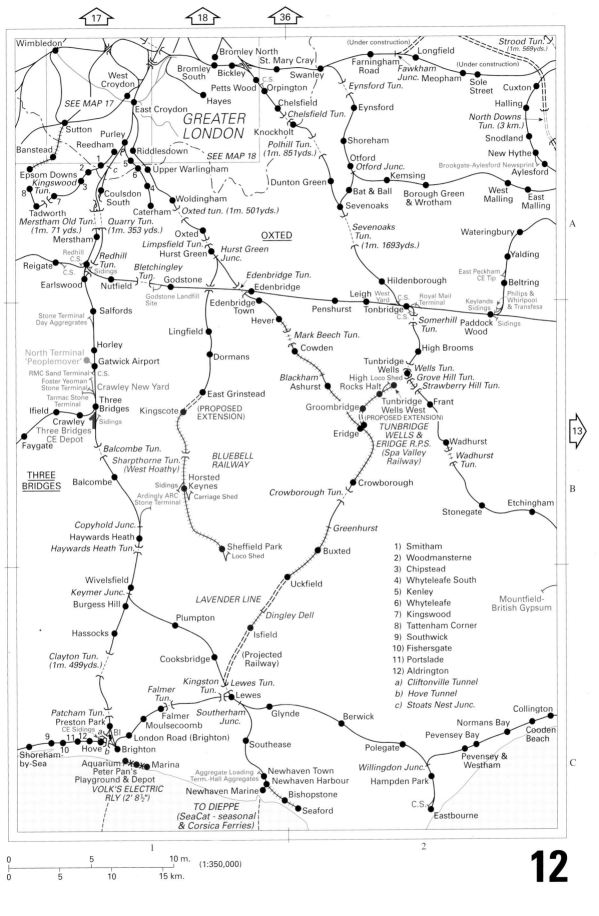

Wimbledon

Bromley North
St. Mary Cray
(Under construction)
Longfield
Strood Tun.
(1m. 569yds.)

West
Croydon
Bromley
South
Bickley
C.S.
Swanley
Farningham
Road
*Fawkham
Junc.* Meopham
(Under construction)
Sole
Street
Cuxton

SEE MAP 17
East Croydon
Petts Wood
Orpington
Chelsfield
Eynsford Tun.
Halling

*GREATER
LONDON*
Hayes
Chelsfield
Chelsfield Tun.
Eynsford
*North Downs
Tun. (3 km.)*
Snodland

Sutton
Purley
Knockholt
Shoreham
New Hythe

Banstead
Reedham
Riddlesdown
SEE MAP 18
*Polhill Tun.
(1m. 851yds.)*
Otford
Otford Junc.
Kemsing
Brookgate-Aylesford Newsprint
Aylesford

Epsom Downs
*Kingswood
Tun.*
Upper Warlingham
Dunton Green
Bat & Ball
Borough Green
& Wrotham
West
Malling
East
Malling

Tadworth
Coulsdon
South
Caterham
Woldingham
Sevenoaks
A

*Merstham Old Tun.
(1m. 71 yds.)*
*Quarry Tun.
(1m. 353 yds.)*
Oxted tun. (1m. 501yds.)
*Sevenoaks
Tun.
(1m. 1693yds.)*
Wateringbury

Merstham
Oxted
OXTED
Yalding

Redhill
C.S.
*Redhill
Tun.*
Sidings
Limpsfield Tun.
Hurst Green
*Hurst Green
Junc.*
Hildenborough
*East Peckham
CE Tip*
Beltring

Reigate
C.S.
*Bletchingley
Tun.*
Godstone
Edenbridge Tun.
Edenbridge
Leigh
West
Yard
C.S.
Royal Mail
Terminal
*Keylands
Sidings*
*Philips &
Whirlpool
& Transfesa*

Earlswood
Nutfield
*Godstone Landfill
Site*
Edenbridge
Town
Penshurst
Tonbridge
C.S.
Sidings

*Stone Terminal
Day Aggregates*
Salfords
Lingfield
Hever
*Somerhill
Tun.*
Paddock
Wood

*North Terminal
'Peoplemover'*
Horley
Mark Beech Tun.
Cowden
High Brooms

RMC Sand Terminal
Gatwick Airport
C.S.
Dormans
Tunbridge
Wells
Wells Tun.

Foster Yeoman
Stone Terminal
Crawley New Yard
Blackham
Ashurst
High
Rocks Halt
Loco Shed
Grove Hill Tun.
Strawberry Hill Tun.

Ifield
Three
Bridges
East Grinstead
Groombridge
Tunbridge
Wells West
Frant
13

Crawley
Three Bridges
CE Depot
Sidings
Kingscote
*(PROPOSED
EXTENSION)*
(PROPOSED EXTENSION)
Eridge
*TUNBRIDGE
WELLS &
ERIDGE R.P.S.
(Spa Valley
Railway)*
Wadhurst

Faygate
Balcombe Tun.
*BLUEBELL
RAILWAY*
*Wadhurst
Tun.*

*Sharpthorne Tun.
(West Hoathy)*
Horsted
Keynes
Crowborough
B

*THREE
BRIDGES*
Balcombe
Sidings
*Ardingly ARC
Stone Terminal*
Carriage Shed
Crowborough Tun.
Stonegate
Etchingham

Copyhold Junc.
Haywards Heath
Haywards Heath Tun.
Sheffield Park
Loco Shed
Greenhurst

Wivelsfield
Buxted
1) Smitham
*Mountfield-
British Gypsum*

Keymer Junc.
Burgess Hill
Uckfield
2) Woodmansterne
3) Chipstead

Hassocks
LAVENDER LINE
4) Whyteleafe South
5) Kenley

*Clayton Tun.
(1m. 499yds.)*
Plumpton
Dingley Dell
6) Whyteleafe
7) Kingswood
8) Tattenham Corner

Cooksbridge
Isfield
9) Southwick
10) Fishersgate

Patcham Tun.
*Falmer
Tun.*
*Kingston
Tun.*
Lewes Tun.
*(Projected
Railway)*
11) Portslade
12) Aldrington
a) Cliftonville Tunnel

Preston Park
Falmer
Moulsecoomb
*Southerham
Junc.*
Glynde
Berwick
b) Hove Tunnel
c) Stoats Nest Junc.

9
11
10
CE Sidings
a
Bl
London Road (Brighton)
Southease
Normans Bay
Cooden
Beach

Shoreham-
by-Sea
Hove
b
Brighton
Southease
Polegate
Pevensey Bay
Pevensey &
Westham

Aquarium
Peter Pan's
Playground & Depot
Marina
*Aggregate Loading
Term.-Hall Aggregates*
Newhaven Town
Newhaven Harbour
Willingdon Junc.
Hampden Park
C

*VOLK'S ELECTRIC
RLY (2' 8½")*
Newhaven Marine
Bishopstone
C.S.
Eastbourne

*TO DIEPPE
(SeaCat - seasonal
& Corsica Ferries)*
Seaford

0   5   10 m. (1:350,000)
0   5   10   15 km.
1
2

12

Strood
Rochester
Gillingham Tun.
Gillingham
Gl
Chatham Tun.
Chatham
Fort Pitt Tun.
Rainham
Newington

King's Ferry Bridge
Swale
Ridham Dock Scrapyard-Ridham Sea Terminals
Kemsley
Kemsley Down
Sittingbourne
d
b' c'
Sittingbourne
Teynham

SITTINGBOURNE & KEMSLEY LT. RLY. (2' 6")

Chestfield & Swalecliffe
Herne Bay
Whitstable

Barming
Allington-ARC Stone Terminal
Maidstone East
Bearsted
Wheeler St. Tun.
Hollingbourne Tun.
Hollingbourne
Maidstone Barracks
Maidstone West
East Farleigh

MAIDSTONE WEST

1) Freight Terminals-Wood & Victa Railfreight
2) Grovehurst Paper Mill
3) Maintenance Depot
4) Chatham Docks-Medway Ports (Disused)

a) Rochester Bridge Junc.
b) Western Junc.
c) Eastern Junc.
d) Middle Junc.
e) Saltwood Junc.
f) Continental Junc.

Faversham C.S.
Selling
Selling Tun.

Sturry
Canterbury West
Canterbury East
Bekesbourne
Adisham
Aylesham
Snowdown
Chartham
Chilham

Harrietsham
Lenham
Harrietsham Tun.
Sandway Tun.
Charing
Beechbrook Construction Site (Proposed)

Channel Tunnel Rail Link - High Speed Line under construction from Cheriton to Fawkham Junction

Westwell Leacon Tun.
Hothfield - Tarmac Stone Term.
Ashford Tun.
Wye

(See inset below for final Ashford layout)

FOLKESTONE EAST
Folkestone (Cheriton) Shuttle Terminal
Martello Tun.

Marden
Staplehurst
Headcorn
Pluckley

Chart Leacon Works-Adtranz (AF)
Ashford International
Sidings
C.S.
CE Depot C.S.
CE Plant Depot

ASHFORD

Sevington Aggregate Terminal
Westenhanger
Sandling
Sandling Tun.
Saltwood Tun. f
e
Folkestone West
Folkestone Central
Folkestone Harbour (Seasonal)
Folkestone East Junc.

KENT & EAST SUSSEX RAILWAY
Depot
Rolvenden
Tenterden Town

Ham Street

Hythe

(See inset p14 for final Folkestone network)

ROTHER VALLEY RAILWAY (PROPOSED EXTENSION)

Wittersham Road
Northiam
Bodiam
Robertsbridge

Appledore

Burmarsh Road Halt*
Dymchurch
St Mary's Bay

ROMNEY, HYTHE & DYMCHURCH RAILWAY (1' 3")

C.S.
Loco Depot
New Romney
P.W. Depot

Mountfield Tun.
Mountfield Sidings

Rye
Winchelsea
Doleham
Three Oaks

Romney Sands

Battle
Crowhurst
Mount Pleasant Tun.
Ore Tun.
West St. Leonards
Hastings Tun.
Ore
Spoil Term.
Hastings
St.Leonards Warrior Sq.
Bexhill
Bopeep Junc. & Tun.
St. Leonards Depot - St. Leonards Rail Engineering Ltd

Dungeness Nuclear Electric
Dungeness

(Inset)
(CTRL)
Ashford Tun.
Chart Leacon-Adtranz(AF)
Ashford International
Sidings
C.S.
CE Plant Depot
CE Depot
C.S.
ASHFORD
(CTRL to Folkestone)
(Ashford - final layout after CTRL completion)
(1:70,000)

A

12

B

C

13

1

2

0   5   10 m.   (1:350,000)
0   5   10   15 km.

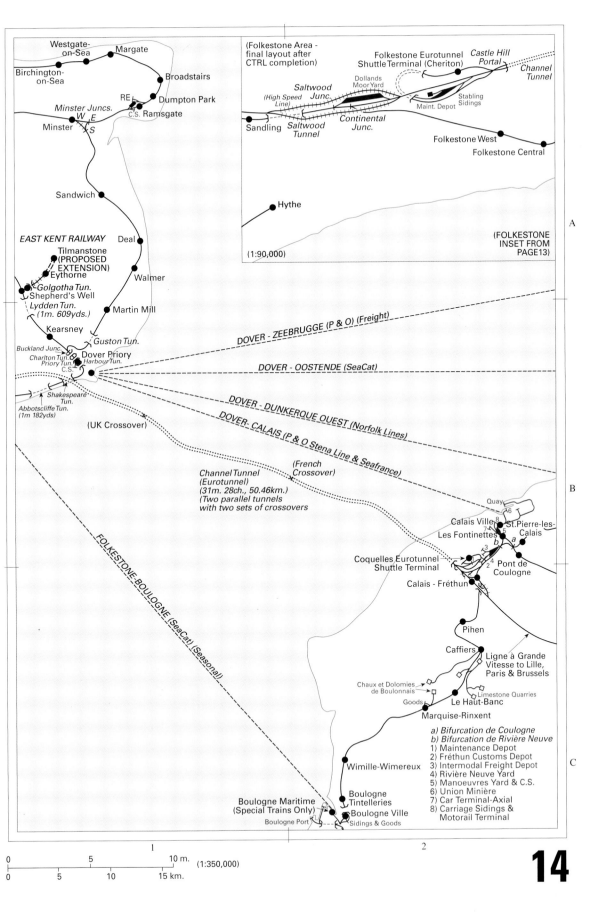

Westgate-on-Sea / Margate area

Birchington-on-Sea
Westgate-on-Sea
Margate
Broadstairs
Dumpton Park
RE
Minster Juncs.
c.s. Ramsgate
W E
Minster
S
Sandwich

EAST KENT RAILWAY
Deal
Tilmanstone
(PROPOSED
EXTENSION)
Eythorne
Golgotha Tun.
Shepherd's Well
Lydden Tun.
(1m. 609yds.)
Walmer
Martin Mill
Kearsney
Guston Tun.
Buckland Junc.
Charlton Tun.
Priory Tun.
C.S.
Dover Priory
Harbour Tun.
Shakespeare
Tun.
Abbotscliffe Tun.
(1m 182yds)
(UK Crossover)

DOVER – ZEEBRUGGE (P & O) (Freight)

DOVER – OOSTENDE (SeaCat)

DOVER – DUNKERQUE OUEST (Norfolk Lines)

DOVER– CALAIS (P & O Stena Line & Seafrance)

(French Crossover)

Channel Tunnel
(Eurotunnel)
(31m. 28ch., 50.46km.)
(Two parallel tunnels
with two sets of crossovers

FOLKESTONE–BOULOGNE (SeaCat) (Seasonal)

Folkestone inset

(Folkestone Area -
final layout after
CTRL completion)

Folkestone Eurotunnel
Shuttle Terminal (Cheriton)
Castle Hill
Portal
Channel
Tunnel
Saltwood
Junc.
(High Speed
Line)
Dollands
Moor Yard
Stabling
Sidings
Maint. Depot
Sandling
Saltwood
Tunnel
Continental
Junc.
Folkestone West
Folkestone Central

Hythe

(1:90,000)

A

(FOLKESTONE
INSET FROM
PAGE 13)

B

Calais / Boulogne area

Quay
6
Calais Ville
St.Pierre-les-
Calais
Les Fontinettes
b
a
3
Coquelles Eurotunnel
Shuttle Terminal
2 4
Pont de
Coulogne
Calais - Fréthun

Pihen

Caffiers
Ligne à Grande
Vitesse to Lille,
Paris & Brussels

Chaux et Dolomies
de Boulonnais
Limestone Quarries
Goods
Le Haut-Banc
Marquise-Rinxent

C

Wimille-Wimereux

Boulogne
Tintelleries
Boulogne Maritime
(Special Trains Only)
Boulogne Ville
Boulogne Port
Sidings & Goods

a) Bifurcation de Coulogne
b) Bifurcation de Rivière Neuve
1) Maintenance Depot
2) Fréthun Customs Depot
3) Intermodal Freight Depot
4) Rivière Neuve Yard
5) Manoeuvres Yard & C.S.
6) Union Minière
7) Car Terminal-Axial
8) Carriage Sidings &
   Motorail Terminal

0   5   10 m.   (1:350,000)
0   5   10   15 km.

1   2

14

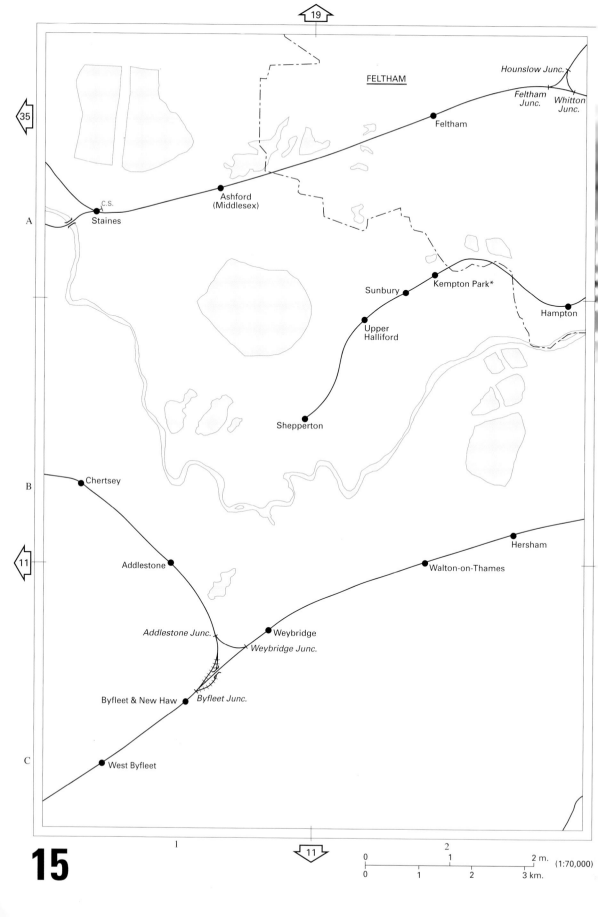

35

FELTHAM

Hounslow Junc.

Feltham Junc.

Whitton Junc.

Feltham

C.S.

Ashford
(Middlesex)

A

Staines

Sunbury

Kempton Park*

Hampton

Upper
Halliford

Shepperton

B

Chertsey

Hersham

11

Addlestone

Walton-on-Thames

Addlestone Junc.

Weybridge

Weybridge Junc.

Byfleet & New Haw

Byfleet Junc.

C

West Byfleet

15

0   2 m.
0   1   2   3 km.   (1:70,000)

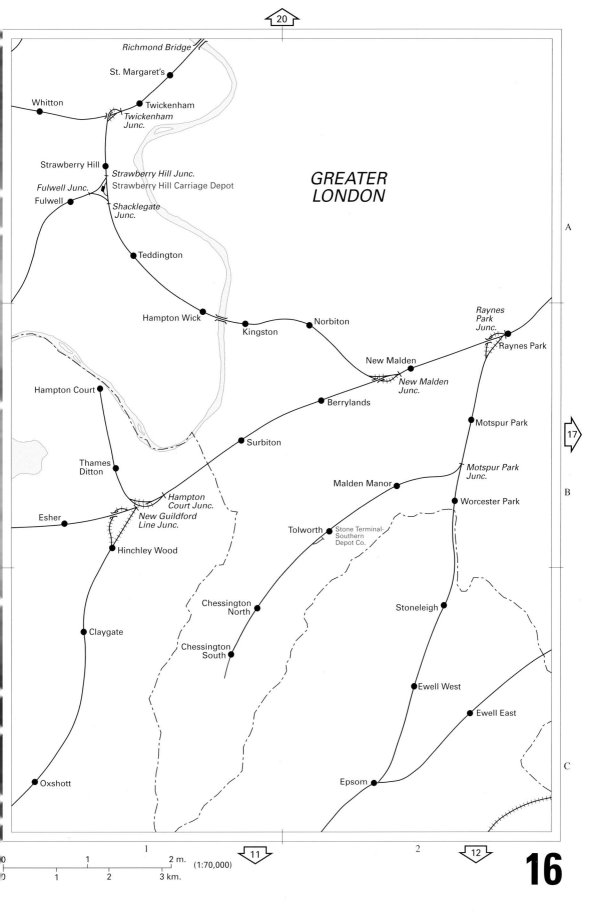

Richmond Bridge

St. Margaret's

Whitton

Twickenham

Twickenham Junc.

Strawberry Hill

Strawberry Hill Junc.
Strawberry Hill Carriage Depot

Fulwell Junc.

Fulwell

Shacklegate Junc.

Teddington

GREATER LONDON

A

Hampton Wick

Kingston

Norbiton

Raynes Park Junc.

Raynes Park

New Malden

New Malden Junc.

Hampton Court

Berrylands

Motspur Park

Surbiton

Thames Ditton

Malden Manor

Motspur Park Junc.

17

Hampton Court Junc.

New Guildford Line Junc.

Worcester Park

B

Esher

Tolworth

Stone Terminal-Southern Depot Co.

Hinchley Wood

Chessington North

Stoneleigh

Claygate

Chessington South

Ewell West

Ewell East

C

Oxshott

Epsom

I

1

2 m.

(1:70,000)

1

2

3 km.

1

2

16

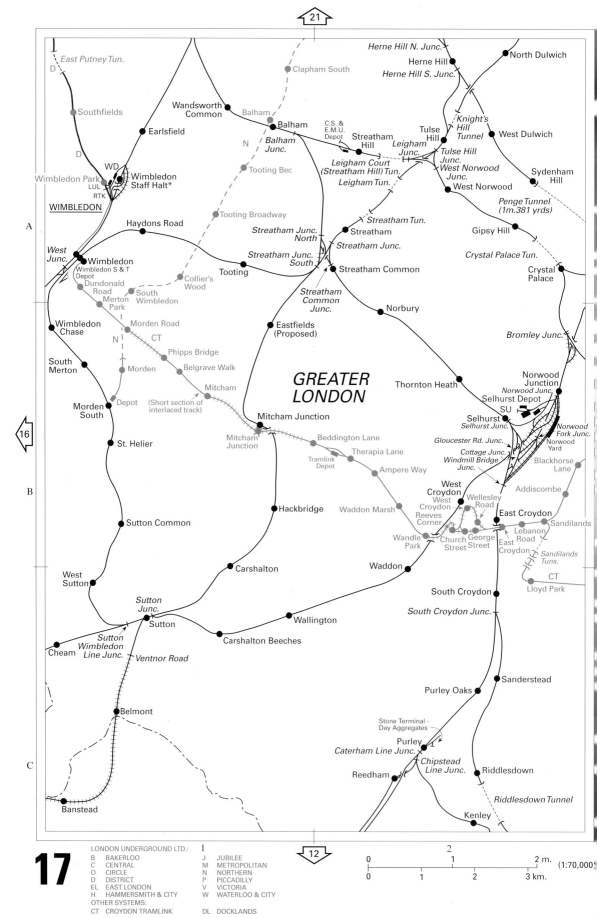

East Putney Tun.

Southfields

Wandsworth Common

Clapham South

Herne Hill N. Junc.

Herne Hill

Herne Hill S. Junc.

North Dulwich

D

Earlsfield

Balham

Balham

C.S. & E.M.U. Depot

Streatham Hill

Knight's Hill Tunnel

Tulse Hill

West Dulwich

D

Balham Junc.

N

Leigham Junc.

Tulse Hill Junc.

WD

Wimbledon Park

LUL

RTK

Wimbledon Staff Halt*

Tooting Bec

Leigham Court (Streatham Hill) Tun.

West Norwood Junc.

Sydenham Hill

WIMBLEDON

Leigham Tun.

West Norwood

Penge Tunnel (1m.381 yrds)

A

Haydons Road

Tooting Broadway

Streatham Tun.

Gipsy Hill

West Junc.

Wimbledon S & T Depot

Wimbledon

Streatham Junc. North

Streatham

Crystal Palace Tun.

Dundonald Road

Collier's Wood

Tooting

Streatham Junc. South

Streatham Junc.

Crystal Palace

South Wimbledon

Streatham Common

Wimbledon Chase

Merton Park

N

CT

Morden Road

Phipps Bridge

Eastfields (Proposed)

Streatham Common Junc.

Norbury

Bromley Junc.

South Merton

Morden

Belgrave Walk

GREATER LONDON

Norwood Junction

Norwood Junc.

Selhurst Depot

Morden South

Depot

Mitcham

(Short section of interlaced track)

Thornton Heath

SU

Mitcham Junction

Beddington Lane

Gloucester Rd. Junc.

Norwood Fork Junc.

St. Helier

Mitcham Junction

Tramlink Depot

Therapia Lane

Cottage Junc.

Windmill Bridge Junc.

Selhurst

Selhurst Junc.

Norwood Yard

Blackhorse Lane

Ampere Way

Addiscombe

B

Sutton Common

Hackbridge

Waddon Marsh

West Croydon

West Croydon

Wellesley Road

East Croydon

Sandilands

Lebanon Road

West Sutton

Wandle Park

Reeves Corner

Church Street

George Street

East Croydon

Sandilands Tuns.

Carshalton

Waddon

South Croydon

Lloyd Park

CT

Sutton Junc.

Wallington

South Croydon Junc.

Sutton

Cheam

Sutton Wimbledon Line Junc.

Carshalton Beeches

Ventnor Road

Sanderstead

Purley Oaks

Belmont

Stone Terminal - Day Aggregates

Purley

Caterham Line Junc.

Riddlesden

C

Chipstead Line Junc.

Reedham

Riddlesdown Tunnel

Banstead

Kenley

17

LONDON UNDERGROUND LTD.:
B   BAKERLOO
C   CENTRAL
O   CIRCLE
D   DISTRICT
EL   EAST LONDON
H   HAMMERSMITH & CITY
OTHER SYSTEMS:
CT   CROYDON TRAMLINK

I   JUBILEE
J   JUBILEE
M   METROPOLITAN
N   NORTHERN
P   PICCADILLY
V   VICTORIA
W   WATERLOO & CITY

DL   DOCKLANDS

2

0   1   2 m.

0   1   2   3 km.

(1:70,000)

16

A

B

C

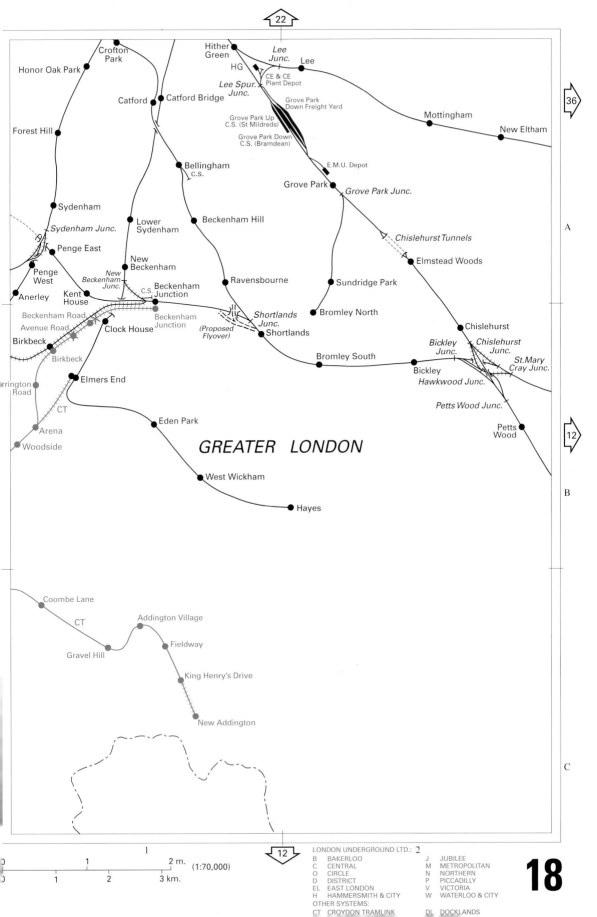

36

Hither
Green
*Lee
Junc.*   Lee
HG
CE & CE
Plant Depot
*Lee Spur.
Junc.*

Crofton
Park
Honor Oak Park
Catford   Catford Bridge

Grove Park
Down Freight Yard
Grove Park Up
C.S. (St Mildreds)
Grove Park Down
C.S. (Bramdean)

Mottingham
New Eltham

Forest Hill

Bellingham
c.s.

E.M.U. Depot

Grove Park   *Grove Park Junc.*

A

Sydenham
Sydenham Junc.
Penge East

Lower
Sydenham

Beckenham Hill

Chislehurst Tunnels

Elmstead Woods

New
Beckenham
*New
Beckenham
Junc.*

Ravensbourne

Sundridge Park

Penge
West
Anerley
Kent
House
C.S.
Beckenham
Junction
Beckenham
Junction

Bromley North

Chislehurst

Beckenham Road
Avenue Road
Birkbeck
Birkbeck

Clock House

*Shortlands
Junc.*
Shortlands
(Proposed
Flyover)

Bromley South

*Bickley
Junc.*   *Chislehurst
Junc.*
Bickley   *St.Mary
Cray Junc.*
Hawkwood Junc.

rrington
Road
CT
Arena
Woodside

Elmers End

Eden Park

GREATER LONDON

Petts Wood Junc.

Petts
Wood

12

B

West Wickham

Hayes

Coombe Lane
CT
Addington Village
Fieldway
Gravel Hill
King Henry's Drive

New Addington

C

I
0   1   2 m.   (1:70,000)
0   1   2   3 km.

LONDON UNDERGROUND LTD.: 2
B   BAKERLOO   J   JUBILEE
C   CENTRAL   M   METROPOLITAN
O   CIRCLE   N   NORTHERN
D   DISTRICT   P   PICCADILLY
EL EAST LONDON   V   VICTORIA
H   HAMMERSMITH & CITY W   WATERLOO & CITY
OTHER SYSTEMS:
CT CROYDON TRAMLINK   DL DOCKLANDS

18

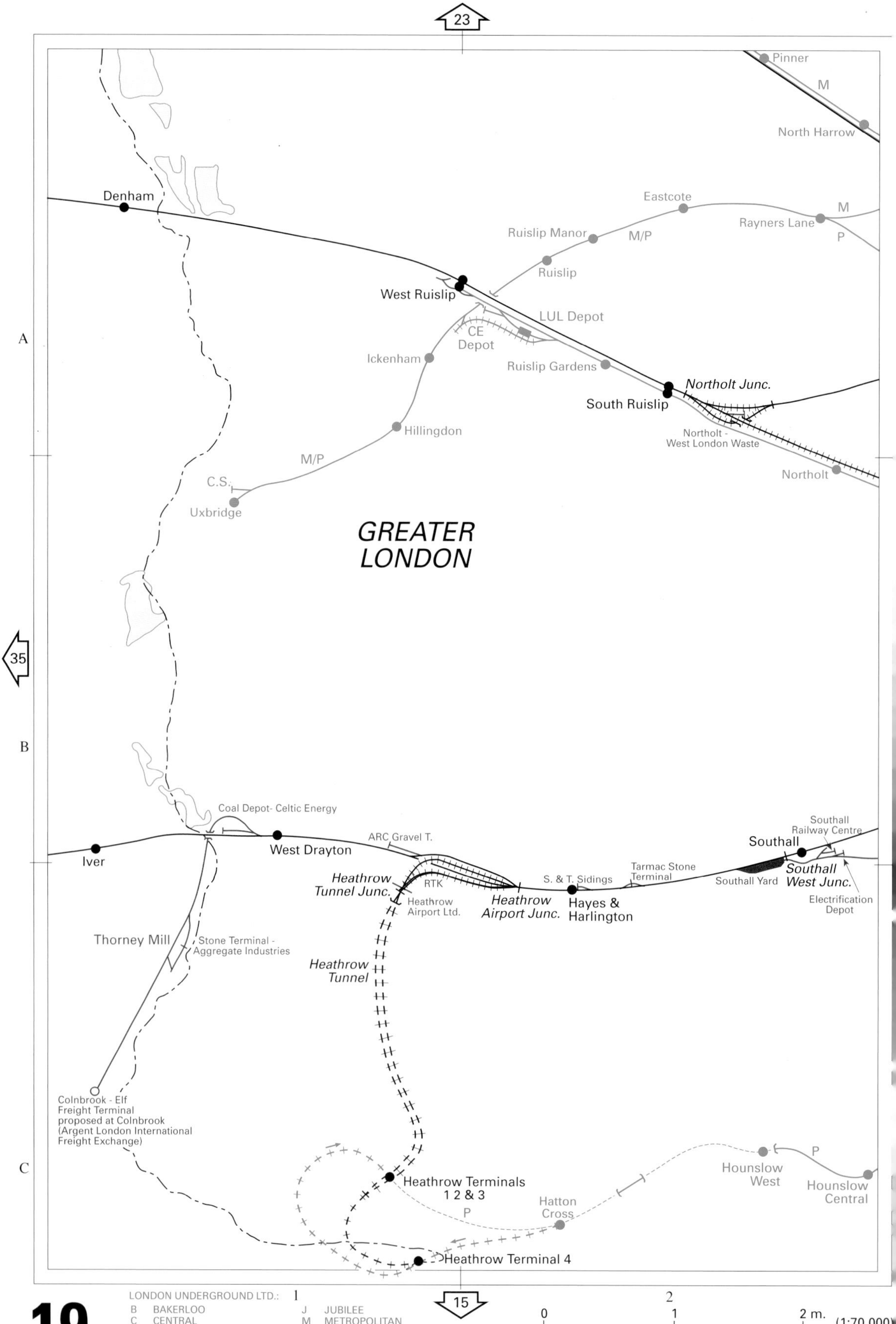

GREATER
LONDON

Pinner
M
North Harrow

Denham

Eastcote
Ruislip Manor
M/P
Rayners Lane
M
P

West Ruislip
Ruislip
LUL Depot
CE Depot
Northolt Junc.
Ickenham
Ruislip Gardens
South Ruislip
Hillingdon
Northolt - West London Waste
M/P
Northolt
C.S.
Uxbridge

35

Coal Depot- Celtic Energy
Southall Railway Centre
Iver
West Drayton
ARC Gravel T.
Southall
Southall West Junc.
Heathrow Tunnel Junc.
RTK
Heathrow Airport Ltd.
S. & T. Sidings
Tarmac Stone Terminal
Southall Yard
Electrification Depot
Heathrow Airport Junc.
Hayes & Harlington
Thorney Mill
Stone Terminal - Aggregate Industries
Heathrow Tunnel

Colnbrook - Elf Freight Terminal proposed at Colnbrook (Argent London International Freight Exchange)

Hounslow West
P
Hounslow Central
Heathrow Terminals 1 2 & 3
P
Hatton Cross
Heathrow Terminal 4

19

LONDON UNDERGROUND LTD.:
B   BAKERLOO
C   CENTRAL
O   CIRCLE
D   DISTRICT
EL EAST LONDON
H   HAMMERSMITH & CITY
OTHER SYSTEMS:
CT CROYDON TRAMLINK

J   JUBILEE
M   METROPOLITAN
N   NORTHERN
P   PICCADILLY
V   VICTORIA
W   WATERLOO & CITY

DL DOCKLANDS

0   1   2 m.
0   1   2   3 km.
2
(1:70,000)

a) Willesden H.L. Junc.
b) West London Junc.
c) Old Oak West Junc.
d) Cricklewood Curve Junc.
e) Mitre Bridge Junc.

1) Willesden S.W. Sidings - CE
2) Scrapyard - Mayer Parry Recycling
3) Brent Waste Terminal (Hendon) Shanks & McEwan
4) Acton - Foster Yeoman Stone Terminal
5) Willesden - FLT & Euroterminal
6) CE Yard
7) Heathrow Express Depot

(Possible route for Crossrail to Aylesbury line trains shown at *)

Harrow & Wealdstone
Harrow North Junc.
Harrow-on-the-Hill
West Harrow
LUL RTK
Kenton
Northwick Park
South Kenton
Preston Road
Kingsbury
Hendon Central
Burroughs Tun.
Silkstream Junc.
Hendon
Brent Cross
Cricklewood Freight Depot Sidings
Brent Curve Junc.
Cricklewood Recess Sdgs.
Dudding Hill Junc.
Cricklewood
Redland Stone Term.
South Harrow Sidings
Sudbury Hill Harrow
S. Harrow Tun.
Northolt Park
Sudbury Hill
North Wembley
Wembley Park
Sudbury & Harrow Road
Sudbury Town
Wembley Stadium
Wembley Central
Neasden Freight Term.-Tibbett & Britten
Neasden Depot
Neasden
Neasden Junc. Stone Terminal-Aggregate Industries
Dollis Hill
Willesden Green
Depot
LUL Depot
Sidings
Wembley Heavy Repair Shops
Wembley InterCity Carriage Depot (WB)
Stonebridge Park
Wembley European Freight Yard RFD
Neasden Junc.
WILLESDEN JUNC.(WEMBLEY)(MAIN LINES)
WILLESDEN (LOCAL LINES)
Reversing Siding
Harlesden
Willesden Royal Mail Terminal
Sudbury Junc.
Willesden 'F' Sidings-'Virtual Quarry'
Willesden Brent Yard
MG Gas Products
Willesden Junc.
Kensal Green Junc.
Kensal Rise
Greenford
Greenford W. Junc.
E. Junc.
LTE Bay Junc.
South Junc.
South Greenford
Perivale
Alperton
Park Royal-Guinness (Disused)
Stone Term.-Marcon Topmix
North Acton *
Acton Canal Wharf Junc.
Acton Wells Junc.
Kensal Green
Kensal Green Tuns.
WN
Hanger Lane
Park Royal
Park Royal Branch Junc.
North Acton
Acton Yard
North Pole Junc.
North Pole Servicing Depot (European Services) (NP)
Maintenance Depot
Castle Bar Park
Castle Bar Tunnel
Drayton Green Junc.
North Ealing
West Acton
East Acton
Latimer Road
Drayton Green
Plasser Wks.
Ealing Broadway
Hanger Lane Junc.
Acton Main Line
Acton East Junc.
White City
Hanwell
CE Sidings
West Ealing
West Ealing Junc.
Hanwell Junc.
Ealing Common
Acton Central
White City LUL Depot
Shepherd's Bush
Goldhawk Road
Shepherd's Bush Depot
LUL Depot
South Ealing
Acton Town North Junc.
Acton Town
LUL Acton Works
South Acton
Acton Central
Stamford Brook
Ravenscourt Park
Hammersmith
Northfields
Depot
Boston Manor
Chiswick Park
South Acton Junc.
Turnham Green
Bedford Park Junc.
Brentford Goods
Stone Term.-Aggregate Industries
Old Kew Junc.
Kew East Junc.
Gunnersbury Junc.
New Kew Junc.
LUL RTK
Gunnersbury
Osterley
Waste Terminal West London Waste
Kew Bridge
Kew Bridge
Brentford
Chiswick
Syon Lane
Kew Gardens
Barnes Bridge
Barnes Bridge
Isleworth
Barnes
Hounslow East
Mortlake
Barnes Junc.
Barnes
Hounslow
North Sheen
Richmond
Putney

21
B

LONDON UNDERGROUND LTD.:
B   BAKERLOO
C   CENTRAL
O   CIRCLE
D   DISTRICT
EL   EAST LONDON
H   HAMMERSMITH & CITY
J   JUBILEE
M   METROPOLITAN
N   NORTHERN
P   PICCADILLY
V   VICTORIA
W   WATERLOO & CITY
OTHER SYSTEMS:
CT   CROYDON TRAMLINK
DL   DOCKLANDS

1   2 m. (1:70,000)
1   2   3 km.

16

20

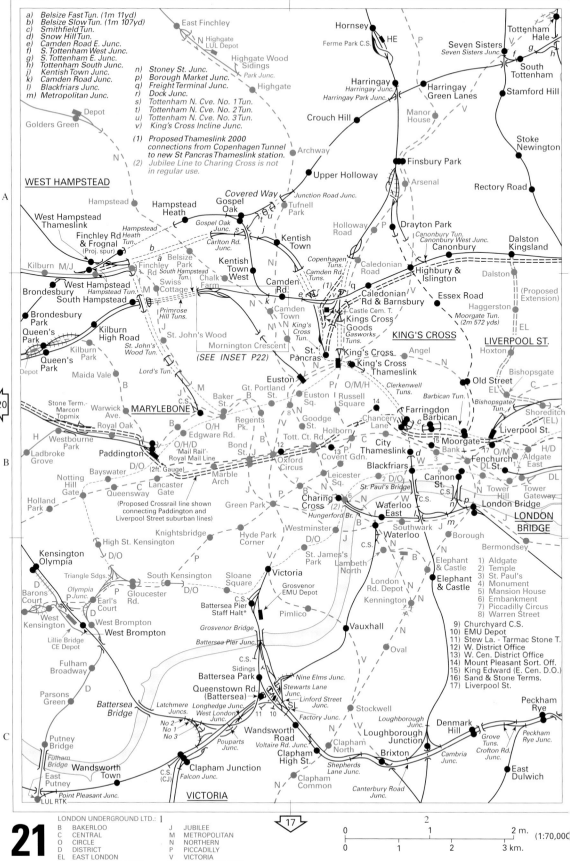

a) Belsize Fast Tun. (1m 11yd)
b) Belsize Slow Tun. (1m 107yd)
c) Smithfield Tun.
d) Snow Hill Tun.
e) Camden Road E. Junc.
f) S. Tottenham West Junc.
g) S. Tottenham E. Junc.
h) Tottenham South Junc.
j) Kentish Town Junc.
k) Camden Road Junc.
l) Blackfriars Junc.
m) Metropolitan Junc.

n) Stoney St. Junc.
p) Borough Market Junc.
q) Freight Terminal Junc.
r) Dock Junc.
s) Tottenham N. Cve. No. 1 Tun.
t) Tottenham N. Cve. No. 2 Tun.
u) Tottenham N. Cve. No. 3 Tun.
v) King's Cross Incline Junc.

(1) Proposed Thameslink 2000 connections from Copenhagen Tunnel to new St Pancras Thameslink station.
(2) Jubilee Line to Charing Cross is not in regular use.

1) Aldgate
2) Temple
3) St. Paul's
4) Monument
5) Mansion House
6) Embankment
7) Piccadilly Circus
8) Warren Street
9) Churchyard C.S.
10) EMU Depot
11) Stew La. - Tarmac Stone T.
12) W. District Office
13) W. Cen. District Office
14) Mount Pleasant Sort. Off.
15) King Edward (E. Cen. D.O.)
16) Sand & Stone Terms.
17) Liverpool St.

21

LONDON UNDERGROUND LTD.:
B   BAKERLOO
C   CENTRAL
O   CIRCLE
D   DISTRICT
EL EAST LONDON
H   HAMMERSMITH & CITY
OTHER SYSTEMS:
CT CROYDON TRAMLINK

J   JUBILEE
M   METROPOLITAN
N   NORTHERN
P   PICCADILLY
V   VICTORIA
W   WATERLOO & CITY

DL DOCKLANDS

0   1   2   2 m.
0   1   2   3 km.

(1:70,000)

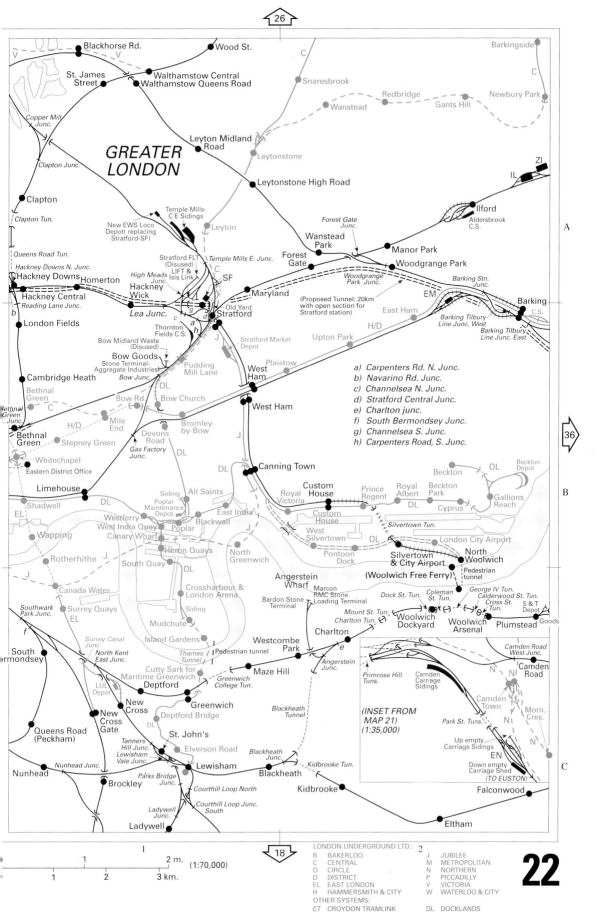

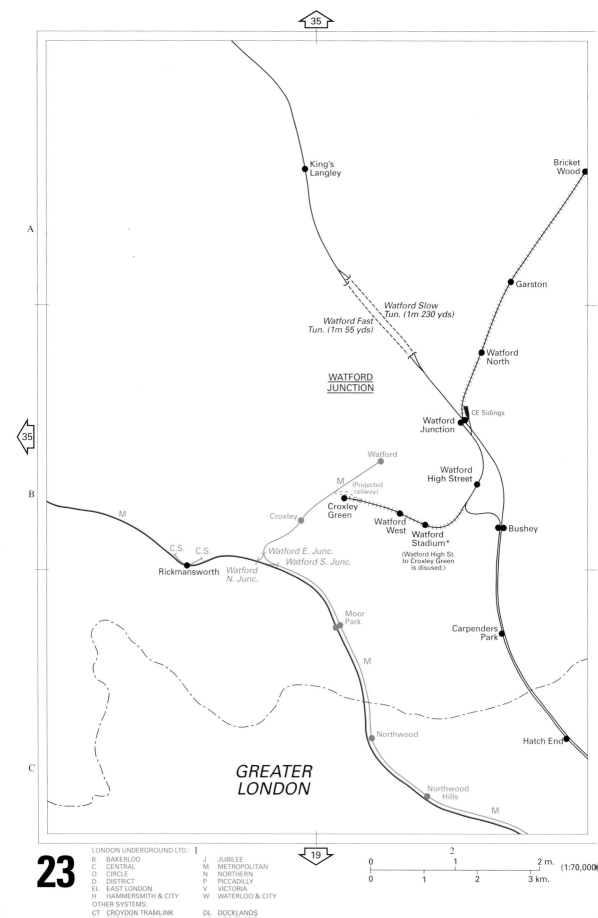

King's
Langley

Bricket
Wood

Garston

*Watford Slow
Tun. (1m 230 yds)*

*Watford Fast
Tun. (1m 55 yds)*

Watford
North

WATFORD
JUNCTION

CE Sidings

Watford
Junction

Watford

Watford
High Street

M

(Projected
railway)

Croxley

Croxley
Green

Bushey

Watford
West

Watford
Stadium*

C.S.   C.S.

Watford E. Junc.
Watford S. Junc.

Rickmansworth   *Watford
N. Junc.*

(Watford High St.
to Croxley Green
is disused.)

Carpenders
Park

Moor
Park

M

Northwood

Hatch End

*GREATER
LONDON*

Northwood
Hills

M

23

LONDON UNDERGROUND LTD.: |
B   BAKERLOO
C   CENTRAL
O   CIRCLE
D   DISTRICT
EL   EAST LONDON
H   HAMMERSMITH & CITY
OTHER SYSTEMS:
CT   CROYDON TRAMLINK

J   JUBILEE
M   METROPOLITAN
N   NORTHERN
P   PICCADILLY
V   VICTORIA
W   WATERLOO & CITY

DL   DOCKLANDS

2

0   1   2 m.

0   1   2   3 km.

(1:70,000)

A

B

C

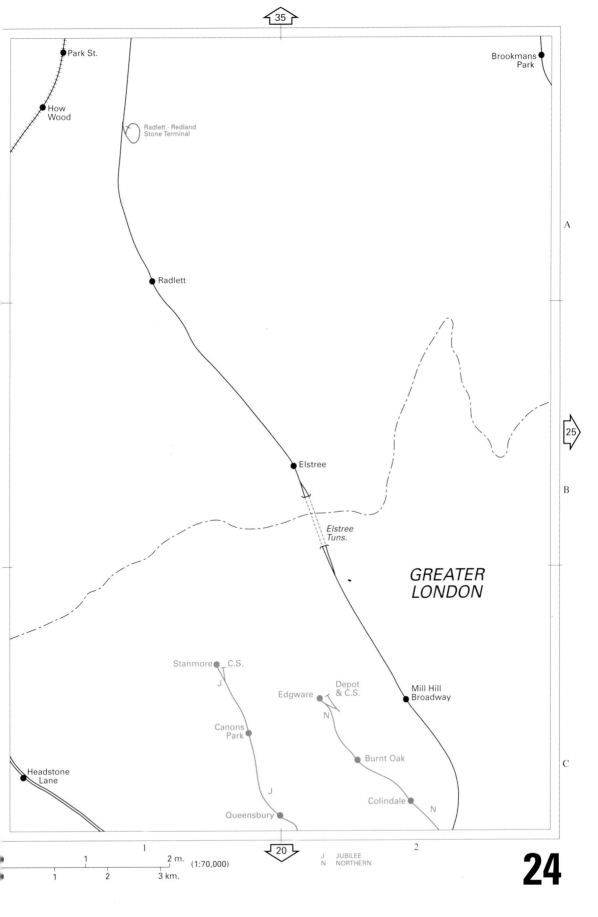

Park St.

Brookmans
Park

How
Wood

Radlett - Redland
Stone Terminal

A

Radlett

25

Elstree

B

Elstree
Tuns.

GREATER
LONDON

Stanmore ● C.S.

Depot
& C.S.

Mill Hill
Broadway

J

Edgware

N

Canons
Park

Burnt Oak

C

Headstone
Lane

J

Colindale

N

Queensbury

1

2

2 m. (1:70,000)

1

2

3 km.

J   JUBILEE
N   NORTHERN

24

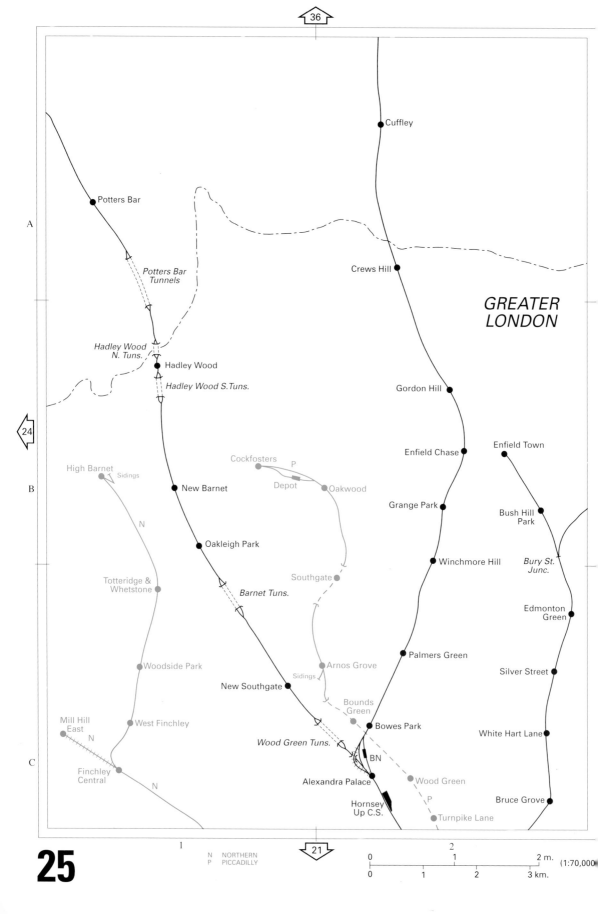

Cuffley

Potters Bar

A

Potters Bar
Tunnels

Crews Hill

*GREATER
LONDON*

Hadley Wood
N. Tuns.

Hadley Wood

Hadley Wood S.Tuns.

Gordon Hill

24

B

High Barnet   Sidings

Cockfosters   P

Depot   Oakwood

New Barnet

Enfield Chase

Enfield Town

Grange Park

Bush Hill
Park

N

Oakleigh Park

Winchmore Hill

*Bury St.
Junc.*

Totteridge &
Whetstone

Barnet Tuns.

Southgate

Edmonton
Green

Woodside Park

Arnos Grove

Palmers Green

Silver Street

Sidings

Mill Hill
East

West Finchley

New Southgate

Bounds
Green

Bowes Park

White Hart Lane

C

N

Wood Green Tuns.

BN

Finchley
Central   N

Alexandra Palace

Wood Green

Bruce Grove

Hornsey
Up C.S.

P

Turnpike Lane

25

1

N   NORTHERN
P   PICCADILLY

2

0   1   2 m.

0   1   2   3 km.

(1:70,000)

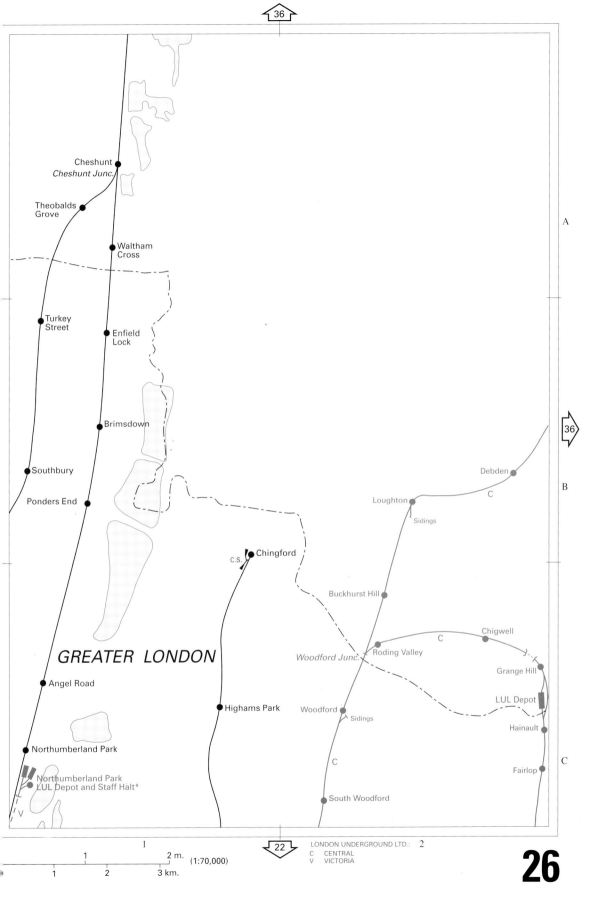

Cheshunt
Cheshunt Junc.

Theobalds
Grove

Waltham
Cross

A

Turkey
Street

Enfield
Lock

36

Brimsdown

Debden

Loughton

B

C

Sidings

Southbury

Ponders End

C.S. Chingford

Buckhurst Hill

Chigwell

C

Woodford Junc. Roding Valley

GREATER LONDON

Grange Hill

LUL Depot

Angel Road

Highams Park

Woodford

Hainault

Sidings

Northumberland Park

Fairlop

C

Northumberland Park
LUL Depot and Staff Halt*

C

V

South Woodford

1

1

2 m. (1:70,000)

1

2

3 km.

LONDON UNDERGROUND LTD.: 2
C CENTRAL
V VICTORIA

26

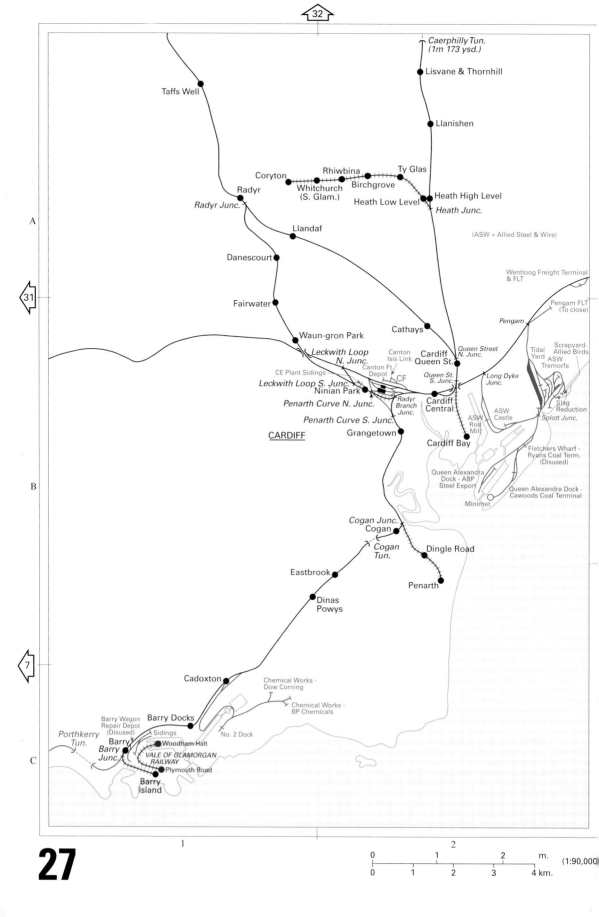

Caerphilly Tun.
(1m 173 ysd.)

Lisvane & Thornhill

Llanishen

Taffs Well

Coryton   Rhiwbina   Ty Glas
              Whitchurch   Birchgrove
Radyr   (S. Glam.)   Heath High Level
Radyr Junc.   Heath Low Level
                                      Heath Junc.

A

Llandaf

Danescourt   (ASW = Allied Steel & Wire)

Wentloog Freight Terminal
& FLT

31

Pengam FLT
(To close)

Fairwater   *Pengam*

Cathays   *Queen Street*   Tidal Yard   Scrapyard-
Waun-gron Park   *N. Junc.*   Allied Birds
       Leckwith Loop   Canton   Cardiff   ASW
         N. Junc.   Isis Link   Queen St.   Tremorfa
    CE Plant Sidings   Canton Ft.   *Queen St.*   Long Dyke
Leckwith Loop S. Junc. Depot   CF   *S. Junc.*   *Junc.*   Slag
              Ninian Park   Cardiff   Reduction
     Penarth Curve N. Junc. Radyr Central   ASW   *Splott Junc.*
                         Branch   Rod   ASW
        Penarth Curve S. Junc. Junc. Mill   Castle
                                      Cardiff Bay
CARDIFF   Grangetown   Fletchers Wharf -
                                          Ryans Coal Term.
                                          (Disused)
B   Queen Alexandra
                            Dock - ABP   Queen Alexandra Dock -
                            Steel Export   Cawoods Coal Terminal
                                   Minimet

Cogan Junc.
Cogan
Cogan   Dingle Road
Eastbrook   *Tun.*
                  Penarth
Dinas
Powys

7

Cadoxton   Chemical Works -
                  Dow Corning
                         Chemical Works -
Barry Wagon   BP Chemicals
Repair Depot   Barry Docks
(Disused)   Sidings   No. 2 Dock
Porthkerry Barry   Woodham Halt
Tun.   *Junc.* *VALE OF GLAMORGAN*
                 RAILWAY
C   Barry   Plymouth Road
          Island

27

1   2

0   1   2   m.
                                      (1:90,000)
0   1   2   3   4 km.

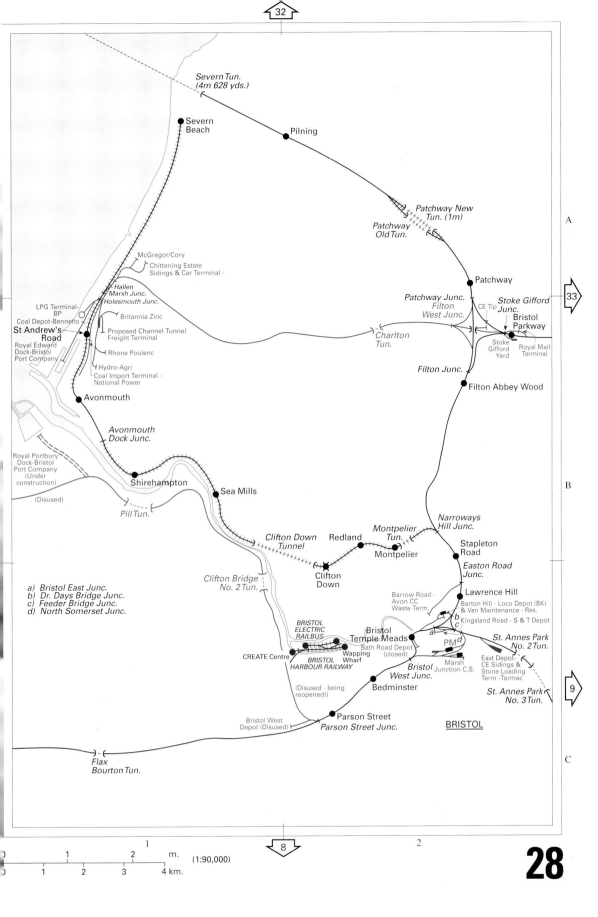

Severn Tun.
(4m 628 yds.)

Severn
Beach

Pilning

Patchway New
Tun. (1m)

Patchway
Old Tun.

A

Patchway

McGregor/Cory
Chittening Estate
Sidings & Car Terminal -

Hallen
Marsh Junc.
Holesmouth Junc.

Patchway Junc.
Filton
West Junc.

CE Tip

Stoke Gifford
Junc.

Bristol
Parkway

33

LPG Terminal-
BP
Coal Depot-Bennetts

Britannia Zinc

Charlton
Tun.

Stoke
Gifford
Yard

Royal Mail
Terminal

St Andrew's
Road

Proposed Channel Tunnel
Freight Terminal

Royal Edward
Dock-Bristol
Port Company

Rhone Poulenc

Filton Junc.

Hydro-Agri

Avonmouth

Coal Import Terminal -
National Power

Filton Abbey Wood

Avonmouth
Dock Junc.

B

Royal Portbury
Dock-Bristol
Port Company
(Under
construction)

Shirehampton

Sea Mills

(Disused)

Pill Tun.

Narroways
Hill Junc.

Montpelier
Tun.

Stapleton
Road

Clifton Down
Tunnel

Redland

Montpelier

Easton Road
Junc.

Clifton Bridge
No. 2 Tun.

Clifton
Down

Lawrence Hill

Barrow Road -
Avon CC
Waste Term.

Barton Hill - Loco Depot (BK)
& Van Maintenance - Res.

Kingsland Road - S & T Depot

a) Bristol East Junc.
b) Dr. Days Bridge Junc.
c) Feeder Bridge Junc.
d) North Somerset Junc.

BRISTOL
ELECTRIC
RAILBUS

CREATE Centre

BRISTOL
HARBOUR RAILWAY

Wapping
Wharf

Bristol
Temple Meads

Bath Road Depot
(closed)

b

c

a

PM

d

St. Annes Park
No. 2 Tun.

East Depot-
CE Sidings &
Stone Loading
Term -Tarmac

Marsh
Junction C.S.

Bristol
West Junc.

(Disused - being
reopened))

Bedminster

St. Annes Park
No. 3 Tun.

9

Bristol West
Depot (Disused)

Parson Street
Parson Street Junc.

BRISTOL

C

Flax
Bourton Tun.

1

m.

(1:90,000)

2

1   1   2

1   2   3   4 km.

28

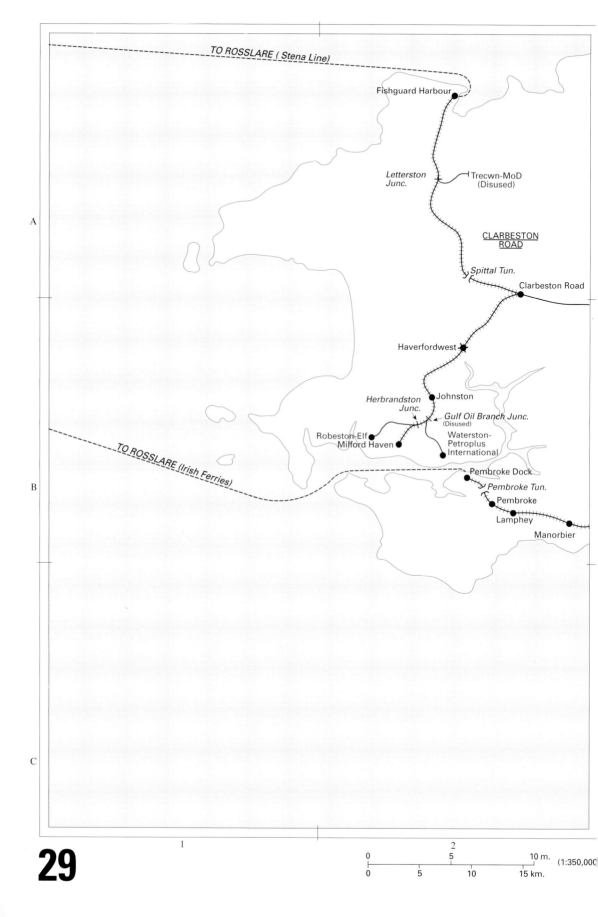

TO ROSSLARE (Stena Line)

Fishguard Harbour

Letterston Junc. ⊢ Trecwn-MoD
(Disused)

CLARBESTON
ROAD

Spittal Tun. Clarbeston Road

Haverfordwest

Herbrandston Junc. Johnston

Gulf Oil Branch Junc.
(Disused)

Robeston-Elf Waterston-
Milford Haven Petroplus
International

Pembroke Dock

TO ROSSLARE (Irish Ferries) *Pembroke Tun.*

Pembroke
Lamphey

Manorbier

A

B

C

1

29

0
0

2
5

10 m.

(1:350,000

0
0

5
5

10
15 km.

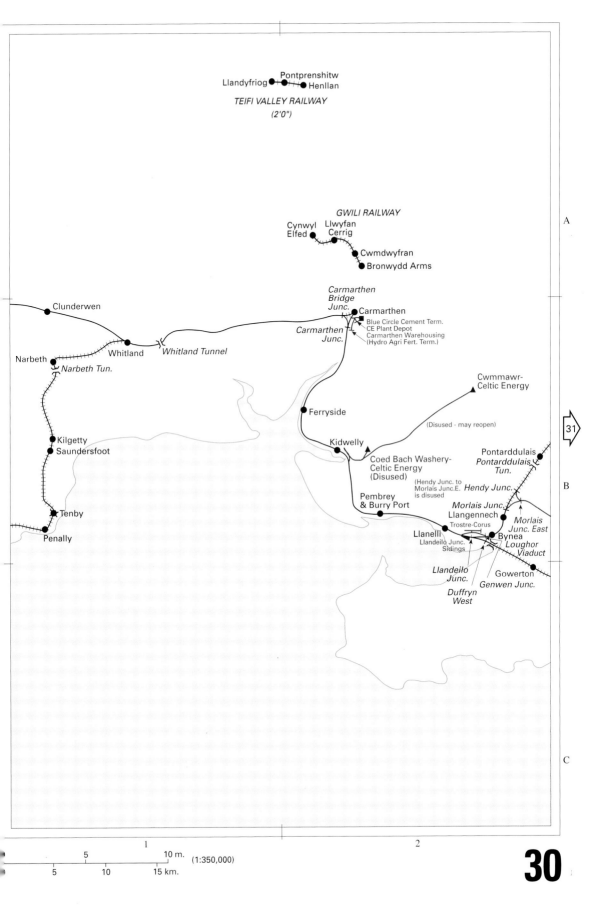

Llandyfriog ● Pontprenshitw
● ● ● Henllan

TEIFI VALLEY RAILWAY
(2'0")

GWILI RAILWAY

Cynwyl ● Llwyfan
Elfed Cerrig
● Cwmdwyfran
● Bronwydd Arms

Clunderwen ●

Carmarthen Bridge Junc.
● Carmarthen
■ Blue Circle Cement Term.
CE Plant Depot
Carmarthen Warehousing
(Hydro Agri Fert. Term.)

Carmarthen Junc.

Narbeth ● Whitland ● *Whitland Tunnel*
Narbeth Tun.

Cwmmawr-
Celtic Energy ▲

(Disused - may reopen)

● Ferryside

Kidwelly ● ▲

Coed Bach Washery-
Celtic Energy
(Disused)

(Hendy Junc. to
Morlais Junc.E.
is disused)

Pontarddulais ●
Pontarddulais Tun.

● Kilgetty
● Saundersfoot

Pembrey
& Burry Port ●

Morlais Junc.
Llangennech ●
Trostre-Corus
Llanelli ●
Llandeilo Junc.
Sidings

Morlais Junc. East
● Bynea
Loughor Viaduct

● Tenby
Penally ●

Llandeilo Junc.
Gowerton ●
Genwen Junc.
Duffryn West

A

31

B

C

1   2

5   10 m.
‖‖‖‖ ‖‖‖ (1:350,000)
5   10   15 km.

30

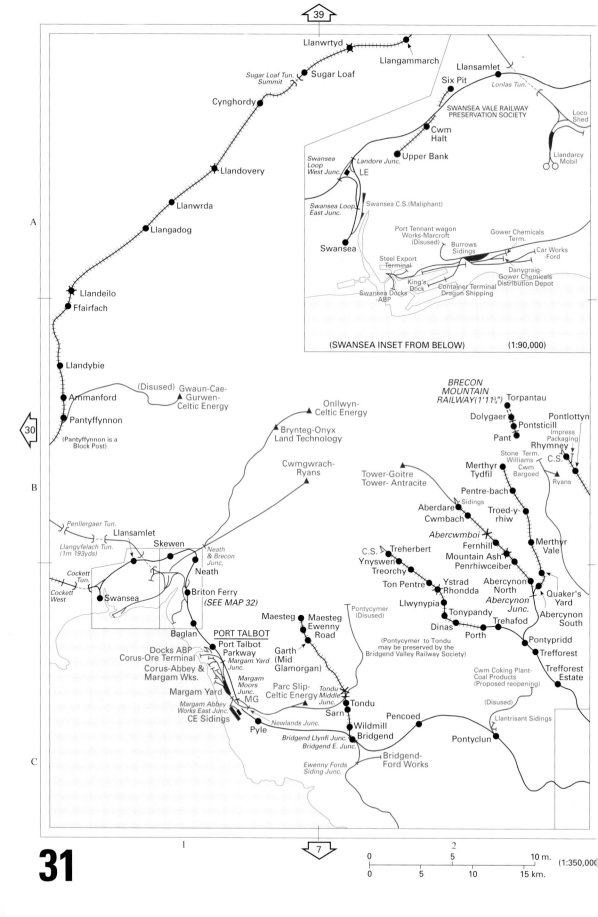

Llanwrtyd

Llangammarch

Llansamlet

Six Pit

Lonlas Tun.

Sugar Loaf Tun. Summit

Sugar Loaf

Loco Shed

Swansea Loop West Junc.

LE

Landore Junc.

Cwm Halt

Upper Bank

SWANSEA VALE RAILWAY PRESERVATION SOCIETY

Llandarcy Mobil

Cynghordy

Swansea Loop East Junc.

Swansea C.S.(Maliphant)

Swansea

Llandovery

Port Tennant wagon Works-Marcroft (Disused)

Burrows Sidings

Gower Chemicals Term.

Car Works -Ford

Steel Export Terminal

King's Dock

Container Terminal Dragon Shipping

Danygraig- Gower Chemicals Distribution Depot

Swansea Docks -ABP

(SWANSEA INSET FROM BELOW) (1:90,000)

Llanwrda

A

Llangadog

BRECON MOUNTAIN RAILWAY(1'11¾") Torpantau

Llandeilo

Ffairfach

(Disused) Gwaun-Cae- ▲ Gurwen- Celtic Energy

Onllwyn- ▲ Celtic Energy

Dolygaer

Pontsticill

Pontlottyn

Pant

Impress Packaging

Rhymney C.S.

Stone Term. Williams

Cwm Bargoed

Llandybie

Brynteg-Onyx ▲ Land Technology

Merthyr Tydfil

Ryans

Ammanford

Pantyffynnon

30

Cwmgwrach- ▲ Ryans

Pentre-bach

Tower-Goitre ▲ Tower- Antracite

Aberdare ↗ Sidings

Cwmbach

Troed-y- rhiw

(Pantyffynnon is a Block Post)

Abercwmboi ✦

Merthyr Vale

Fernhill

B

C.S. ✦ Treherbert

Mountain Ash Penrhiwceiber

Penllergaer Tun.

Ynyswen

Treorchy

Llangyfelach Tun. (1m 193yds)

Llansamlet

Skewen

Neath & Brecon Junc.

Ton Pentre

Ystrad Rhondda

Abercynon North

Abercynon Junc.

Quaker's Yard

Neath

Llwynypia

Cockett Tun.

Cockett West

Swansea

Briton Ferry

(SEE MAP 32)

Tonypandy

Dinas

Porth

Trehafod

Abercynon South

Maesteg

Maesteg Ewenny Road

Pontycymer (Disused)

Pontypridd

Trefforest

Baglan

PORT TALBOT

Garth (Mid Glamorgan)

(Pontycymer to Tondu may be preserved by the Bridgend Valley Railway Society)

Trefforest Estate

Port Talbot Parkway

Docks ABP Corus-Ore Terminal

Margam Yard Junc.

Cwm Coking Plant- Coal Products (Proposed reopening)

Corus-Abbey & Margam Wks.

Margam Moors Junc.

Parc Slip- ▲ Celtic Energy

Tondu Middle Junc.

Llantrisant Sidings

Margam Yard

MG

Tondu

(Disused)

Margam Abbey Works East Junc.

CE Sidings

Sarn

Pencoed

Newlands Junc.

Pyle

Wildmill

Bridgend

Pontyclun

C

Bridgend Llynfi Junc.

Bridgend E. Junc.

Bridgend- Ford Works

Ewenny Fords Siding Junc.

| 0 | | 5 | | 10 m. | (1:350,000 |

| 0 | 5 | 10 | 15 km. |

31

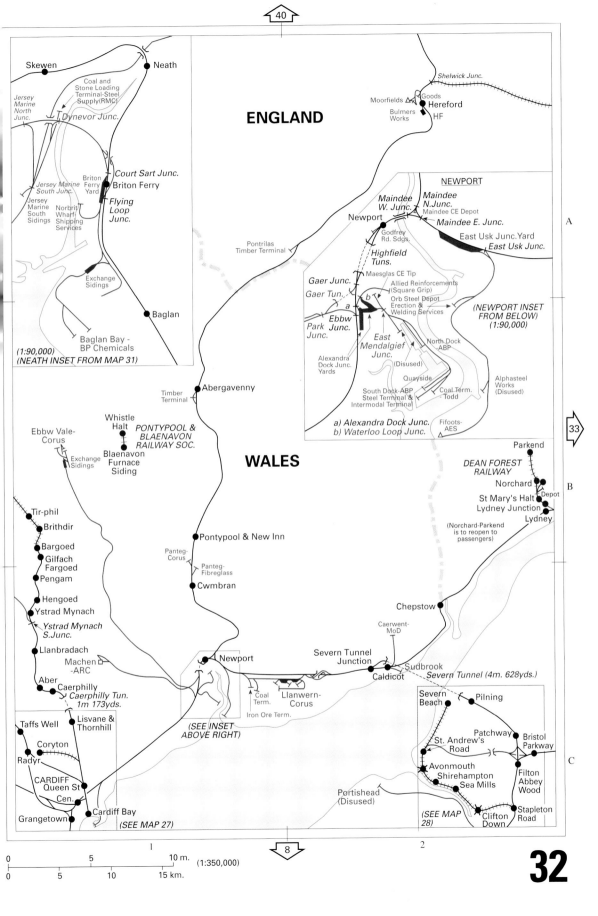

ENGLAND

Skewen Neath

Shelwick Junc.

Coal and
Stone Loading
Terminal-Steel
Supply(RMC)

Moorfields △ Goods
Hereford
Bulmers HF
Works

Jersey
Marine
North
Junc.

Dynevor Junc.

NEWPORT

Briton
Ferry Yard
Court Sart Junc.
Briton Ferry

Maindee Maindee
W. Junc. N.Junc.
Maindee CE Depot

Jersey Marine
South Junc.

Flying
Loop
Junc.

Newport Maindee E. Junc.

Jersey
Marine
South
Sidings

Norbrit
Wharf-
Shipping
Services

Godfrey
Rd. Sdgs.
East Usk Junc.Yard
East Usk Junc.

A

Pontrilas
Timber Terminal

Highfield
Tuns.

Exchange
Sidings

Maesglas CE Tip

Gaer Junc. Allied Reinforcements
(Square Grip)

Gaer Tun. Orb Steel Depot
Erection &
Welding Services

Baglan

a

b

Ebbw
Park Junc.
Junc.

East
Mendalgief
Junc.

North Dock
-ABP

(NEWPORT INSET
FROM BELOW)
(1:90,000)

Baglan Bay -
BP Chemicals

Alexandra
Dock Junc.
Yards

(Disused)

Quayside

Alphasteel
Works
(Disused)

(1:90,000)
(NEATH INSET FROM MAP 31)

South Dock-ABP
Steel Terminal &
Intermodal Terminal

Coal Term.
Todd

33

Timber
Terminal
Abergavenny

a) Alexandra Dock Junc.
b) Waterloo Loop Junc.

Fifoots-
AES △

Whistle
Halt

Parkend

WALES

*PONTYPOOL &
BLAENAVON
RAILWAY SOC.*

*DEAN FOREST
RAILWAY*

Ebbw Vale-
Corus

Norchard

B

Exchange
Sidings

Blaenavon
Furnace
Siding

Depot
St Mary's Halt
Lydney Junction

Lydney

(Norchard-Parkend
is to reopen to
passengers)

Tir-phil

Pontypool & New Inn

Brithdir

Bargoed

Panteg-
Corus

Gilfach
Fargoed

Panteg-
Fibreglass

Pengam

Cwmbran

Hengoed

Ystrad Mynach

Chepstow

Ystrad Mynach
S.Junc.

Caerwent-
MoD

Llanbradach

Machen
-ARC

Newport

Severn Tunnel
Junction

Sudbrook

Aber

Severn Tunnel (4m. 628yds.)

Caerphilly

Coal
Term.
Llanwern-
Corus

Caldicot

Caerphilly Tun.
1m 173yds.

Lisvane &
Thornhill

Severn
Beach

Pilning

Iron Ore Term.

Taffs Well

Patchway

Bristol
Parkway

Coryton

St. Andrew's
Road

(SEE INSET
ABOVE RIGHT)

Radyr

Avonmouth
Shirehampton
Sea Mills

Filton
Abbey
Wood

C

CARDIFF
Queen St
Cen.

Portishead
(Disused)

Stapleton
Road

Grangetown Cardiff Bay

(SEE MAP
28)

Clifton
Down

(SEE MAP 27)

I 10 m.
0 5
(1:350,000)
0 5 10 15 km.

2

32

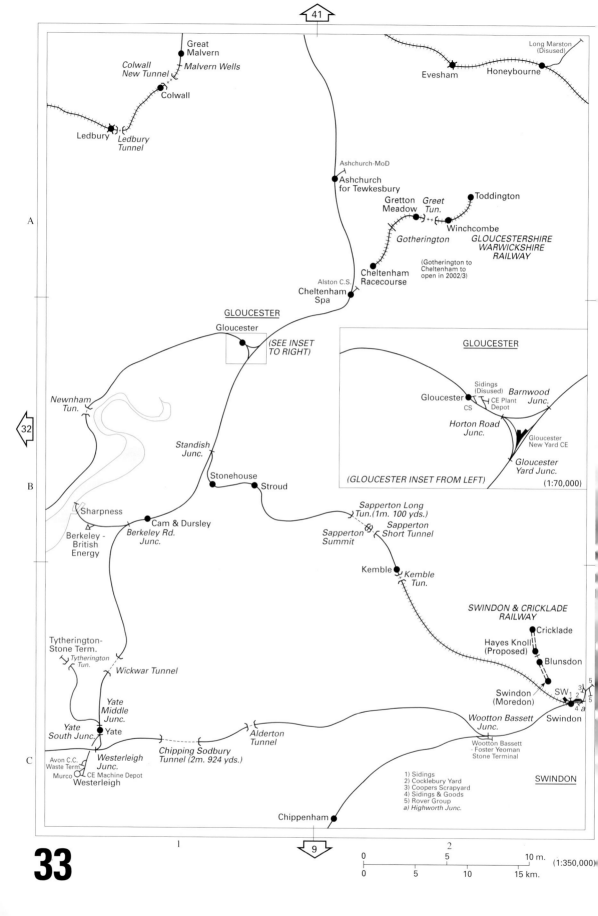

Great Malvern
Malvern Wells
Colwall New Tunnel
Colwall
Ledbury
Ledbury Tunnel

Long Marston (Disused)
Evesham
Honeybourne

Ashchurch-MoD
Ashchurch for Tewkesbury
Gretton Meadow
Greet Tun.
Toddington
Winchcombe
Gotherington

A

GLOUCESTERSHIRE WARWICKSHIRE RAILWAY
(Gotherington to Cheltenham to open in 2002/3)

Cheltenham Racecourse
Alston C.S.
Cheltenham Spa

GLOUCESTER

Gloucester
(SEE INSET TO RIGHT)

GLOUCESTER

Gloucester
CS
Sidings (Disused)
CE Plant Depot
Barnwood Junc.

Horton Road Junc.
Gloucester New Yard CE

Newnham Tun.

32

Gloucester Yard Junc.

(GLOUCESTER INSET FROM LEFT)
(1:70,000)

B

Standish Junc.
Stonehouse
Stroud

Sharpness
Berkeley - British Energy

Cam & Dursley
Berkeley Rd. Junc.

Sapperton Long Tun.(1m. 100 yds.)
Sapperton Short Tunnel
Sapperton Summit
Kemble
Kemble Tun.

SWINDON & CRICKLADE RAILWAY

Cricklade
Hayes Knoll (Proposed)
Blunsdon

Tytherington-Stone Term.
Tytherington Tun.
Wickwar Tunnel

Yate Middle Junc.
Yate South Junc.
Yate

Swindon (Moredon)
SW 1 2 3 4 5
a
Swindon

Wootton Bassett Junc.
Wootton Bassett - Foster Yeoman Stone Terminal

C

Avon C.C. Waste Term.
Murco
CE Machine Depot
Westerleigh Junc.
Westerleigh

Chipping Sodbury Tunnel (2m. 924 yds.)
Alderton Tunnel

1) Sidings
2) Cocklebury Yard
3) Coopers Scrapyard
4) Sidings & Goods
5) Rover Group
a) Highworth Junc.

SWINDON

Chippenham

0   5 — 2 — 10 m.   (1:350,000)
0   5   10   15 km.

33

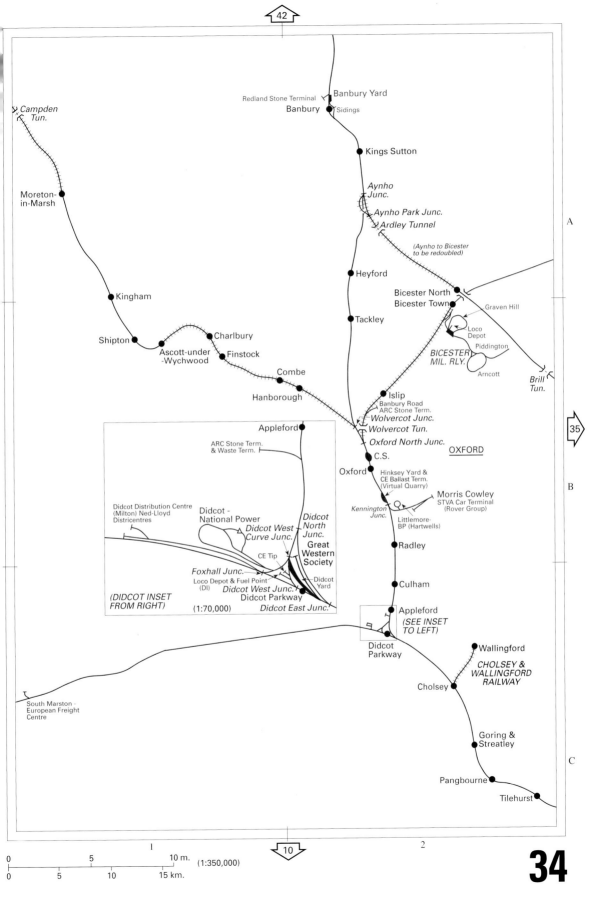

42

Redland Stone Terminal
Banbury Yard
Banbury · Sidings

Kings Sutton

Aynho Junc.
Aynho Park Junc.
Ardley Tunnel

(Aynho to Bicester
to be redoubled)

Heyford

Bicester North
Bicester Town · Graven Hill
Loco Depot
Piddington
BICESTER MIL. RLY.
Arncott

Tackley

Brill Tun.

A

Campden Tun.

Moreton-in-Marsh

Kingham

Charlbury

Shipton · Ascott-under-Wychwood · Finstock

Combe

Hanborough

Islip
Banbury Road
ARC Stone Term.
Wolvercot Junc.
Wolvercot Tun.
Oxford North Junc.
C.S.
OXFORD

Oxford · Hinksey Yard &
CE Ballast Term.
(Virtual Quarry)

Morris Cowley
STVA Car Terminal
(Rover Group)

Kennington Junc.
Littlemore-
BP (Hartwells)

35

B

Appleford

Radley

Culham

Didcot Distribution Centre
(Milton) Ned-Lloyd
Districentres

ARC Stone Term.
& Waste Term.

Didcot -
National Power

Didcot
Didcot West Curve Junc.

Didcot North Junc.

Great Western Society

CE Tip
Foxhall Junc.
Loco Depot & Fuel Point
(DI)
Didcot West Junc.
Didcot Parkway
Didcot East Junc.

Didcot Yard

(DIDCOT INSET FROM RIGHT)
(1:70,000)

Appleford
(SEE INSET TO LEFT)

Didcot Parkway

Wallingford
CHOLSEY & WALLINGFORD RAILWAY

South Marston -
European Freight
Centre

Cholsey

Goring & Streatley

C

Pangbourne

Tilehurst

0   5   10 m. (1:350,000)
0   5   10   15 km.

1   10   2

34

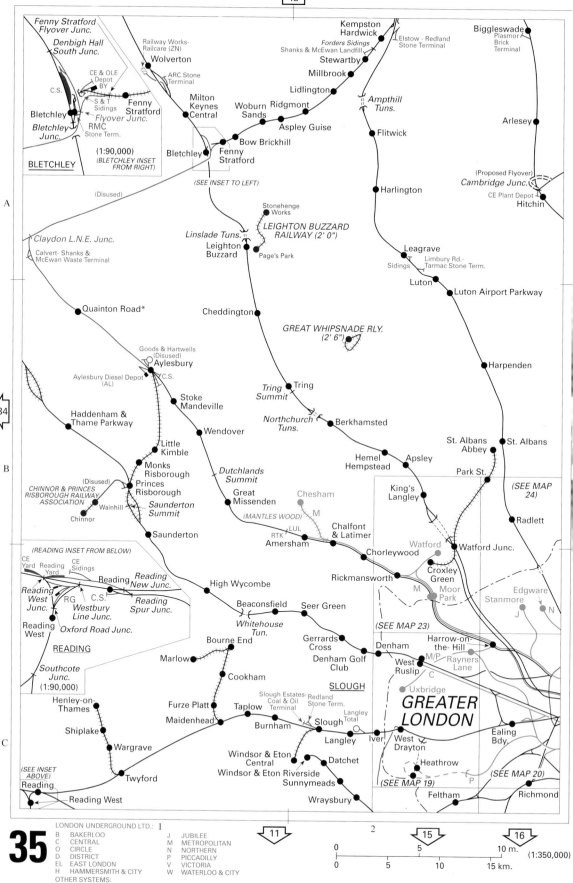

BLETCHLEY (inset)

Fenny Stratford
Flyover Junc.
Denbigh Hall
South Junc.
Railway Works-
Railcare (ZN)
Wolverton
CE & OLE
Depot
BY
ARC Stone
Terminal
C.S.
S & T
Sidings
Fenny
Stratford
Flyover Junc.
Bletchley
RMC
Bletchley
Junc.
Stone Term.
(1:90,000)
(BLETCHLEY INSET
FROM RIGHT)
BLETCHLEY

Kempston
Hardwick
Forders Sidings
Shanks & McEwan Landfill
Elstow - Redland
Stone Terminal
Stewartby
Millbrook
Milton
Keynes
Central
Lidlington
Woburn
Sands
Ridgmont
Ampthill
Tuns.
Aspley Guise
Flitwick
Bow Brickhill
Bletchley
Fenny
Stratford
(SEE INSET TO LEFT)
Harlington

Bigglesswade
Plasmor
Brick
Terminal
Arlesey
(Proposed Flyover)
Cambridge Junc.
CE Plant Depot
Hitchin
(Disused)
Claydon L.N.E. Junc.
Calvert- Shanks &
McEwan Waste Terminal

Stonehenge
Works
LEIGHTON BUZZARD
RAILWAY (2' 0")
Linslade Tuns.
Leighton
Buzzard
Page's Park
Leagrave
Limbury Rd.-
Sidings Tarmac Stone Term.
Luton
Luton Airport Parkway
Quainton Road*
Cheddington
GREAT WHIPSNADE RLY.
(2' 6")
Harpenden
Goods & Hartwells
(Disused)
Aylesbury
Aylesbury Diesel Depot
(AL)
C.S.
Stoke
Mandeville
Tring
Summit
Tring
Haddenham &
Thame Parkway
Wendover
Northchurch
Tuns.
Berkhamsted
St. Albans
Abbey
St. Albans
Little
Kimble
Monks
Risborough
Dutchlands
Summit
Hemel
Hempstead
Apsley
Park St.
(Disused)
CHINNOR & PRINCES
RISBOROUGH RAILWAY
ASSOCIATION
Wainhill
Chinnor
Princes
Risborough
Saunderton
Summit
Great
Missenden
Chesham
M
(MANTLES WOOD)
RTK
LUL
Chalfont
& Latimer
King's
Langley
(SEE MAP
24)
Radlett
Saunderton
Amersham
Chorleywood
Watford
Watford Junc.
Edgware
Stanmore
J   N
(READING INSET FROM BELOW)
CE
Yard
Reading
Yard
CE
Sidings
Reading
New Junc.
Reading
West Junc.
RG
C.S.
Westbury
Line Junc.
Reading
Spur Junc.
Reading
West
Oxford Road Junc.
READING
Southcote
Junc.
(1:90,000)
High Wycombe
Beaconsfield
Whitehouse
Tun.
Seer Green
Rickmansworth
Croxley
Green
Moor
Park
M
(SEE MAP 23)
Harrow-on-
the- Hill
M/P
Rayners
Lane
Gerrards
Cross
Denham
C
Denham Golf
Club
West
Ruslip
Uxbridge
GREATER
LONDON
Henley-on-
Thames
Bourne End
Marlow
Cookham
Furze Platt
Maidenhead
Taplow
Slough Estates
Coal & Oil
Terminal
Redland
Stone Term.
SLOUGH
Langley
Total
Shiplake
Wargrave
Burnham
Slough
Langley
Iver
West
Drayton
Ealing
Bdy.
Twyford
Windsor & Eton
Central
Windsor & Eton Riverside
Datchet
Heathrow
(SEE MAP 20)
(SEE INSET
ABOVE)
Reading
Sunnymeads
(SEE MAP 19)
P
Reading West
Wraysbury
Feltham
Richmond

LONDON UNDERGROUND LTD.:
B   BAKERLOO   J   JUBILEE
C   CENTRAL   M   METROPOLITAN
O   CIRCLE   N   NORTHERN
D   DISTRICT   P   PICCADILLY
EL   EAST LONDON   V   VICTORIA
H   HAMMERSMITH & CITY W   WATERLOO & CITY
OTHER SYSTEMS:
CT   CROYDON TRAMLINK   DL   DOCKLANDS

0   5   10 m.
0   5   10   15 km.
(1:350,000)

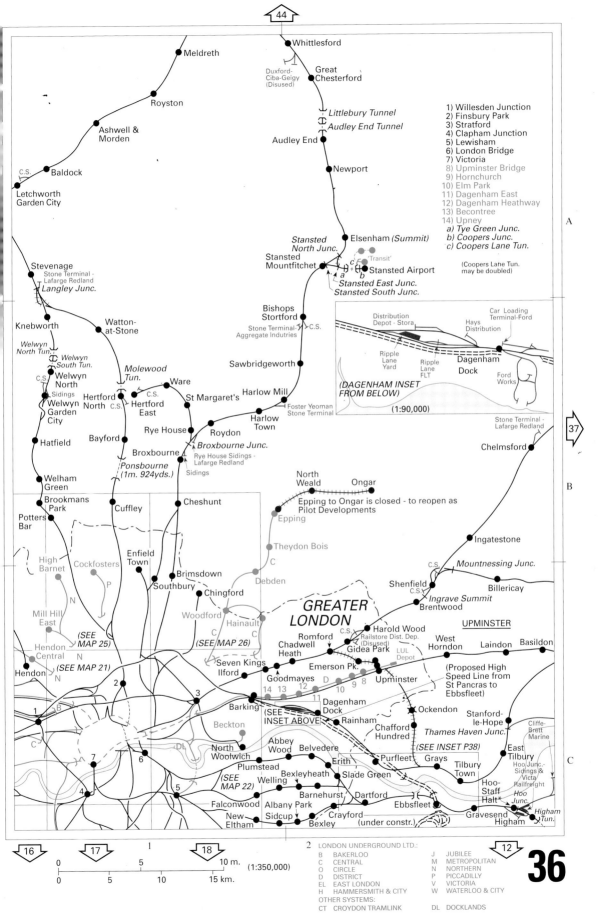

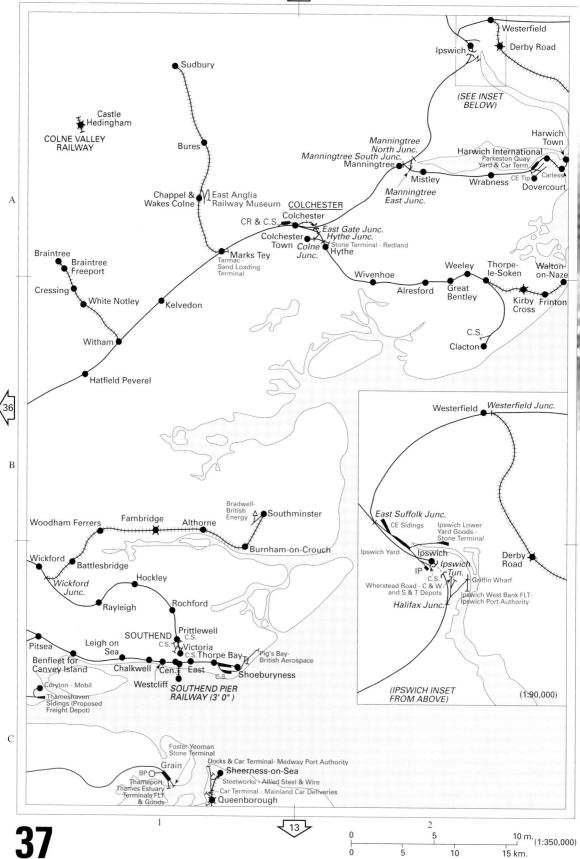

Westerfield

Ipswich

Derby Road

(SEE INSET BELOW)

Sudbury

Castle
Hedingham
COLNE VALLEY
RAILWAY

Bures

Chappel &
Wakes Colne

East Anglia
Railway Museum

COLCHESTER

Colchester

CR & C.S.

Colchester
Town

East Gate Junc.

Hythe Junc.

Stone Terminal - Redland

*Colne
Junc.*

Hythe

*Manningtree
North Junc.*

Manningtree South Junc.

Manningtree

*Manningtree
East Junc.*

Mistley

Harwich
Town

Harwich International

Parkeston Quay
Yard & Car Term.

Wrabness

CE Tip

Carless

Dovercourt

Marks Tey

Tarmac -
Sand Loading
Terminal

Braintree

Braintree
Freeport

Cressing

White Notley

Kelvedon

Wivenhoe

Alresford

Great
Bentley

Weeley

Thorpe-
le-Soken

Walton-
on-Naze

Kirby
Cross

Frinton

Witham

Hatfield Peverel

C.S.

Clacton

A

B

Westerfield

Westerfield Junc.

Bradwell-
British Energy

Southminster

East Suffolk Junc.

CE Sidings

Ipswich Lower
Yard Goods -
Stone Terminal

Woodham Ferrers

Fambridge

Althorne

Ipswich Yard

Ipswich

IP

Derby
Road

Burnham-on-Crouch

*Ipswich
Tun.*

Wickford

Battlesbridge

Hockley

C.S.

Griffin Wharf

Wherstead Road - C & W
and S & T Depots

Ipswich West Bank FLT-
Ipswich Port Authority

*Wickford
Junc.*

Rayleigh

Rochford

Halifax Junc.

Pitsea

Leigh on
Sea

SOUTHEND

Prittlewell

C.S.

C.S.

Victoria

Benfleet for
Canvey Island

Chalkwell

Cen.

C.S.Thorpe Bay

East

*Pig's Bay-
British Aerospace*

Westcliff

*SOUTHEND PIER
RAILWAY (3' 0")*

Shoeburyness

C.S.

Coryton - Mobil

Thameshaven
Sidings (Proposed
Freight Depot)

*(IPSWICH INSET
FROM ABOVE)*

(1:90,000)

C

Foster Yeoman
Stone Terminal

Grain

BP

Thameport
Thames Estuary
Terminals FLT
& Goods

Docks & Car Terminal- Medway Port Authority

Sheerness-on-Sea

Steelworks - Allied Steel & Wire

Car Terminal - Mainland Car Deliveries

Queenborough

1

2

0   5   10 m.

(1:350,000)

0   5   10   15 km.

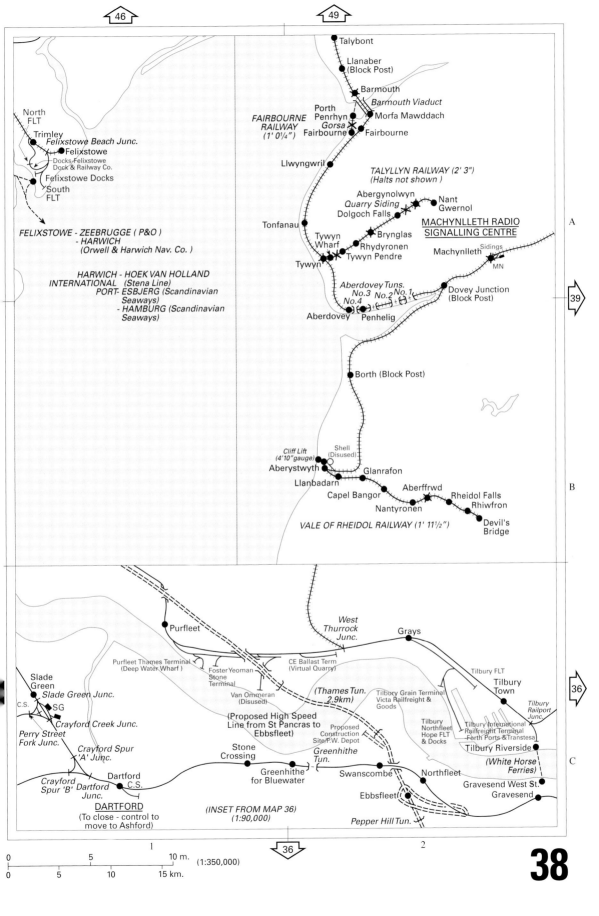

Talybont
Llanaber
(Block Post)
Barmouth
Barmouth Viaduct
Porth
Penrhyn
Morfa Mawddach
FAIRBOURNE
RAILWAY
(1' 0¼")
Gorsa
Fairbourne
Fairbourne

North
FLT
Trimley
Felixstowe Beach Junc.
Felixstowe
Docks-Felixstowe
Dock & Railway Co.
Felixstowe Docks
South
FLT

Llwyngwril

TALYLLYN RAILWAY (2' 3")
(Halts not shown)

Abergynolwyn
Quarry Siding
Nant
Gwernol
Dolgoch Falls

Tonfanau

MACHYNLLETH RADIO
SIGNALLING CENTRE

A

Brynglas
Tywyn
Wharf
Rhydyronen
Machynlleth
Sidings

FELIXSTOWE - ZEEBRUGGE (P&O)
- HARWICH
(Orwell & Harwich Nav. Co.)

Tywyn
Tywyn Pendre
MN

HARWICH - HOEK VAN HOLLAND
INTERNATIONAL   (Stena Line)
PORT- ESBJERG (Scandinavian
Seaways)
- HAMBURG (Scandinavian
Seaways)

Aberdovey Tuns.
No.3 No.2 *No.1*
No.4
Dovey Junction
(Block Post)

39

Aberdovey
Penhelig

Borth (Block Post)

Cliff Lift
(4'10"gauge)
Shell
(Disused)
Aberystwyth
Glanrafon

B

Llanbadarn
Aberffrwd
Rheidol Falls
Capel Bangor
Rhiwfron
Nantyronen
Devil's
Bridge

VALE OF RHEIDOL RAILWAY (1' 11½")

Purfleet
West
Thurrock
Junc.
Grays

Tilbury FLT

Purfleet Thames Terminal
(Deep Water Wharf)
Foster Yeoman
Stone
Terminal
CE Ballast Term
(Virtual Quarry)
Tilbury
Town

Slade
Green
Slade Green Junc.
C.S.
SG
Crayford Creek Junc.
Van Ommeran
(Disused)
(Thames Tun.
2.9km)
Tilbury Grain Terminal
Victa Railfreight &
Goods
Tilbury
Railport
Junc.

Perry Street
Fork Junc.
Crayford Spur
'A' Junc.
(Proposed High Speed
Line from St Pancras to
Ebbsfleet)
Proposed
Construction
Site/P.W. Depot
Tilbury
Northfleet
Hope FLT
& Docks
Tilbury International
Railfreight Terminal
Ferth Ports & Transtesa
Tilbury Riverside

Dartford
C.S.
Stone
Crossing
Greenhithe
Tun.
(White Horse
Ferries)

C

Crayford
Spur 'B'
Dartford
Junc.
Greenhithe
for Bluewater
Swanscombe
Northfleet
Gravesend West St.
Gravesend

DARTFORD
(To close - control to
move to Ashford)
(INSET FROM MAP 36)
(1:90,000)
Ebbsfleet
Pepper Hill Tun.

36

1   10 m.   (1:350,000)

0   5
0   5   10   15 km.

1

2

38

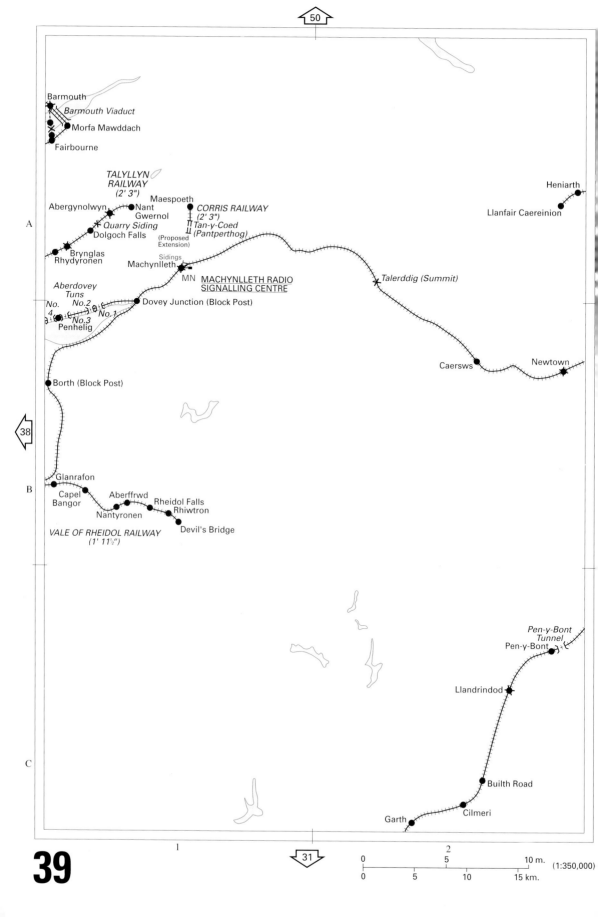

Barmouth
Barmouth Viaduct
Morfa Mawddach
Fairbourne

*TALYLLYN
RAILWAY
(2' 3")*

Maespoeth

*CORRIS RAILWAY
(2' 3")*

Abergynolwyn
Nant
Gwernol
Quarry Siding
Dolgoch Falls
Tan-y-Coed
(Pantperthog)
(Proposed
Extension)

Heniarth

Llanfair Caereinion

A

Brynglas
Rhydyronen

Sidings
Machynlleth

MN **MACHYNLLETH RADIO
SIGNALLING CENTRE**

Talerddig (Summit)

*Aberdovey
Tuns*
No. *No.2*
No.1
No.
4
No.3
Penhelig

Dovey Junction (Block Post)

38

Borth (Block Post)

Caersws

Newtown

B

Glanrafon
Capel
Bangor
Aberffrwd
Rheidol Falls
Nantyronen
Rhiwtron
Devil's Bridge

*VALE OF RHEIDOL RAILWAY
(1' 11½")*

Pen-y-Bont
Tunnel
Pen-y-Bont

Llandrindod

C

Builth Road

Garth
Cilmeri

39

1

0   2
          5
              10 m.   (1:350,000)

0   5   10
           15 km.

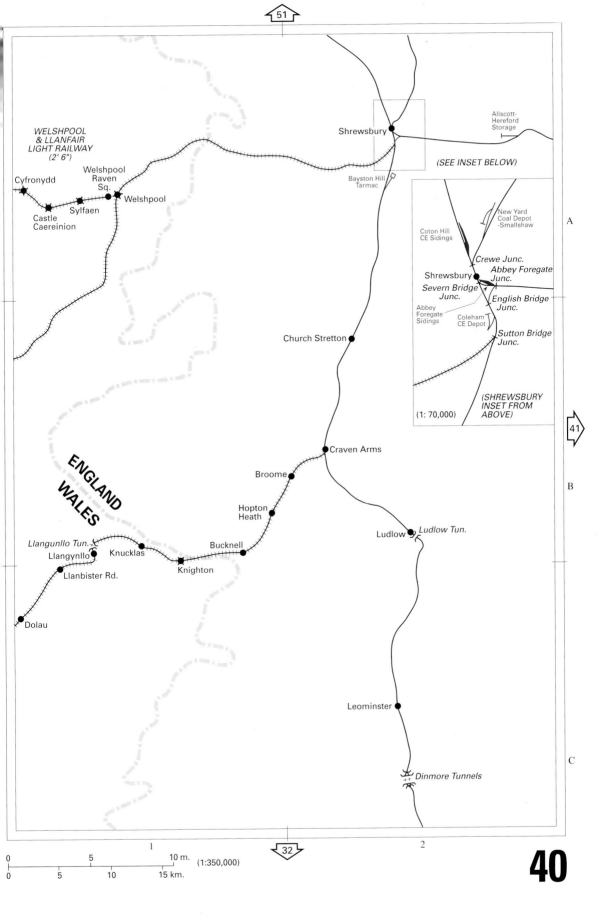

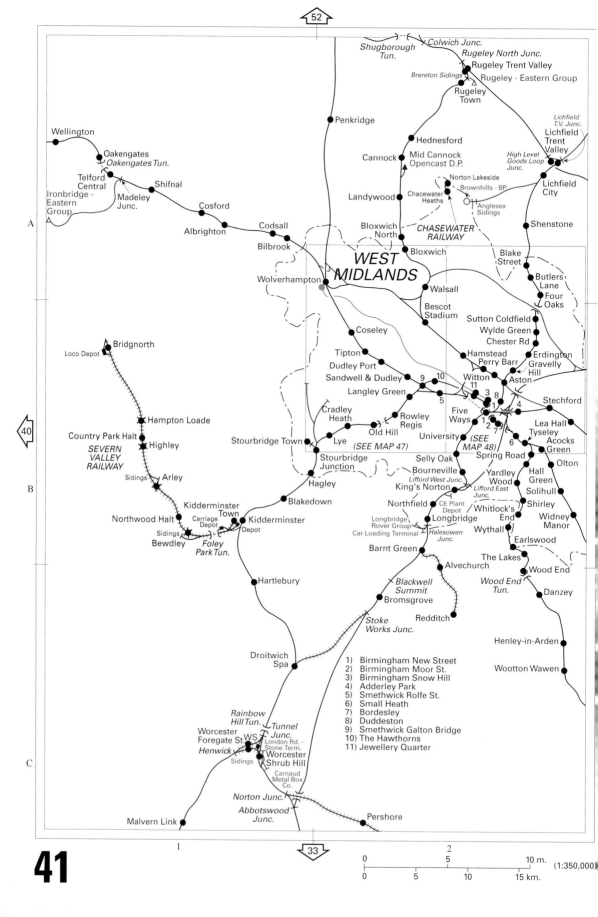

Shugborough Tun.
Colwich Junc.
Rugeley North Junc.
Rugeley Trent Valley
Brereton Sidings
Rugeley - Eastern Group
Rugeley Town
Penkridge
Hednesford
Cannock
Mid Cannock Opencast D.P.
Landywood
Norton Lakeside
Brownhills - BP
Chacewater Heaths
Anglesea Sidings
Lichfield T.V. Junc.
Lichfield Trent Valley
High Level Goods Loop Junc.
Lichfield City
Wellington
Oakengates
Oakengates Tun.
Telford Central
Madeley Junc.
Shifnal
Ironbridge - Eastern Group
Cosford
Albrighton
Codsall
Bilbrook
Bloxwich North
CHASEWATER RAILWAY
Shenstone
Bloxwich
Blake Street
WEST MIDLANDS
Walsall
Butlers Lane
Four Oaks
Wolverhampton
Bescot Stadium
Sutton Coldfield
Wylde Green
Chester Rd
Coseley
Hamstead
Perry Barr
Erdington
Gravelly Hill
Aston
Bridgnorth
Loco Depot
Tipton
Dudley Port
Sandwell & Dudley
9
10
Witton
11
8
3
Stechford
Langley Green
5
Five Ways
1
4
Hampton Loade
Country Park Halt
Highley
SEVERN VALLEY RAILWAY
Arley
Sidings
Cradley Heath
Rowley Regis
Old Hill
Lye
University
(SEE MAP 47)
(SEE MAP 48)
2
6
7
Lea Hall
Tyseley
Acocks Green
Olton
Stourbridge Town
6
Kidderminster Town
Carriage Depot
Kidderminster
Depot
Northwood Halt
Sidings
Bewdley
Foley Park Tun.
Hagley
Blakedown
Stourbridge Junction
Selly Oak
Bourneville
Lifford West Junc.
King's Norton
Northfield
CE Plant Depot
Lifford East Junc.
Whitlock's End
Spring Road
Hall Green
Solihull
Shirley
Widney Manor
Hartlebury
Longbridge Rover Group
Car Loading Terminal
Longbridge
Halesowen Junc.
Wythall
Earlswood
Barnt Green
Alvechurch
The Lakes
Wood End
Blackwell Summit
Bromsgrove
Redditch
Wood End Tun.
Danzey
Stoke Works Junc.
Droitwich Spa
1) Birmingham New Street
2) Birmingham Moor St.
3) Birmingham Snow Hill
4) Adderley Park
5) Smethwick Rolfe St.
6) Small Heath
7) Bordesley
8) Duddeston
9) Smethwick Galton Bridge
10) The Hawthorns
11) Jewellery Quarter
Henley-in-Arden
Wootton Wawen
Rainbow Hill Tun.
Tunnel Junc.
Worcester Foregate St. WS
London Rd. - Stone Term.
Henwick
Sidings
Worcester Shrub Hill
Carnaud Metal Box Co.
Norton Junc.
Abbotswood Junc.
Malvern Link
Pershore

1
0
2
5
10 m.
(1:350,000)
0
5
10
15 km.

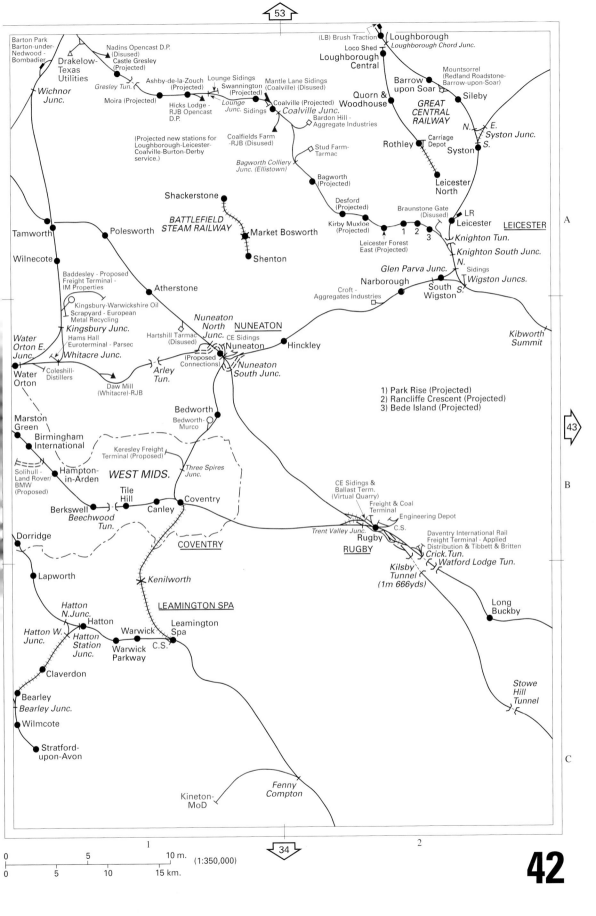

Barton Park
Barton-under-
Nedwood -
Bombardier

Drakelow-
Texas
Utilities

*Wichnor
Junc.*

Nadins Opencast D.P.
(Disused)
Castle Gresley
(Projected)

Gresley Tun.

Moira (Projected)

Ashby-de-la-Zouch
(Projected)

Lounge Sidings
(Projected)
Swannington
(Projected)

Hicks Lodge -
RJB Opencast
D.P.

*Lounge
Junc.* Sidings

Mantle Lane Sidings
(Coalville) (Disused)

Coalville (Projected)
Coalville Junc.

Bardon Hill -
Aggregate Industries

(LB) Brush Traction

Loco Shed

Loughborough
Loughborough Chord Junc.

Loughborough
Central

Barrow
upon Soar

Quorn &
Woodhouse

Mountsorrel
(Redland Roadstone-
Barrow-upon-Soar)

Sileby

GREAT
CENTRAL
RAILWAY

Rothley

Carriage
Depot

N. E.
Syston Junc.
S.

Syston

Leicester
North

(Projected new stations for
Loughborough-Leicester-
Coalville-Burton-Derby
service.)

Coalfields Farm
-RJB (Disused)

Stud Farm-
Tarmac

*Bagworth Colliery
Junc. (Ellistown)*

Bagworth
(Projected)

Shackerstone

BATTLEFIELD
STEAM RAILWAY

★ Market Bosworth

Shenton

Desford
(Projected)

Kirby Muxloe
(Projected)

Leicester Forest
East (Projected)

Braunstone Gate
(Disused)

LR

1 2
3

Leicester

LEICESTER

A

Knighton Tun.

Knighton South Junc.
N.

Tamworth

Polesworth

Wilnecote

Atherstone

Baddesley - Proposed
Freight Terminal -
IM Properties

Kingsbury-Warwickshire Oil
Scrapyard - European
Metal Recycling

Kingsbury Junc.

*Water
Orton E.
Junc.*

Whitacre Junc.

Water
Orton

Coleshill-
Distillers

Daw Mill
(Whitacre)-RJB

Hams Hall
Euroterminal - Parsec

*Nuneaton
North
Junc.*

NUNEATON

Hartshill Tarmac
(Disused)

CE Sidings

Nuneaton

(Proposed
Connections)

*Nuneaton
South Junc.*

*Arley
Tun.*

Hinckley

Narborough

Croft -
Aggregates Industries

Glen Parva Junc.

South
Wigston

Sidings
Wigston Juncs.
S.

*Kibworth
Summit*

1) Park Rise (Projected)
2) Rancliffe Crescent (Projected)
3) Bede Island (Projected)

43

B

Marston
Green

Birmingham
International

Solihull -
Land Rover/
BMW
(Proposed)

Hampton-
in-Arden

WEST MIDS.

Bedworth

Bedworth-
Murco

Keresley Freight
Terminal (Proposed)

*Three Spires
Junc.*

Berkswell
*Beechwood
Tun.*

Tile
Hill

Canley

Coventry

CE Sidings &
Ballast Term.
(Virtual Quarry)

Freight & Coal
Terminal

Engineering Depot

Trent Valley Junc.
C.S.

Rugby

RUGBY

Daventry International Rail
Freight Terminal - Applied
Distribution & Tibbett & Britten

Crick. Tun.

Watford Lodge Tun.

*Kilsby
Tunnel
(1m 666yds)*

Dorridge

COVENTRY

Lapworth

× Kenilworth

LEAMINGTON SPA

Long
Buckby

*Hatton
N. Junc.*

Hatton

*Hatton W.
Junc.*

*Hatton
Station
Junc.*

Warwick

Warwick
Parkway

C.S.

Leamington
Spa

Claverdon

Bearley
Bearley Junc.

Wilmcote

Stratford-
upon-Avon

*Stowe
Hill
Tunnel*

C

Kineton-
MoD

*Fenny
Compton*

1

0   5   10 m.
0   5   10   15 km.

(1:350,000)

2

42

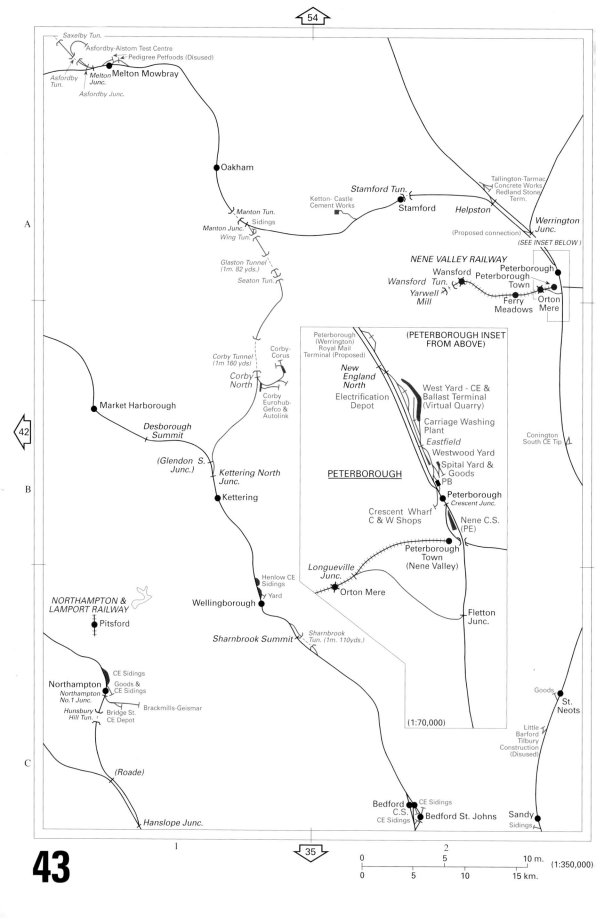

Saxelby Tun.
Asfordby-Alstom Test Centre
Pedigree Petfoods (Disused)
Asfordby Tun.
Melton Junc.
Asfordby Junc.
Melton Mowbray

Oakham

Stamford Tun.
Ketton- Castle Cement Works
Stamford
Helpston
Tallington-Tarmac Concrete Works Redland Stone Term.
Werrington Junc.
(Proposed connection)
(SEE INSET BELOW)

Manton Tun.
Sidings
Manton Junc.
Wing Tun.

Glaston Tunnel (1m. 82 yds.)
Seaton Tun.

A

NENE VALLEY RAILWAY
Wansford Tun.
Wansford
Yarwell Mill
Peterborough
Peterborough Town
Ferry Meadows
Orton Mere

42

Corby Tunnel (1m 160 yds)
Corby-Corus
Corby North
Corby Eurohub-Gefco & Autolink

Market Harborough

Desborough Summit

(Glendon S. Junc.)
Kettering North Junc.
Kettering

(PETERBOROUGH INSET FROM ABOVE)

Peterborough (Werrington) Royal Mail Terminal (Proposed)
New England North
Electrification Depot
West Yard - CE & Ballast Terminal (Virtual Quarry)
Carriage Washing Plant
Eastfield
Westwood Yard
Spital Yard & Goods
PB
Peterborough
Crescent Junc.
Coningsby South CE Tip
Nene C.S. (PE)

B

PETERBOROUGH

Crescent Wharf C & W Shops

Peterborough Town (Nene Valley)
Longueville Junc.
Orton Mere
Fletton Junc.

NORTHAMPTON & LAMPORT RAILWAY
Pitsford

Henlow CE Sidings
Yard
Wellingborough

Sharnbrook Summit
Sharnbrook Tun. (1m. 110yds.)

(1:70,000)

CE Sidings
Goods & CE Sidings
Northampton
Northampton No.1 Junc.
Hunsbury Hill Tun.
Bridge St. CE Depot
Brackmills-Geismar

Goods
St. Neots

Little Barford Tilbury Construction (Disused)

C

(Roade)

Hanslope Junc.

Bedford
C.S.
CE Sidings
CE Sidings
Bedford St. Johns

Sandy
Sidings

43

1   2

0   5   10 m.   (1:350,000)

0   5   10   15 km.

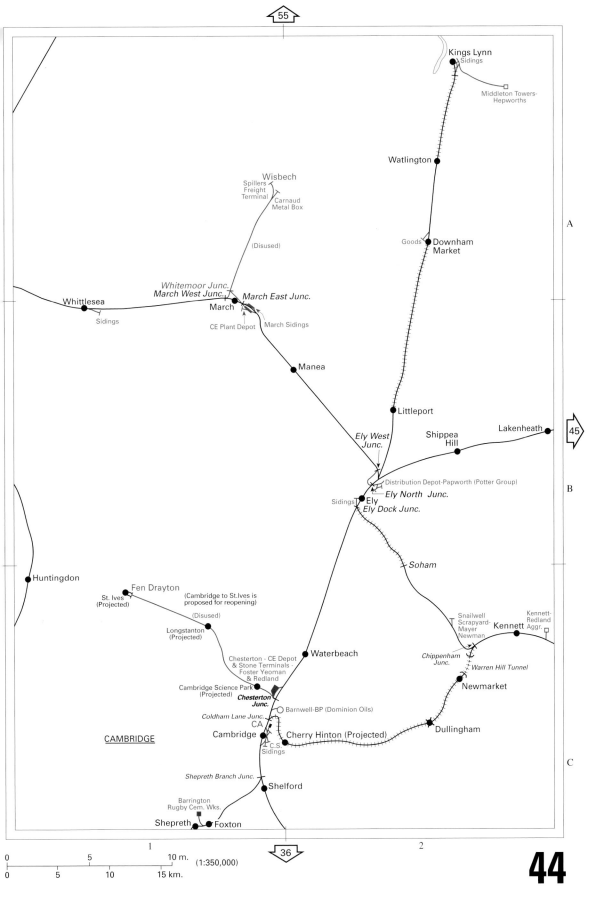

Kings Lynn
Sidings

Middleton Towers-
Hepworths

Watlington

A

Wisbech
Spillers
Freight
Terminal
Carnaud
Metal Box

(Disused)

Goods   Downham
Market

Whitemoor Junc.
March West Junc.   *March East Junc.*
Whittlesea   March
Sidings   CE Plant Depot   March Sidings

Manea

Littleport

*Ely West
Junc.*

Lakenheath

Shippea
Hill

45

Distribution Depot-Papworth (Potter Group)
Ely North Junc.

B

Sidings Ely
Ely Dock Junc.

Soham

Huntingdon

Fen Drayton
St. Ives
(Projected)   (Cambridge to St.Ives is
proposed for reopening)
(Disused)
Longstanton
(Projected)

Snailwell
Scrapyard-
Mayer
Newman   Kennett-
Redland
Aggr.   Kennett

Waterbeach

*Chippenham
Junc.*

Chesterton - CE Depot
& Stone Terminals -
Foster Yeoman
& Redland
Cambridge Science Park
(Projected)   *Warren Hill Tunnel*
*Chesterton
Junc.*   Newman

Barnwell-BP (Dominion Oils)

Coldham Lane Junc.
CA   Dullingham
CAMBRIDGE   Cambridge   Cherry Hinton (Projected)

C.S
Sidings

C

Shepreth Branch Junc.
Shelford

Barrington
Rugby Cem. Wks.
Shepreth   Foxton

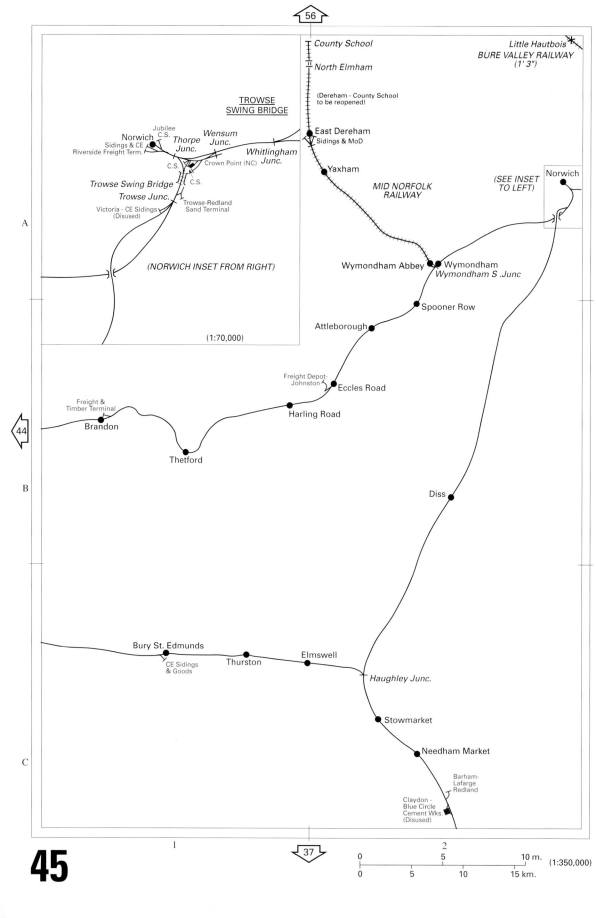

County School

North Elmham

Little Hautbois
BURE VALLEY RAILWAY
(1' 3")

(Dereham - County School
to be reopened)

**TROWSE
SWING BRIDGE**

East Dereham
Sidings & MoD

Jubilee
C.S.
Norwich *Thorpe* *Wensum*
Junc. *Junc.*
Sidings & CE
Riverside Freight Term. *Whitlingham*
Junc.
C.S.
Crown Point (NC)
C.S.

Yaxham

*MID NORFOLK
RAILWAY*

*(SEE INSET
TO LEFT)*

Norwich

Trowse Swing Bridge

Trowse Junc.

Victoria - CE Sidings Trowse-Redland
(Disused) Sand Terminal

(NORWICH INSET FROM RIGHT)

(1:70,000)

A

Wymondham Abbey Wymondham
Wymondham S .Junc

Spooner Row

Attleborough

Freight Depot-
Johnston
Eccles Road

Freight &
Timber Terminal

B
44
Brandon Harling Road

Thetford

Diss

C

Bury St. Edmunds

CE Sidings
& Goods Thurston Elmswell

Haughley Junc.

Stowmarket

Needham Market

Barham-
Lafarge
Redland

Claydon -
Blue Circle
Cement Wks.
(Disused)

45

1

2
5
10 m. *(1:350,000)*

0
0 5 10 15 km.

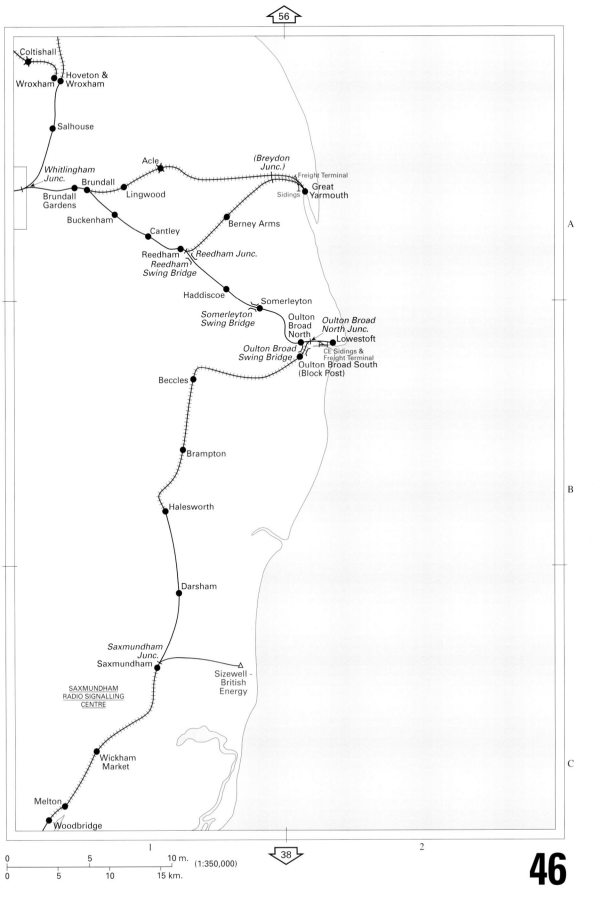

Coltishall

Hoveton &
Wroxham

Wroxham

Salhouse

*Whitlingham
Junc.*

Acle

Brundall

Brundall
Gardens

Lingwood

Buckenham

*(Breydon
Junc.)*

Freight Terminal

Sidings

Great
Yarmouth

Berney Arms

Cantley

Reedham

Reedham Junc.

*Reedham
Swing Bridge*

Haddiscoe

Somerleyton

*Somerleyton
Swing Bridge*

Oulton
Broad
North

*Oulton Broad
North Junc.*

Lowestoft

CE Sidings &
Freight Terminal

*Oulton Broad
Swing Bridge*

Oulton Broad South
(Block Post)

Beccles

Brampton

Halesworth

Darsham

*Saxmundham
Junc.*

Saxmundham

Sizewell -
British
Energy

SAXMUNDHAM
RADIO SIGNALLING
CENTRE

Wickham
Market

Melton

Woodbridge

A

B

C

1

2

0   5   10 m.   (1:350,000)

0   5   10   15 km.

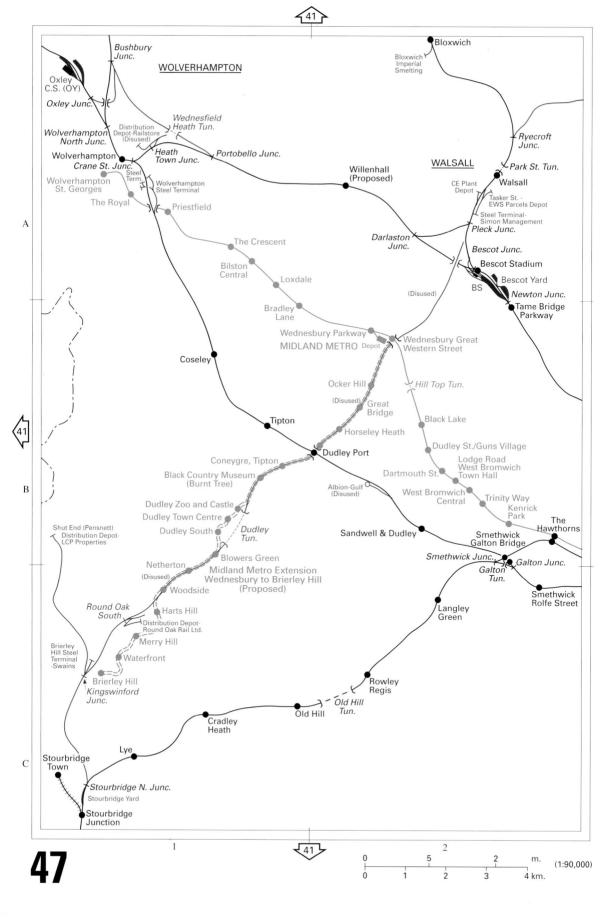

Bushbury
Junc.

WOLVERHAMPTON

Bloxwich

Bloxwich
Imperial
Smelting

Oxley
C.S. (OY)

Oxley Junc.

Wednesfield
Heath Tun.

Ryecroft
Junc.

WALSALL

Wolverhampton
North Junc.

Distribution
Depot-Railstore
(Disused)

Heath
Town Junc.

Portobello Junc.

Park St. Tun.

Wolverhampton
Crane St. Junc.

Steel
Term.

Willenhall
(Proposed)

Walsall

Wolverhampton
St. Georges

Wolverhampton
Steel Terminal

CE Plant
Depot

Tasker St. -
EWS Parcels Depot

The Royal

Priestfield

Steel Terminal-
Simon Management

Pleck Junc.

A

The Crescent

Darlaston
Junc.

Bescot Junc.

Bilston
Central

Bescot Stadium

Loxdale

Bescot Yard

BS

Newton Junc.

Bradley
Lane

(Disused)

Tame Bridge
Parkway

Wednesbury Parkway

MIDLAND METRO   Depot

Wednesbury Great
Western Street

Coseley

Ocker Hill

Hill Top Tun.

(Disused)

Great
Bridge

Black Lake

Tipton

Horseley Heath

Dudley St./Guns Village

Dudley Port

Coneygre, Tipton

Dartmouth St.

Lodge Road
West Bromwich
Town Hall

Black Country Museum
(Burnt Tree)

Albion-Gulf
(Disused)

West Bromwich
Central

Trinity Way

B

Dudley Zoo and Castle

Kenrick
Park

Dudley Town Centre

The
Hawthorns

Dudley South

Dudley
Tun.

Sandwell & Dudley

Smethwick
Galton Bridge

Netherton

Blowers Green

Smethwick Junc.

Galton Junc.

(Disused)

Midland Metro Extension
Wednesbury to Brierley Hill
(Proposed)

Galton
Tun.

Woodside

Round Oak
South

Harts Hill

Smethwick
Rolfe Street

Distribution Depot-
Round Oak Rail Ltd.

Langley
Green

Brierley
Hill Steel
Terminal
-Swains

Merry Hill

Waterfront

Brierley Hill
Kingswinford
Junc.

Shut End (Pensnett)
Distribution Depot-
LCP Properties

Rowley
Regis

Old Hill
Tun.

Old Hill

Cradley
Heath

Lye

Stourbridge
Town

C

Stourbridge N. Junc.

Stourbridge Yard

Stourbridge
Junction

47

1

2

0   5   2   m.

0   1   2   3   4 km.

(1:90,000)

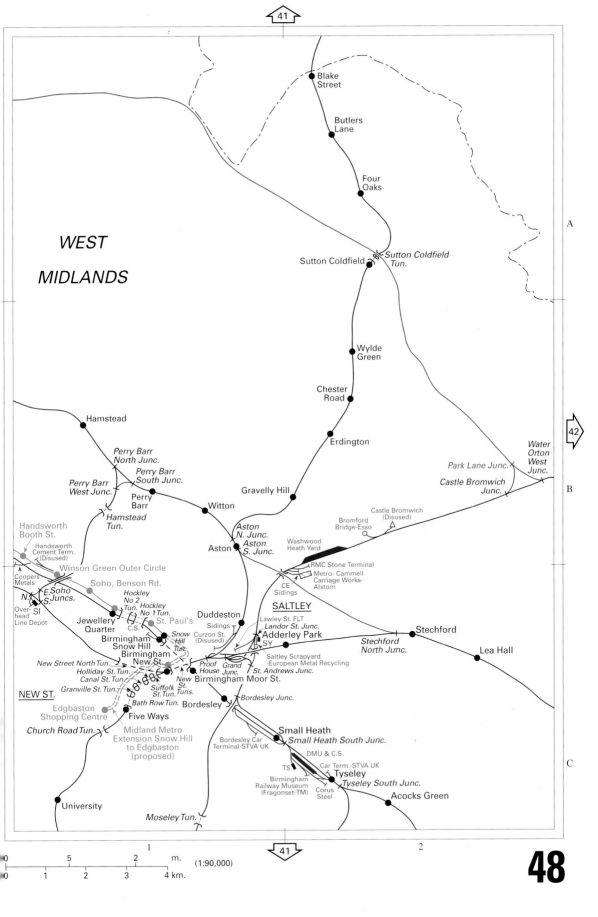

A

WEST

MIDLANDS

Blake Street

Butlers Lane

Four Oaks

Sutton Coldfield Tun.

Sutton Coldfield

42

B

Hamstead

Wylde Green

Chester Road

Erdington

Water Orton West Junc.

Perry Barr North Junc.

Perry Barr South Junc.

Park Lane Junc.

Castle Bromwich Junc.

Perry Barr West Junc.

Perry Barr

Gravelly Hill

Hamstead Tun.

Witton

Aston N. Junc.

Aston S. Junc.

Handsworth Booth St.

Handsworth Cement Term. (Disused)

Castle Bromwich (Disused)

Bromford Bridge-Esso

Winson Green Outer Circle

Aston

Washwood Heath Yard

Coopers Metals

Soho, Benson Rd.

RMC Stone Terminal

Metro- Cammell Carriage Works-Alstom

E.Soho S. Juncs.

N.

Hockley No 2 Tun.

CE Sidings

Over-head Line Depot

SI

Hockley No 1 Tun.

SALTLEY

Stechford

Jewellery Quarter

St. Paul's

Duddeston

Lawley St. FLT

Landor St. Junc.

C.S.

Sidings

Adderley Park

Lea Hall

Birmingham Snow Hill

Snow Hill Tun.

Curzon St. (Disused)

SY

Stechford North Junc.

Birmingham New St.

Proof House

Grand Junc.

Saltley Scrapyard -European Metal Recycling

New Street North Tun.

St. Andrews Junc.

Holliday St. Tun.

New Birmingham Moor St.

Canal St. Tun.

Suffolk St. Tuns.

NEW ST.

Granville St. Tun.

St. Tun.

Bordesley Junc.

Bath Row Tun.

Bordesley

Edgbaston Shopping Centre

Five Ways

Small Heath

Church Road Tun.

Small Heath South Junc.

Midland Metro Extension Snow Hill to Edgbaston (proposed)

Bordesley Car Terminal-STVA UK

DMU & C.S.

Car Term.-STVA UK

C

TS

Tyseley

Tyseley South Junc.

Birmingham Railway Museum (Fragonset-TM)

Corus Steel

University

Acocks Green

Moseley Tun.

1   m.   (1:90,000)   2

0   5   2

0   1   2   3   4 km.

48

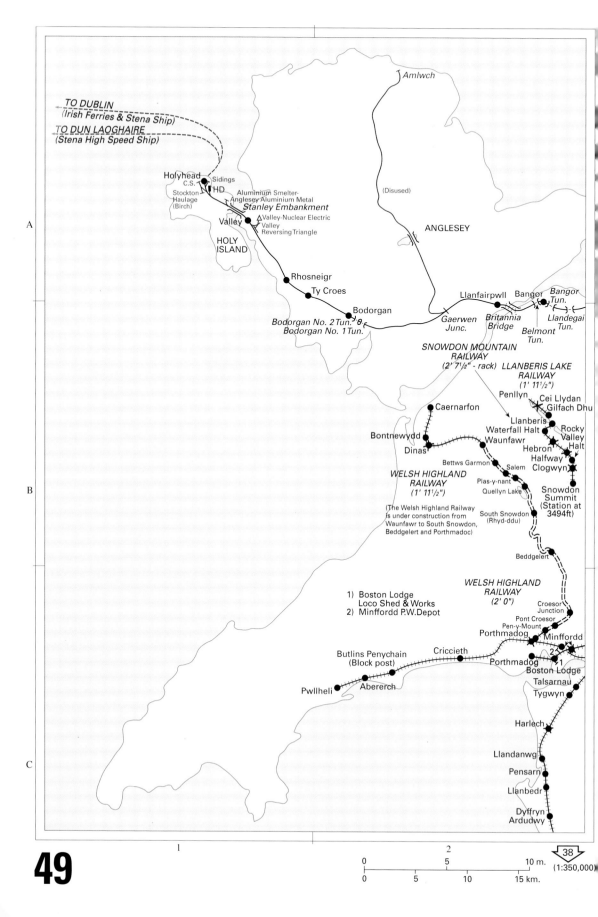

TO DUBLIN
(Irish Ferries & Stena Ship)

TO DUN LAOGHAIRE
(Stena High Speed Ship)

Amlwch

Holyhead
C.S. Sidings
HD
Stockton
Haulage
(Birch)
Aluminium Smelter-
Anglesey Aluminium Metal
Stanley Embankment

Valley

Valley-Nuclear Electric
Valley
Reversing Triangle

(Disused)

ANGLESEY

HOLY
ISLAND

A

Rhosneigr

Ty Croes

Bodorgan

Bodorgan No. 2 Tun. &
Bodorgan No. 1 Tun.

Llanfairpwll

Bangor

*Bangor
Tun.*

Gaerwen
Junc.

Britannia
Bridge

Belmont
Tun.

*Llandegai
Tun.*

*SNOWDON MOUNTAIN
RAILWAY*
(2' 7½" - rack)

LLANBERIS LAKE
RAILWAY
(1' 11½")

Penllyn

Cei Llydan
Gilfach Dhu

Caernarfon

Llanberis

Waterfall Halt

Rocky
Valley
Halt

Bontnewydd

Waunfawr

Dinas

Hebron
Halfway

Bettws Garmon

Salem

Clogwyn

*WELSH HIGHLAND
RAILWAY*
(1' 11½")

Plas-y-nant

Quellyn Lake

Snowdon
Summit
(Station at
3494ft)

(The Welsh Highland Railway
is under construction from
Waunfawr to South Snowdon,
Beddgelert and Porthmadoc)

South Snowdon
(Rhyd-ddu)

B

Beddgelert

*WELSH HIGHLAND
RAILWAY*
(2' 0")

Croesor
Junction

Pont Croesor
Pen-y-Mount

1) Boston Lodge
   Loco Shed & Works
2) Minffordd P.W.Depot

Porthmadog

Minffordd

Butlins Penychain
(Block post)

Criccieth

Porthmadog

2   1

Boston Lodge

Talsarnau

Pwllheli

Abererch

Tygwyn

Harlech

C

Llandanwg

Pensarn

Llanbedr

Dyffryn
Ardudwy

49

2

0   5   10 m.

0   5   10   15 km.

⬇ 38

(1:350,000)

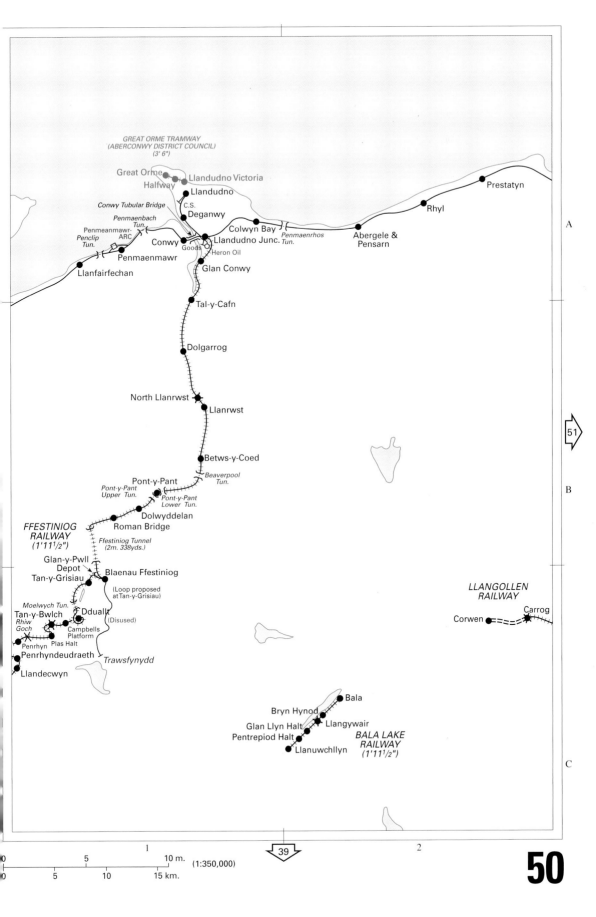

GREAT ORME TRAMWAY
(ABERCONWY DISTRICT COUNCIL)
(3' 6")

Great Orme
Halfway

Llandudno Victoria

Llandudno

Prestatyn

Conwy Tubular Bridge

C.S.

Deganwy

Rhyl

Penmaenbach
Tun.

Colwyn Bay

Penmaenmawr-
ARC

Penmeanrhos
Tun.

Penclip
Tun.

Conwy

Llandudno Junc.

Abergele &
Pensarn

Goods

Penmaenmawr

Heron Oil

Llanfairfechan

Glan Conwy

A

Tal-y-Cafn

Dolgarrog

North Llanrwst

Llanrwst

51

Betws-y-Coed

Pont-y-Pant

Beaverpool
Tun.

B

Pont-y-Pant
Upper Tun.

Pont-y-Pant
Lower Tun.

Dolwyddelan

Roman Bridge

FFESTINIOG
RAILWAY
(1'11½")

Ffestiniog Tunnel
(2m. 338yds.)

Glan-y-Pwll
Depot

Blaenau Ffestiniog

Tan-y-Grisiau

(Loop proposed
at Tan-y-Grisiau)

LLANGOLLEN
RAILWAY

Moelwych Tun.

Tan-y-Bwlch

Dduallt

(Disused)

Carrog

Rhiw
Goch

Campbells
Platform

Corwen

Penrhyn

Plas Halt

Penrhyndeudraeth

Trawsfynydd

Llandecwyn

Bala

Bryn Hynod

Glan Llyn Halt

Llangywair

Pentrepiod Halt

BALA LAKE
RAILWAY
(1'11½")

Llanuwchllyn

C

I

10 m.

(1:350,000)

5

10

15 km.

39

2

50

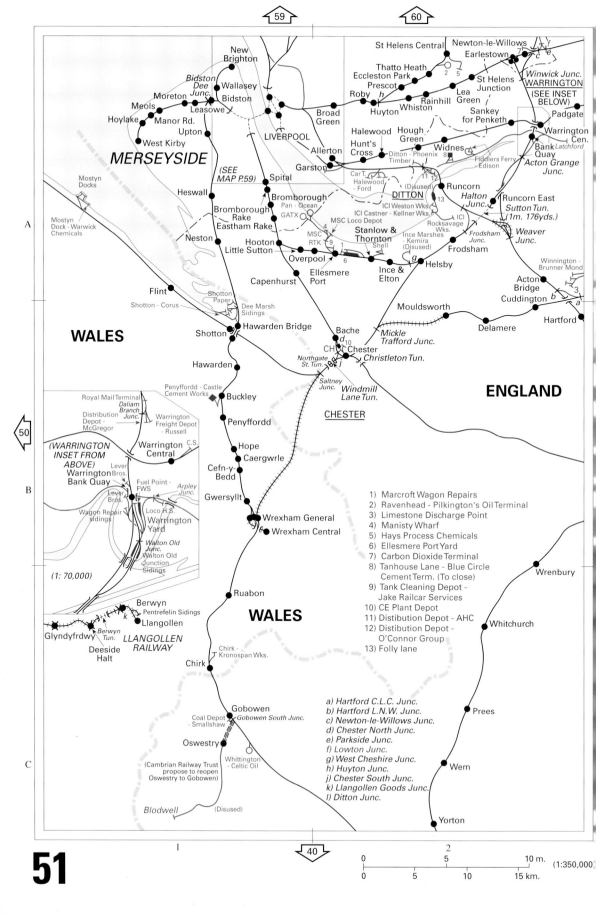

New Brighton
Wallasey
Bidston Dee Junc.
Bidston
Moreton
Leasowe
Meols
Manor Rd.
Hoylake
Upton
West Kirby

MERSEYSIDE

Heswall

(SEE MAP P.59)
Spital
Bromborough
Pan - Ocean
GATX
Bromborough Rake
Eastham Rake
Neston
Hooton
Little Sutton
Overpool
Capenhurst
Ellesmere Port

LIVERPOOL
Broad Green
Allerton
Garston
Hunt's Cross
Halewood
Ditton - Phoenix
Car T. Halewood - Ford

St Helens Central
Thatto Heath
Eccleston Park
Prescot
Roby *h*
Huyton
Whiston
Rainhill
Lea Green
Halewood
Hough Green
Widnes *8*
Ditton Timber
DITTON
ICI Weston Wks.
ICI Castner - Kellner Wks.
MSC Loco Depot
MSC RTK *9*
Stanlow & Thornton
Shell
Ince & Elton
Helsby
g
Ince Marshes - Kemira (Disused)
Frodsham
Rocksavage Wks.
13
ICI
Runcorn
Halton Junc.
Runcorn East
Sutton Tun. (1m. 176yds.)
Frodsham Junc.
Weaver Junc.

Newton-le-Willows
Earlestown *7* *f* *e* *c*
Winwick Junc.
WARRINGTON (SEE INSET BELOW)
St Helens Junction
Sankey for Penketh
Padgate
Warrington Cen.
Bank Quay
Latchford
Acton Grange Junc.
Fiddlers Ferry Edison

Mostyn Docks
Mostyn Dock - Warwick Chemicals

Winnington - Brunner Mond
Acton Bridge
Cuddington *b* *a* *3*
Hartford
Mouldsworth
Delamere
Mickle Trafford Junc.

Flint
Shotton Paper
Shotton - Corus
Dee Marsh Sidings
Shotton
Hawarden Bridge
Hawarden

Bache *d* *10*
CH.
Chester
Northgate St. Tun. *j*
Saltney Junc.
Christleton Tun.
Windmill Lane Tun.

ENGLAND

CHESTER

WALES

Penyfford - Castle Cement Works
Buckley
Penyffordd
Hope
Caergwrle
Cefn-y-Bedd
Gwersyllt
Wrexham General
Wrexham Central

Royal Mail Terminal
Daliam Branch Junc.
Distribution Depot - McGregor
Warrington Freight Depot - Russell
Warrington Central
C.S.
(WARRINGTON INSET FROM ABOVE)
Warrington Bank Quay
Lever Bros.
Fuel Point - FWS
Lever Bros.
Arpley Junc.
Loco H.S.
Warrington Yard
Wagon Repair sidings
Walton Old Junc.
Walton Old Junction Sidings
(1: 70,000)

1) Marcroft Wagon Repairs
2) Ravenhead - Pilkington's Oil Terminal
3) Limestone Discharge Point
4) Manisty Wharf
5) Hays Process Chemicals
6) Ellesmere Port Yard
7) Carbon Dioxide Terminal
8) Tanhouse Lane - Blue Circle Cement Term. (To close)
9) Tank Cleaning Depot - Jake Railcar Services
10) CE Plant Depot
11) Distibution Depot - AHC
12) Distibution Depot - O'Connor Group
13) Folly lane

Berwyn
Pentrefelin Sidings
Llangollen
k
Glyndyfrdwy
Berwyn Tun.
Deeside Halt
LLANGOLLEN RAILWAY

Ruabon

WALES

Chirk - Kronospan Wks.
Chirk

Wrenbury
Whitchurch
Prees
Wem
Yorton

Gobowen
Gobowen South Junc.
Coal Depot - Smallshaw
Oswestry
Whittington - Celtic Oil
(Cambrian Railway Trust propose to reopen Oswestry to Gobowen)

a) Hartford C.L.C. Junc.
b) Hartford L.N.W. Junc.
c) Newton-le-Willows Junc.
d) Chester North Junc.
e) Parkside Junc.
f) Lowton Junc.
g) West Cheshire Junc.
h) Huyton Junc.
j) Chester South Junc.
k) Llangollen Goods Junc.
l) Ditton Junc.

Blodwell
(Disused)

2
0   5   10 m.
0   5   10   15 km.
(1:350,000)

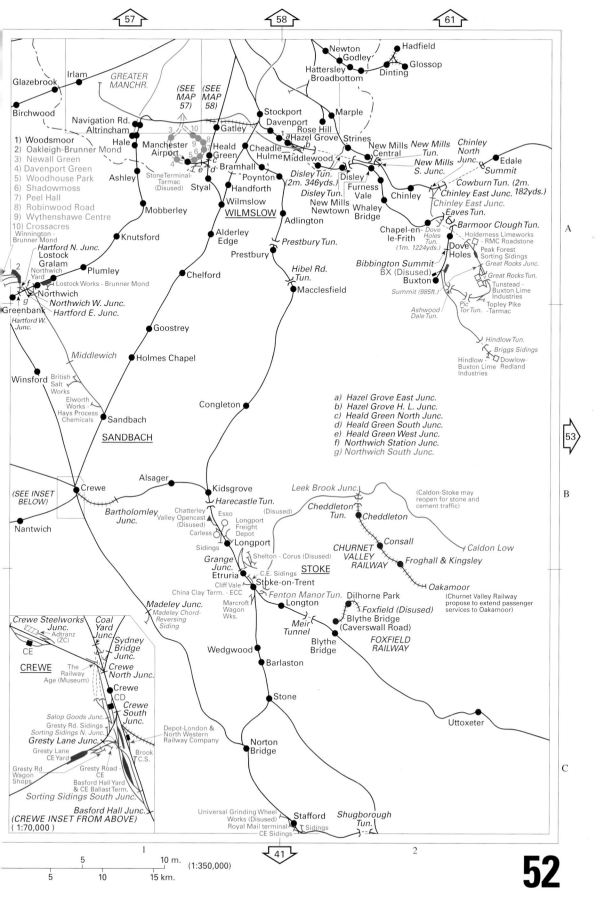

Newton
Godley
Hadfield
Hattersley
Broadbottom
Glossop
Dinting

Glazebrook
Irlam
GREATER MANCHR.
(SEE MAP 57)
(SEE MAP 58)
Marple

Birchwood

Stockport
Davenport
Rose Hill
Strines

Navigation Rd.
Altrincham
Hale
Manchester Airport
Gatley
Hazel Grove
New Mills Central
New Mills Tun.
Chinley North Junc.

1) Woodsmoor
2) Oakleigh-Brunner Mond
3) Newall Green
4) Davenport Green
5) Woodhouse Park
6) Shadowmoss
7) Peel Hall
8) Robinwood Road
9) Wythenshawe Centre
10) Crossacres

Heald Green
Cheadle Hulme
Middlewood
New Mills S. Junc.
Edale
Cowburn Tun. (2m.)
Chinley East Junc. 182yds.

Ashley
Bramhall
Poynton
Disley Tun.
(2m. 346yds.)
Disley
Furness Vale
Chinley East Junc.

Styal
Handforth
Disley Tun.
Eaves Tun.

Winnington - Brunner Mond
Hartford N. Junc.
Lostock Gralam
Mobberley
Wilmslow
New Mills Newtown
Whaley Bridge
Chinley
Barmoor Clough Tun.
Holderness Limeworks - RMC Roadstone

Northwich Yard
Plumley
WILMSLOW
Adlington
Chapel-en-le-Frith
Dove Holes Tun.
(1m. 1224yds.)
Peak Forest Sorting Sidings
Great Rocks Junc.

Lostock Works - Brunner Mond
Knutsford
Alderley Edge
Prestbury Tun.
Bibbington Summit
BX (Disused)
Dove Holes
Great Rocks Tun.

Northwich W. Junc.
Hartford E. Junc.
Prestbury
Buxton
Tunstead - Buxton Lime Industries

Greenbank
Hartford W. Junc.
Chelford
Hibel Rd. Tun.
Macclesfield
Summit (985ft.)
Ashwood Dale Tun.
Pic Tor Tun.
Topley Pike -Tarmac

Goostrey
Hindlow Tun.
Briggs Sidings

Winsford
British Salt Works
Holmes Chapel
Hindlow - Buxton Lime Industries
Dowlow- Redland

Elworth Works - Hays Process Chemicals
Congleton

Middlewich
Sandbach
a) Hazel Grove East Junc.
b) Hazel Grove H. L. Junc.
c) Heald Green North Junc.
d) Heald Green South Junc.
e) Heald Green West Junc.
f) Northwich Station Junc.
g) Northwich South Junc.

SANDBACH

Alsager
Kidsgrove
Leek Brook Junc.
(Caldon-Stoke may reopen for stone and cement traffic)

Crewe
Harecastle Tun.
Cheddleton Tun.
Cheddleton

(SEE INSET BELOW)
Chatterley Valley Opencast (Disused)
Esso
(Disused)
Consall
Caldon Low

Nantilwich
Bartholomley Junc.
Carless
Longport Freight Depot
CHURNET VALLEY RAILWAY
Froghall & Kingsley

Sidings
Longport
Grange Junc.
Etruria
Shelton - Corus (Disused)
STOKE
Oakamoor
(Churnet Valley Railway propose to extend passenger services to Oakamoor)

Madeley Junc.
Madeley Chord-Reversing Siding
Cliff Vale
China Clay Term. - ECC
C.E. Sidings
Stoke-on-Trent
Fenton Manor Tun.
Longton
Dilhorne Park
Foxfield (Disused)

Marcroft Wagon Wks.
Meir Tunnel
Blythe Bridge (Caverswall Road)
FOXFIELD RAILWAY

Wedgwood
Blythe Bridge

Crewe Steelworks Junc.
Coal Yard Junc.
Adtranz (ZC)
Sydney Bridge Junc.
Barlaston

CE
The Railway Age (Museum)
Crewe North Junc.

CREWE
Crewe
CD
Crewe South Junc.
Stone

Salop Goods Junc.
Gresty Rd. Sidings
Sorting Sidings N. Junc.
Depot-London & North Western Railway Company
Uttoxeter

Gresty Lane Junc.
Gresty Lane CE Yard
Brook C.S.
Norton Bridge

Gresty Rd Wagon Shops
Gresty Road CE
Basford Hall Yard & CE Ballast Term.

Sorting Sidings South Junc.
Basford Hall Junc.
(CREWE INSET FROM ABOVE)
(1:70,000)

Universal Grinding Wheel Works (Disused)
Royal Mail terminal
CE Sidings
Stafford
Sidings
Shugborough Tun.

1
5
10 m.
(1:350,000)
5
10
15 km.
2

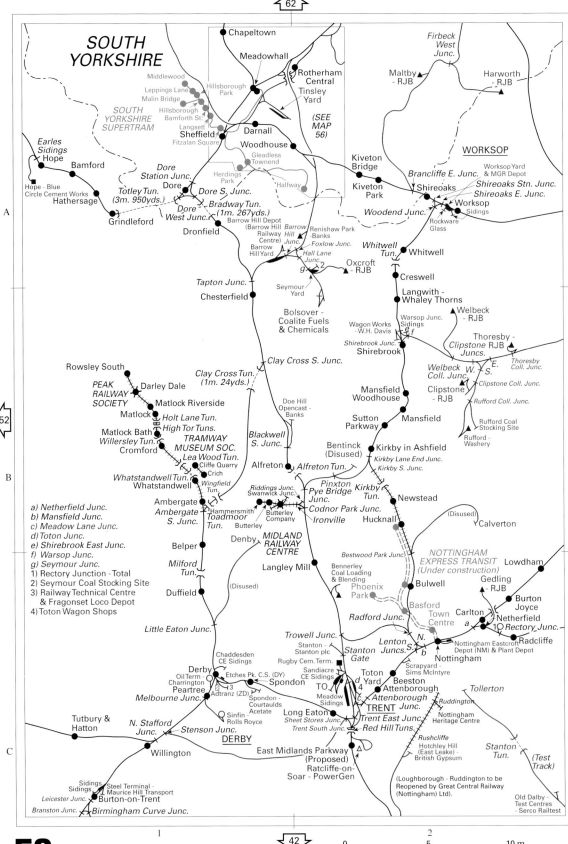

SOUTH YORKSHIRE

Chapeltown

Meadowhall

Middlewood
Leppings Lane
Malin Bridge
Hillsborough Park
Rotherham Central
Tinsley Yard

SOUTH YORKSHIRE SUPERTRAM

Hillsborough
Bamforth St.
Langsett
Sheffield
Fitzalan Square

Darnall

Woodhouse

(SEE MAP 56)

WORKSOP

Maltby - RJB

Firbeck West Junc.

Harworth - RJB

Kiveton Bridge
Kiveton Park

Worksop Yard & MGR Depot

Brancliffe E. Junc.

Shireoaks Stn. Junc.
Shireoaks E. Junc.

Shireoaks

Worksop
Sidings

Rockware Glass

Earles Sidings
Hope

Bamford

Hope - Blue
Circle Cement Works

Hathersage

Dore Station Junc.
Dore

Totley Tun.
(3m. 950yds.)

Grindleford

Dore S. Junc.

Dore West Junc.

Bradway Tun.
(1m. 267yds.)

Gleadless
Townend

Herdings

Halfway

Woodend Junc.

Whitwell Tun.

Whitwell

Dronfield

Barrow Hill Depot
(Barrow Hill
Railway Centre)
Barrow Hill Yard

Barrow Hill Junc.

Renishaw Park
- Banks

Foxlow Junc.

Hall Lane Junc.

g

Oxcroft - RJB

2

Creswell

Tapton Junc.

Chesterfield

Seymour Yard

Bolsover - Coalite Fuels & Chemicals

Langwith - Whaley Thorns

Welbeck - RJB

Wagon Works - W.H. Davis

Warsop Junc.
Sidings

e f

Thoresby - Clipstone RJB Juncs.

Rowsley South

PEAK RAILWAY SOCIETY

Darley Dale

Matlock Riverside

Matlock

Matlock Bath

Cromford

Clay Cross S. Junc.

Clay Cross Tun.
(1m. 24yds.)

Shirebrook Junc.

Shirebrook

Mansfield Woodhouse

Sutton Parkway

Mansfield

Welbeck W. S.
Coll. Junc.

E.

Thoresby Coll. Junc.

Clipstone Coll. Junc.

Rufford Coll. Junc.

Clipstone - RJB

Rufford Coal Stocking Site

Rufford - Washery

Holt Lane Tun.
High Tor Tuns.
Willersley Tun.

TRAMWAY MUSEUM SOC.

Lea Wood Tun.

Cliffe Quarry
Crich

Doe Hill Opencast - Banks

Blackwell S. Junc.

Bentinck (Disused)

Kirkby in Ashfield

Kirkby Lane End Junc.

Kirkby S. Junc.

Whatstandwell Tun.
Whatstandwell

Wingfield Tun.

Alfreton

Alfreton Tun.

Kirkby Tun.

Newstead

(Disused)

Calverton

Ambergate

Ambergate S. Junc.

Hammersmith

Toadmoor Tun.

Butterley

Denby

MIDLAND RAILWAY CENTRE

Riddings Junc.
Swanwick Junc.

Butterley Company

Pinxton
Pye Bridge Junc.

Codnor Park Junc.

Ironville

Kirkby

Hucknall

NOTTINGHAM EXPRESS TRANSIT (Under construction)

Lowdham

Belper

Milford Tun.

Duffield

(Disused)

Langley Mill

Bestwood Park Junc.

Bennerley Coal Loading & Blending

Phoenix Park

Bulwell

Gedling - RJB

Burton Joyce

Little Eaton Junc.

Trowell Junc.

Stanton - Stanton plc

Rugby Cem. Term.

Sandiacre CE Sidings

Radford Junc.

Lenton Juncs.

N.

S.

b

Basford Town Centre

Carlton

Netherfield
Rectory Junc.

Radcliffe

Nottingham Eastcroft Depot (NM) & Plant Depot

Nottingham

Chaddesden CE Sidings

Derby

Oil Term
Charrington

Peartree

Melbourne Junc.

Etches Pk. C.S. (DY)

3

Adtranz (ZD)

Spondon

Spondon - Courtaulds Acetate

Sinfin Rolls Royce

Stanton Gate

Scrapyard - Sims McIntyre

Toton Yard

d

4

Beeston

Attenborough

Attenborough Junc.

Tollerton

Ruddington

Nottingham Heritage Centre

Tutbury & Hatton

N. Stafford Junc.

Stenson Junc.

DERBY

Willington

TO

Meadow Sidings

Long Eaton

Sheet Stores Junc.

Trent South Junc.

TRENT

Trent East Junc.

Red Hill Tuns.

East Midlands Parkway (Proposed)

Ratcliffe-on-Soar - PowerGen

Rushcliffe
Hotchley Hill (East Leake) - British Gypsum

Stanton Tun.

(Test Track)

(Loughborough - Ruddington to be Reopened by Great Central Railway (Nottingham) Ltd).

Old Dalby - Test Centres - Serco Railtest

a) Netherfield Junc.
b) Mansfield Junc.
c) Meadow Lane Junc.
d) Toton Junc.
e) Shirebrook East Junc.
f) Warsop Junc.
g) Seymour Junc.
1) Rectory Junction - Total
2) Seymour Coal Stocking Site
3) Railway Technical Centre & Fragonset Loco Depot
4) Toton Wagon Shops

Sidings
Sidings
Leicester Junc.

Steel Terminal - Maurice Hill Transport

Burton-on-Trent

Branston Junc.

Birmingham Curve Junc.

0   2   5   10 m.   (1:350,000)

0   5   10   15 km.

53

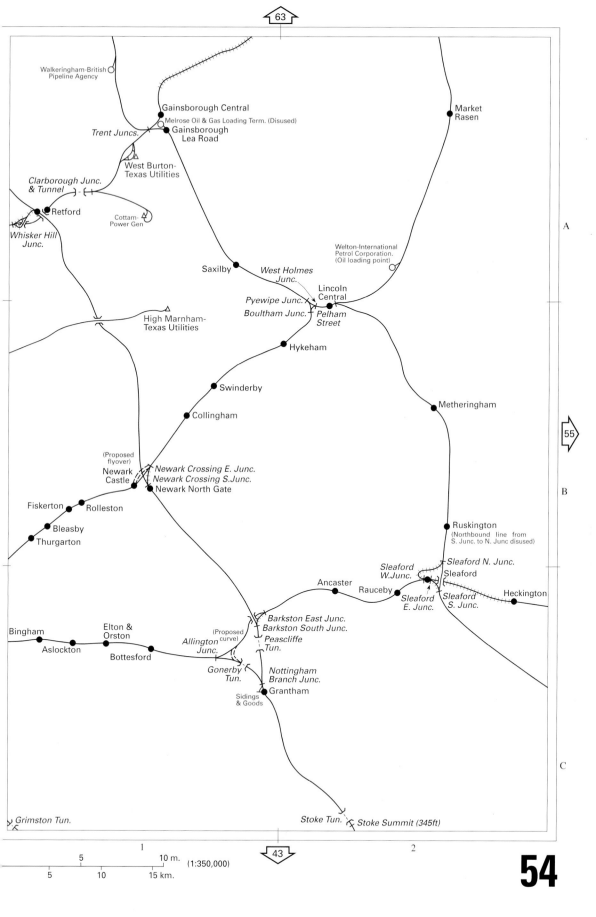

Walkeringham-British
Pipeline Agency

Market
Rasen

Gainsborough Central

Melrose Oil & Gas Loading Term. (Disused)

Trent Juncs.
Gainsborough
Lea Road

Clarborough Junc.
& Tunnel

West Burton-
Texas Utilities

Retford

Cottam-
Power Gen

Whisker Hill
Junc.

Welton-International
Petrol Corporation.
(Oil loading point)

A

Saxilby
West Holmes
Junc.
Lincoln
Central

Pyewipe Junc.
Boultham Junc.
Pelham
Street

High Marnham-
Texas Utilities

Hykeham

Swinderby

Metheringham

55

Collingham

(Proposed
flyover)
Newark
Castle

Newark Crossing E. Junc.
Newark Crossing S.Junc.
Newark North Gate

B

Fiskerton
Rolleston

Bleasby
Thurgarton

Ruskington
(Northbound line from
S. Junc. to N. Junc disused)

Sleaford N. Junc.
Sleaford
W.Junc.
Sleaford

Ancaster
Rauceby
Sleaford
E. Junc.
Sleaford
S. Junc.
Heckington

Bingham

Elton &
Orston

Barkston East Junc.
Barkston South Junc.
Allington (Proposed
curve)
Junc.
Peascliffe
Tun.

Aslockton

Bottesford

Gonerby
Tun.
Nottingham
Branch Junc.
Grantham

C

Sidings
& Goods

Grimston Tun.

Stoke Tun. *Stoke Summit (345ft)*

1
10 m.
5
(1:350,000)
5
10
15 km.

2

54

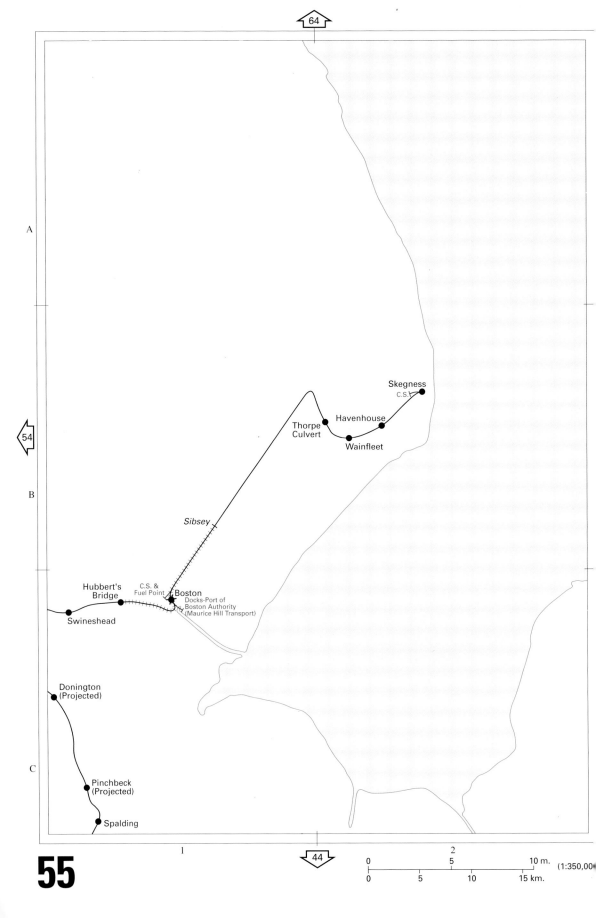

A

54

B

Skegness
C.S.

Thorpe
Culvert

Havenhouse

Wainfleet

Sibsey

Hubbert's
Bridge

C.S. &
Fuel Point

Boston

Docks-Port of
Boston Authority
(Maurice Hill Transport)

Swineshead

Donington
(Projected)

C

Pinchbeck
(Projected)

Spalding

1

2
5
10 m. (1:350,00
0   5   10   15 km.

55

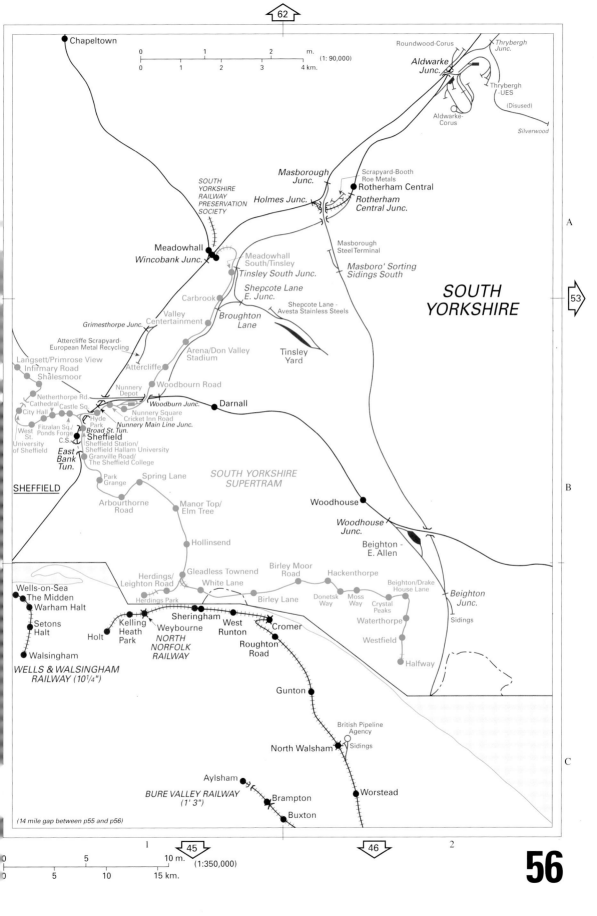

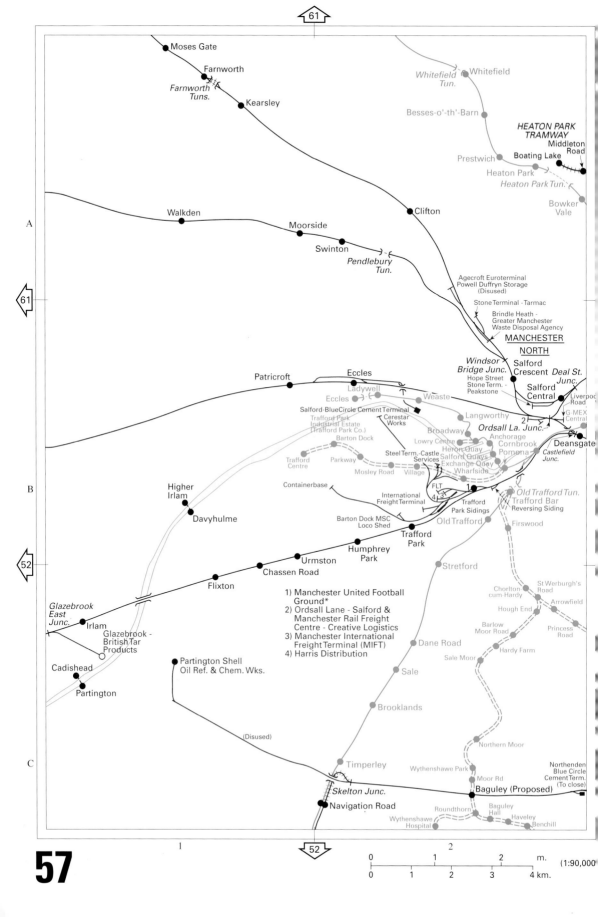

Moses Gate
Farnworth
Farnworth Tuns.
Kearsley

Whitefield
Whitefield Tun.
Besses-o'-th'-Barn

HEATON PARK TRAMWAY
Prestwich
Boating Lake
Middleton Road
Heaton Park
Heaton Park Tun.
Bowker Vale

Walkden
Moorside
Clifton
Swinton
Pendlebury Tun.

A

Agecroft Euroterminal
Powell Duffryn Storage (Disused)
Stone Terminal - Tarmac
Brindle Heath - Greater Manchester Waste Disposal Agency

MANCHESTER NORTH

Windsor Bridge Junc.
Salford Crescent
Deal St. Junc.
Hope Street Stone Term. - Peakstone
Salford Central

Patricroft
Eccles
Ladywell
Eccles
Weaste
Liverpool Road
Salford-BlueCircle Cement Terminal
Cerestar Works
Trafford Park Industrial Estate (Trafford Park Co.)
Langworthy
G-MEX Central
Ordsall La. Junc.
Barton Dock
Broadway
Lowry Centre
Anchorage
Cornbrook
Deansgate
Steel Term.-Castle Services
Heron Quay
Salford Quays
Pomona
Castlefield Junc.
Trafford Centre
Parkway
Mosley Road
Exchange Quay
Village
Wharfside
FLT

B

Higher Irlam
Davyhulme
Containerbase
International Freight Terminal
FLT
Old Trafford Tun.
Trafford Bar
Reversing Siding
Barton Dock MSC Loco Shed
Trafford Park Sidings
Old Trafford
Firswood

Humphrey Park
Urmston
Chassen Road
Trafford Park
Stretford

52

Flixton

1) Manchester United Football Ground*
2) Ordsall Lane - Salford & Manchester Rail Freight Centre - Creative Logistics
3) Manchester International Freight Terminal (MIFT)
4) Harris Distribution

Chorlton cum-Hardy
St Werburgh's Road
Arrowfield
Hough End
Barlow Moor Road
Princess Road

Glazebrook East Junc.
Irlam
Glazebrook - British Tar Products

Dane Road
Sale Moor
Hardy Farm

Cadishead
Partington

Partington Shell Oil Ref. & Chem. Wks.

Sale

Brooklands

Northern Moor

(Disused)

C

Timperley
Wythenshawe Park
Moor Rd
Northenden Blue Circle Cement Term. (To close)
Skelton Junc.
Navigation Road
Baguley (Proposed)
Roundthorn
Baguley Hall
Haveley
Benchill
Wythenshawe Hospital

57

1

2

m.

0   1   2
0   1   2   3   4 km.

(1:90,000)

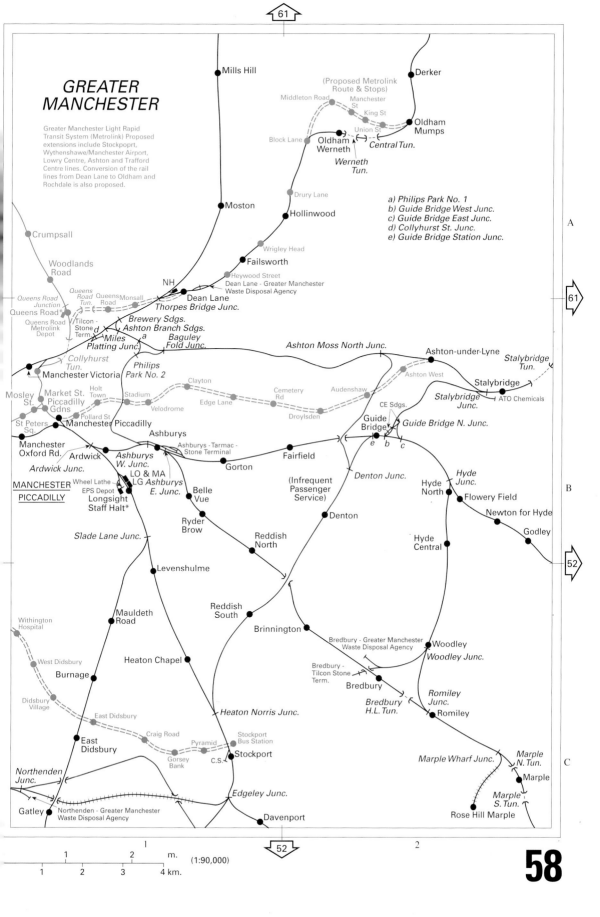

GREATER MANCHESTER

Greater Manchester Light Rapid Transit System (Metrolink) Proposed extensions include Stockpoprt, Wythenshawe/Manchester Airport, Lowry Centre, Ashton and Trafford Centre lines. Conversion of the rail lines from Dean Lane to Oldham and Rochdale is also proposed.

(Proposed Metrolink Route & Stops)

a) Philips Park No. 1
b) Guide Bridge West Junc.
c) Guide Bridge East Junc.
d) Collyhurst St. Junc.
e) Guide Bridge Station Junc.

Mills Hill
Derker
Middleton Road
Manchester St
King St
Oldham Mumps
Block Lane
Union St
Oldham Werneth
Central Tun.
Werneth Tun.
Moston
Drury Lane
Hollinwood
Crumpsall
Woodlands Road
Wrigley Head
Failsworth
Queens Road Junction
Queens Road*
Queens Road Tun.
Queens Road
Monsall
NH
Heywood Street
Dean Lane - Greater Manchester Waste Disposal Agency
Dean Lane
Thorpes Bridge Junc.
Queens Road Metrolink Depot
Tilcon - Stone Term.
d
Brewery Sdgs.
Ashton Branch Sdgs.
a
Baguley Fold Junc.
Ashton Moss North Junc.
Ashton-under-Lyne
Stalybridge Tun.
Collyhurst Tun.
Miles Platting Junc.
Philips Park No. 2
Ashton West
Stalybridge
Manchester Victoria
Clayton
Cemetery Rd
Audenshaw
Stalybridge Junc.
ATO Chemicals
Mosley St.
Market St.
Piccadilly Gdns
Holt Town
Stadium
Edge Lane
Velodrome
Droylsden
CE Sdgs.
Stalybridge Junc.
St Peters Sq.
Pollard St
Manchester Piccadilly
Guide Bridge
Guide Bridge N. Junc.
Ashburys
Ashburys - Tarmac - Stone Terminal
Fairfield
e b c
Manchester Oxford Rd.
Ardwick
Ashburys W. Junc.
Gorton
Denton Junc.
Hyde Junc.
Hyde North
Ardwick Junc.
LO & MA
LG Ashburys E. Junc.
Belle Vue
(Infrequent Passenger Service)
Flowery Field
MANCHESTER PICCADILLY
Wheel Lathe
EPS Depot
Longsight Staff Halt*
Ryder Brow
Denton
Newton for Hyde
Godley
Slade Lane Junc.
Reddish North
Hyde Central
Levenshulme
Withington Hospital
Mauldeth Road
Reddish South
Brinnington
West Didsbury
Bredbury - Greater Manchester Waste Disposal Agency
Woodley
Woodley Junc.
Burnage
Heaton Chapel
Bredbury - Tilcon Stone Term.
Didsbury Village
East Didsbury
Craig Road
Bredbury
Romiley Junc.
Romiley
Heaton Norris Junc.
Pyramid
Stockport Bus Station
Bredbury H.L. Tun.
Gorsey Bank
Stockport
Marple Wharf Junc.
Marple N. Tun.
Northenden Junc.
C.S.
Marple
Gatley
Northenden - Greater Manchester Waste Disposal Agency
Edgeley Junc.
Marple S. Tun.
Davenport
Rose Hill Marple

A

B

C

1   2

m. (1:90,000)

1   2   3   4 km.

1   2

58

MERSEYSIDE

Hall Road Depot (Disused)
Hall Road

Blundellsands & Crosby

Old Roan

Kirkby

Waterloo

TO DOUGLAS (Isle of Man Steam Packet Seaways)
TO BELFAST (Norse Irish Ferries)

Seaforth & Litherland

Excursion Platform *
Aintree

Fazakerley Junc.

Fazakerley

Seaforth FLT & Cawood Coal Export Terminal

(Disused)

Orrell Park

A

TO DUBLIN (Merchant Ferries)
TO DUBLIN (SeaCat)

Walton
Rice Lane

Walton Junc.

Gladstone Dock - Powergen

Bootle New Strand

Alexandra Dock European Metal Recycling

MDHC

Bootle Oriel Rd.

Kirkdale No. 1 Tun.
Kirkdale No. 2 Tun.

1) Pacific Road Depot
2) Egerton Bridge
3) Taylor St. Depot
a) Derby Square Junc.
b) Bootle Junc.
c) Paradise Junc.
d) Mann Island Junc.
e) Canning St. Junc.
f) Bootle Branch Junc.
g) Edge Hill East Junc.
h) Hamilton Sq. Junc.
j) Picko No. 2 Tun.
k) Oriel Road Tun.
l) Bury Street Tun.
m) Alexandra Dock Tun.
n) Haymarket Tun.
p) Canning St. N.

RTK
m
Kirkdale
b
k
Spellow Tun.
Westminster Rd. Tun.
Kirkdale EMU Depot

New Brighton

Bank Hall

Sandhills Junc.

Wallasey Grove Rd.

Wallasey Village

Sandhills

MERSEYRAIL

Bidston E. Junc.
RTK MDHC
BD

(Mersey Ferries)
Seacombe
BIRKENHEAD TRAMWAY

Moorfields

Lime St.
Russell St. Tun.

EDGE HILL

Tuebrook
CE Sidings

j

B

Birkenhead North

LIVERPOOL
Pier Head
d a
c
Central

Edge Hill
g
CE

Wavertree Technology Park

Broad Green

(Disused)

Birkenhead Park

MDHC
p 2 1
3 h e
RTK
n

James St.
JAMES ST.
Mersey Tun.
Woodside
Birkenhead Hamilton Square

Mount Pleasant Tun.
Crown St. Tun.
Overbury St. Tun.

Spekeland Road Goods

Gullet Sidings

Downhill C.S.(LL)

Wavertree Junc.

Conway Park

St. James Tuns.

Birkenhead Central
Depot (Disused)

Hinderton Field Tun.

Green Lane

Brunswick

Dingle Tun.

Mossley Hill

(Disused)

St. Michaels Tun.

Fulwood Tun.

West Allerton

Rock Ferry

Rock Ferry S. Junc.

St. Michaels

Aigburth

Hunts Cross West Junc.
AN

Bebington

Cressington

Allerton

Garston

Speke Junc.

Garston FLT

Garston Junc.

Port Sunlight

Garston Coal Terminal - ABP (Disused)

Speke Yard

Spital

Car Terminal - Axial

59

1

2

0   1   2   m.
0   1   2   3   4 km.

(1:90,000)

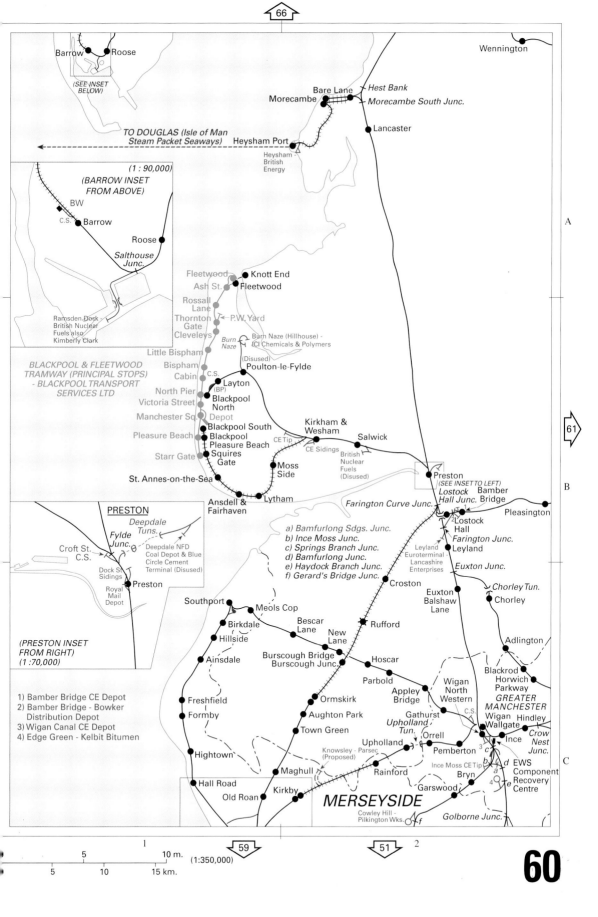

Wennington

Barrow Roose

(SEE INSET BELOW)

TO DOUGLAS (Isle of Man
Steam Packet Seaways)

Bare Lane *Hest Bank*
Morecambe *Morecambe South Junc.*
Lancaster
Heysham Port
Heysham -
British
Energy

**(1 : 90,000)
(BARROW INSET
FROM ABOVE)**

BW

C.S. Barrow

Roose

*Salthouse
Junc.*

Ramsden Dock -
British Nuclear
Fuels also
Kimberly Clark

Fleetwood Knott End
Ash St. Fleetwood
Rossall
Lane
Thornton P.W. Yard
Gate
Cleveleys Burn Naze (Hillhouse) -
Burn (CI) Chemicals & Polymers
Naze
(Disused)
Little Bispham Poulton-le-Fylde
Bispham
Cabin C.S.
Layton
North Pier (BP)
Victoria Street Blackpool
North
Manchester Sq Depot
Blackpool South Kirkham &
Pleasure Beach Blackpool Wesham Salwick
Pleasure Beach CE Tip
Starr Gate Squires CE Sidings British
Gate Nuclear
Moss Fuels
St. Annes-on-the-Sea Side (Disused)

*BLACKPOOL & FLEETWOOD
TRAMWAY (PRINCIPAL STOPS)
- BLACKPOOL TRANSPORT
SERVICES LTD*

Ansdell & Lytham Preston
Fairhaven *(SEE INSET TO LEFT)*
Farington Curve Junc. Lostock Bamber
Hall Junc. Bridge
Lostock Pleasington
Hall
Farington Junc.
Leyland Leyland
Euroterminal -
Lancashire
Enterprises *Euxton Junc.*

PRESTON
*Deepdale
Tuns.*
*Fylde
Junc.*
Croft St.
C.S. Deepdale NFD
Coal Depot & Blue
Circle Cement
Terminal (Disused)
Dock St
Sidings
Royal
Mail
Depot Preston

a) Bamfurlong Sdgs. Junc.
b) Ince Moss Junc.
c) Springs Branch Junc.
d) Bamfurlong Junc.
e) Haydock Branch Junc.
f) Gerard's Bridge Junc.

Croston

Euxton *Chorley Tun.*
Balshaw Chorley
Lane

**(PRESTON INSET
FROM RIGHT)
(1 : 70,000)**

Southport Meols Cop Adlington
Rufford
Birkdale Bescar
Lane New Blackrod
Hillside Lane Horwich
Burscough Bridge Hoscar Parkway
Ainsdale Burscough Junc. *GREATER
Parbold Appley Wigan MANCHESTER*
Freshfield Ormskirk Bridge North
Western Wigan Hindley
Formby Aughton Park Gathurst Wallgate
Upholland C.S. *Crow
Tun.* Orrell *Nest
Town Green Ince Junc.*
Upholland Pemberton
Hightown Knowsley - Parsec Ince Moss CE Tip EWS
(Proposed) Rainford Bryn Component
Maghull Garswood Recovery
Hall Road Centre
Old Roan Kirkby

1) Bamber Bridge CE Depot
2) Bamber Bridge - Bowker
Distribution Depot
3) Wigan Canal CE Depot
4) Edge Green - Kelbit Bitumen

MERSEYSIDE

Cowley Hill -
Pilkington Wks. *Golborne Junc.*

A

61

B

C

1 10 m.
5 *(1:350,000)*
5 10 15 km.

60

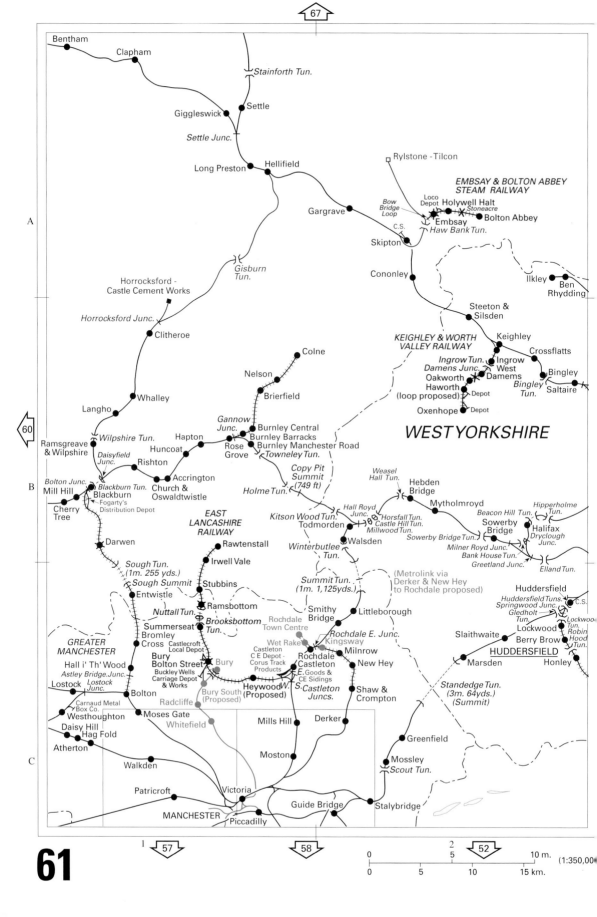

Bentham

Clapham

Stainforth Tun.

Settle

Giggleswick

Settle Junc.

Long Preston Hellifield

Gargrave

Rylstone - Tilcon

**EMBSAY & BOLTON ABBEY
STEAM RAILWAY**

*Bow
Bridge
Loop* Loco
Depot Holywell Halt *Stoneacre*
Embsay Bolton Abbey
C.S. *Haw Bank Tun.*

Skipton

Cononley Ilkley Ben
Rhydding

Steeton &
Silsden

**KEIGHLEY & WORTH
VALLEY RAILWAY** Keighley

Crossflatts

Ingrow Tun. Ingrow
Damens Junc. West
Oakworth Damems Bingley
Haworth Saltaire
(loop proposed) Depot *Bingley
Tun.*

Oxenhope Depot

WEST YORKSHIRE

Horrocksford -
Castle Cement Works

*Gisburn
Tun.*

Horrocksford Junc. Clitheroe

Whalley

Colne

Nelson

Brierfield

Langho

Ramsgreave
& Wilpshire *Wilpshire Tun.* Hapton
*Daisyfield
Junc.* Huncoat
Rishton Rose
Grove

*Gannow
Junc.* Burnley Central
Burnley Barracks
Burnley Manchester Road
Towneley Tun.

*Weasel
Hall Tun.* Hebden
Bridge

Mytholmroyd

*Hipperholme
Tun.*

Beacon Hill Tun.

Mill Hill *Blackburn Tun.*
Blackburn
*Fogarty's
Distribution Depot*

Bolton Junc.

Cherry
Tree

Darwen

*Sough Tun.
(1m. 255 yds.)*
Sough Summit

Entwistle

Nuttall Tun.

Summerseat
Bromley
Cross Castlecroft
Local Depot

**GREATER
MANCHESTER**

Hall i' Th' Wood
Astley Bridge Junc.
Lostock Lostock
Junc.

Bolton

Westhoughton

Daisy Hill
Hag Fold

Atherton

Walkden

Patricroft

Church &
Oswaldtwistle

Accrington

**EAST
LANCASHIRE
RAILWAY**

Rawtenstall

Irwell Vale

Stubbins

Ramsbottom

*Brooksbottom
Tun.*

Bury
Bolton Street
Buckley Wells
Carriage Depot
& Works Bury

Bury South
(Proposed)

Radcliffe

Moses Gate
Whitefield

Carnaud Metal
Box Co.

*Copy Pit
Summit
(749 ft)*
Holme Tun.

Kitson Wood Tun. *Hall Royd
Junc.* *Horsfall Tun.*
Todmorden *Castle Hill Tun.*
Millwood Tun.

Walsden

*Winterbutlee
Tun.*

*Summit Tun.
(1m. 1,125yds.)*

Smithy
Bridge Littleborough

Rochdale
Town Centre
Wet Rake Castleton
C E Depot -
Corus Track
Products Kingsway
Rochdale E. Junc.
Rochdale Milnrow
Castleton
E. Goods &
CE Sidings New Hey

Heywood
(Proposed) *W. &
S. Castleton
Juncs.* Shaw &
Crompton

Mills Hill Derker

Moston

**(Metrolink via
Derker & New Hey
to Rochdale proposed)**

Sowerby
Bridge
Sowerby Bridge Tun. Halifax
*Dryclough
Junc.*

Milner Royd Junc.
Bank House Tun.
Greetland Junc. Elland Tun.

Huddersfield
Huddersfield Tuns. C.S.
Springwood Junc.
*Gledholt
Tun.* Lockwood
Tun. *Robin
Hood
Tun.*

Slaithwaite Lockwood
Berry Brow

HUDDERSFIELD

Marsden Honley

*Standedge Tun.
(3m. 64yds.)
(Summit)*

Greenfield

Mossley
Scout Tun.

Mills Hill

Guide Bridge Stalybridge

MANCHESTER
Piccadilly Victoria

0 5 10 m.
0 5 10 15 km. (1:350,000)

60

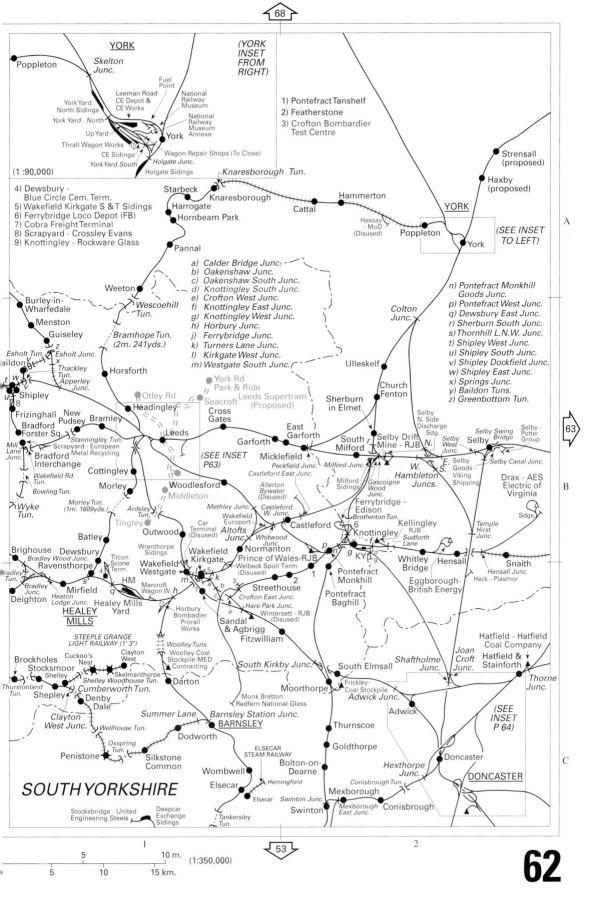

YORK
(YORK INSET FROM RIGHT)

Skelton Junc.

Poppleton

Fuel Point

Leeman Road CE Depot & CE Works

National Railway Museum

National Railway Museum Annexe

York Yard North Sidings

York Yard . North

Up Yard

Thrall Wagon Works

CE Sidings

Wagon Repair Shops (To Close)

York Yard South

Holgate Junc.

Holgate Sidings

York

(1 : 90,000)

1) Pontefract Tanshelf
2) Featherstone
3) Crofton Bombardier Test Centre

4) Dewsbury - Blue Circle Cem. Term.
5) Wakefield Kirkgate S & T Sidings
6) Ferrybridge Loco Depot (FB)
7) Cobra Freight Terminal
8) Scrapyard - Crossley Evans
9) Knottingley - Rockware Glass

a) Calder Bridge Junc.
b) Oakenshaw Junc.
c) Oakenshaw South Junc.
d) Knottingley South Junc.
e) Crofton West Junc.
f) Knottingley East Junc.
g) Knottingley West Junc.
h) Horbury Junc.
j) Ferrybridge Junc.
k) Turners Lane Junc.
l) Kirkgate West Junc.
m) Westgate South Junc.

n) Pontefract Monkhill Goods Junc.
p) Pontefract West Junc.
q) Dewsbury East Junc.
r) Sherburn South Junc.
s) Thornhill L.N.W. Junc.
t) Shipley West Junc.
u) Shipley South Junc.
v) Shipley Dockfield Junc.
w) Shipley East Junc.
x) Springs Junc.
y) Baildon Tuns.
z) Greenbottom Tun.

Knaresborough Tun.

Starbeck

Knaresborough

Hammerton

Cattal

Hessay - MoD (Disused)

Poppleton

York

Strensall (proposed)

Haxby (proposed)

YORK

(SEE INSET TO LEFT)

A

Harrogate

Hornbeam Park

Pannal

Weeton

Wescoehill Tun.

Colton Junc.

Burley-in-Wharfedale

Menston

Guiseley

Esholt Tun. z

Esholt Junc.

aildon x

t w

u Shipley

Thackley Tun.

Apperley Junc.

Bramhope Tun. (2m. 241yds.)

Horsforth

Ulleskelf

Church Fenton

Sherburn in Elmet

Selby N. Side Discharge Sdg.

Selby West Junc.

Selby Swing Bridge

Selby - Potter Group

Selby

Frizinghall

New Pudsey

Bramley

York Rd Park & Ride

Headingley

Seacroft

Leeds Supertram (Proposed)

Cross Gates

East Garforth

South Milford

Selby Drift Mine - RJB

N.

Otley Rd

W. Selby Goods Viking Shipping

E. S.

Selby Canal Junc.

63

Bradford Forster Sq.

Stanningley Tun.

Scrapyard - European Metal Recycling

Leeds

Garforth

Micklefield

Hambleton Juncs.

Drax - AES Electric of Virginia

Mill Lane Junc.

Bradford Interchange

Cottingley

Morley

Woodlesford

Peckfield Junc.

Milford Junc.

Castleford East Junc.

Milford Sidings

Gascoigne Wood Junc.

Sdgs.

B

Wakefield Rd. Tun.

Bowling Tun.

(SEE INSET P63)

Middleton

Allerton Bywater (Disused)

Castleford W. Junc.

Ferrybridge - Edison

Brotherton Tun.

Temple Hirst Junc.

Wyke Tun.

Morley Tun. (1m. 1609yds.)

Ardsley Tun.

Tingley

Outwood

Car Terminal (Disused)

Methley Junc.

Altofts Junc.

Whitwood Junc.

Castleford

6

Knottingley

f

Kellingley RJB

Sudforth Lane

Batley

Wrenthorpe Sidings

Wakefield Kirkgate

Normanton

Prince of Wales-RJB

p

g

KY 9

Whitley Bridge

Hensall

Brighouse

Dewsbury

Tilcon Scone Term.

Welbeck Spoil Term. (Disused)

1

Hensall Junc.

Heck - Plasmor

Snaith

Bradley Wood Junc.

Ravensthorpe

4

Wakefield Westgate

s

HM

m

k

a

3

2

Pontefract Monkhill

Eggborough - British Energy

radley Tun.

Bradley Junc.

Mirfield

q

Marcroft Wagon W.

h

b

c

Streethouse

Pontefract Baghill

Deighton

Heaton Lodge Junc.

Healey Mills Yard

Horbury - Bombardier Prorail Works

Crofton East Junc.

Hare Park Junc.

e

Wintersett - RJB (Disused)

HEALEY MILLS

Sandal & Agbrigg

Fitzwilliam

Hatfield - Hatfield Coal Company

STEEPLE GRANGE LIGHT RAILWAY (1' 3")

Woolley Tuns.

Woolley Coal Stockpile-MED Contracting

South Kirkby Junc.

South Elmsall

Shaftholme Junc.

Joan Croft Junc.

Hatfield & Stainforth

Brockholes

Stocksmoor

Shelley

Cuckoo's Nest

Clayton West

Skelmanthorpe

Shelley Woodhouse Tun.

Darton

Moorthorpe

Frickley - Coal Stockpile

Adwick Junc.

Adwick

Thorne Junc.

Thurstonland Tun.

Shepley

Cumberworth Tun.

Denby Dale

Monk Bretton - Redfern National Glass

(SEE INSET P 64)

Clayton West Junc.

Wellhouse Tun.

Summer Lane

Barnsley Station Junc.

BARNSLEY

Thurnscoe

Hexthorpe Junc.

Doncaster

C

Penistone

Oxspring Tun.

Dodworth

Silkstone Common

ELSECAR STEAM RAILWAY

Goldthorpe

DONCASTER

SOUTH YORKSHIRE

Wombwell

Elsecar

Bolton-on-Dearne

Conisbrough Tun.

Stocksbridge - United Engineering Steels

Deepcar Exchange Sidings

Hemingfield

Elsecar

Swinton Junc.

Mexborough

Conisbrough

Tankersley Tun.

Swinton

Mexborough East Junc.

5   10 m.   (1:350,000)

5   10   15 km.

1

2

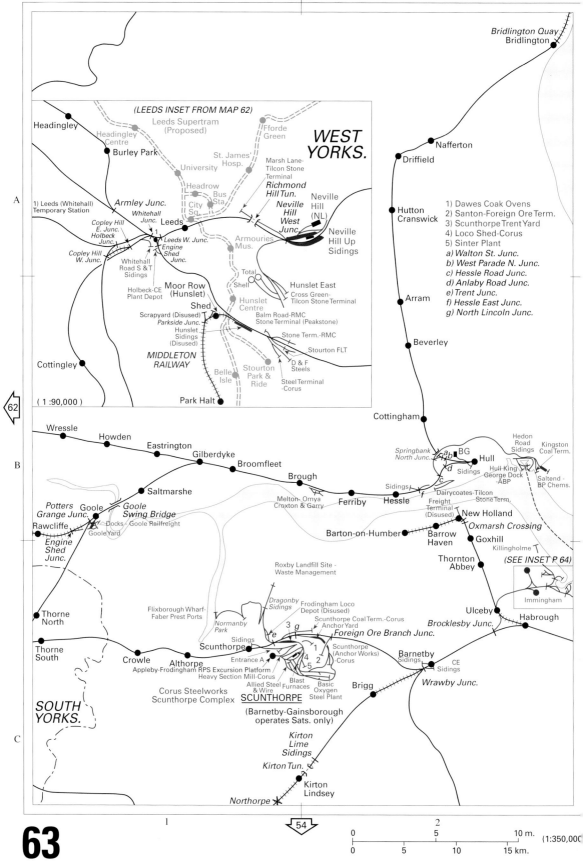

(LEEDS INSET FROM MAP 62)

Leeds Supertram
(Proposed)

WEST
YORKS.

Headingley

Headingley
Centre

Burley Park

University

Fforde
Green

St. James'
Hosp.

Headrow
Bus
Sta.

City
Sq.

Marsh Lane-
Tilcon Stone
Terminal

Richmond
Hill Tun.

Neville
Hill
West
Junc.

Neville
Hill
(NL)

1) Leeds (Whitehall)
Temporary Station

Armley Junc.

Whitehall
Junc.

Leeds

Leeds W. Junc.

Neville
Hill Up
Sidings

Copley Hill
E. Junc.
Holbeck
Junc.

Copley Hill
W. Junc.

Engine
Shed
Junc.

Whitehall
Road S & T
Sidings

Armouries
Mus.

Holbeck-CE
Plant Depot

Total
Shell

Hunslet East

Cottingley

Moor Row
(Hunslet)
Shed

Scrapyard (Disused)
Parkside Junc.

Hunslet
Sidings
(Disused)

MIDDLETON
RAILWAY

Belle
Isle

Hunslet
Centre

Cross Green-
Tilcon Stone Terminal

Balm Road-RMC
Stone Terminal (Peakstone)

Stone Term.-RMC

Stourton FLT

Stourton
Park &
Ride

D & F
Steels

(1:90,000)

Park Halt

Steel Terminal
-Corus

A

1) Dawes Coak Ovens
2) Santon-Foreign Ore Term.
3) Scunthorpe Trent Yard
4) Loco Shed-Corus
5) Sinter Plant
a) Walton St. Junc.
b) West Parade N. Junc.
c) Hessle Road Junc.
d) Anlaby Road Junc.
e) Trent Junc.
f) Hessle East Junc.
g) North Lincoln Junc.

Bridlington Quay
Bridlington

Nafferton

Driffield

Hutton
Cranswick

Arram

Beverley

Cottingham

Springbank
North Junc.

Hedon
Road
Sidings

Kingston
Coal Term.

BG
Hull

Hull King
George Dock
-ABP

Saltend -
BP Chems.

Sidings

Wressle

Howden

Eastrington

Gilberdyke

Broomfleet

Brough

Melton- Omya
Croxton & Garry

Ferriby

Sidings

Hessle

Dairycoates-Tilcon
Freight
Terminal
(Disused)

Stone Term.

B

Saltmarshe

New Holland

Barton-on-Humber

Barrow
Haven

Goxhill

Oxmarsh Crossing

Killingholme

Potters
Grange Junc.

Goole
Goole
Swing Bridge

Rawcliffe

Docks Goole Railfreight
Goole Yard

Thornton
Abbey

(SEE INSET P 64)

Engine
Shed
Junc.

Immingham

Thorne
North

Roxby Landfill Site -
Waste Management

Ulceby

Brocklesby Junc.

Habrough

Thorne
South

Crowle

Flixborough Wharf-
Faber Prest Ports

Normanby
Park

Dragonby
Sidings

Frodingham Loco
Depot (Disused)

Scunthorpe Coal Term.-Corus
Anchor Yard

Foreign Ore Branch Junc.

Scunthorpe
(Anchor Works)
-Corus

Barnetby
Sidings

CE
Sidings

Althorpe

Sidings

Scunthorpe

Entrance A

Appleby-Frodingham RPS Excursion Platform
Heavy Section Mill-Corus

Allied Steel
& Wire

Corus Steelworks
Scunthorpe Complex

SCUNTHORPE

(Barnetby-Gainsborough
operates Sats. only)

Blast
Furnaces

Basic
Oxygen
Steel Plant

Brigg

Wrawby Junc.

SOUTH
YORKS.

Kirton
Lime
Sidings

Kirton Tun.

Kirton
Lindsey

Northorpe

C

0   2
| | | | | 10 m.   (1:350,000)
0   5   10   15 km.

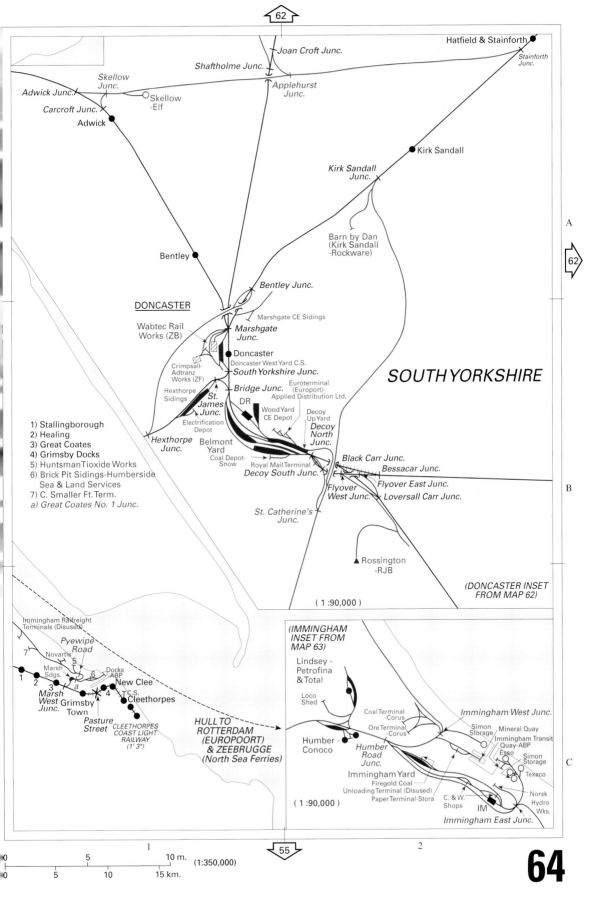

Hatfield & Stainforth

Stainforth Junc.

Joan Croft Junc.

Shaftholme Junc.

Applehurst Junc.

Skellow Junc.

Skellow -Elf

Adwick Junc.

Carcroft Junc.

Adwick

Kirk Sandall

Kirk Sandall Junc.

A

Barn by Dan (Kirk Sandall -Rockware)

Bentley

Bentley Junc.

DONCASTER

Marshgate CE Sidings

Wabtec Rail Works (ZB)

Marshgate Junc.

Doncaster

Doncaster West Yard C.S.

South Yorkshire Junc.

Crimpsall- Adtranz Works (ZF)

Bridge Junc.

Euroterminal (Europort)- Applied Distribution Ltd.

SOUTH YORKSHIRE

Hexthorpe Sidings

St. James Junc.

DR

Wood Yard CE Depot

Decoy Up Yard

Electrification Depot

Decoy North Junc.

Hexthorpe Junc.

Belmont Yard

Coal Depot- Snow

Royal Mail Terminal

Decoy South Junc.

Black Carr Junc.

Bessacar Junc.

Flyover East Junc.

Flyover West Junc.

Loversall Carr Junc.

B

1) Stallingborough
2) Healing
3) Great Coates
4) Grimsby Docks
5) HuntsmanTioxide Works
6) Brick Pit Sidings-Humberside
   Sea & Land Services
7) C. Smaller Ft. Term.
a) Great Coates No. 1 Junc.

St. Catherine's Junc.

▲ Rossington -RJB

(DONCASTER INSET FROM MAP 62)

(1 :90,000)

Immingham Railfreight Terminals (Disused)

Pyewipe Road

Novartis

7

Marsh Sdgs.

5

6

Docks ABP

New Clee

1 2 3 *a* 4 T.C.S. Cleethorpes

Marsh West Junc. Grimsby Town

Pasture Street

CLEETHORPES COAST LIGHT RAILWAY (1' 3")

HULL TO ROTTERDAM (EUROPOORT) & ZEEBRUGGE (North Sea Ferries)

(IMMINGHAM INSET FROM MAP 63)

Lindsey - Petrofina & Total

Loco Shed

Humber - Conoco

Coal Terminal -Corus

Ore Terminal -Corus

Humber Road Junc.

Immingham Yard

Firegold Coal Unloading Terminal (Disused)

Paper Terminal-Stora

Immingham West Junc.

Simon Storage

Mineral Quay

Immingham Transit Quay-ABP

Esso

Simon Storage

Texaco

C. & W. Shops

IM

Norsk Hydro Wks.

Immingham East Junc.

(1 :90,000)

C

0   5   10 m.

(1:350,000)

0   5   10   15 km.

1

2

64

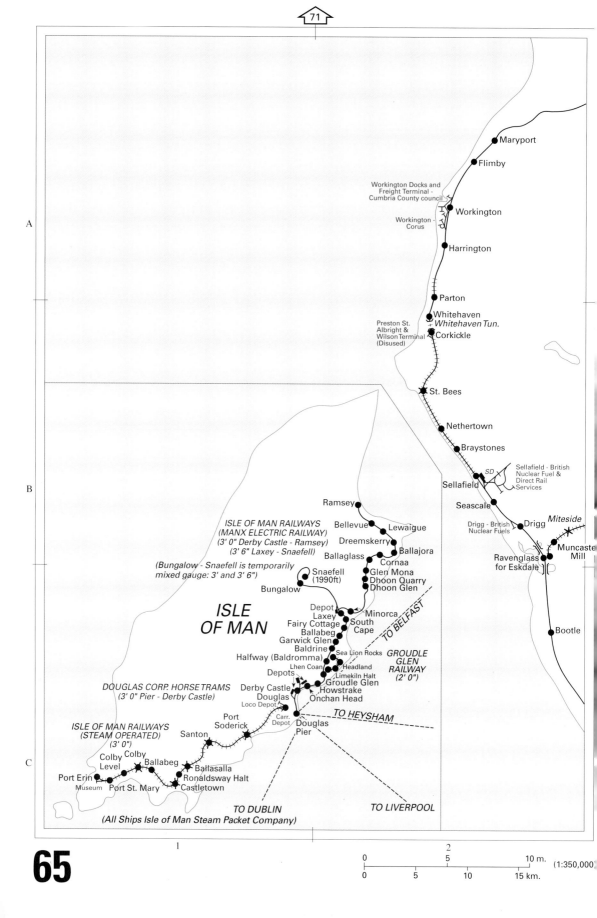

Maryport

Flimby

Workington Docks and
Freight Terminal -
Cumbria County council

Workington -
Corus

Workington

Harrington

Parton

Whitehaven

Whitehaven Tun.

Preston St.
Albright &
Wilson Terminal
(Disused)

Corkickle

St. Bees

Nethertown

Braystones

SD

Sellafield - British
Nuclear Fuel &
Direct Rail
Services

Sellafield

Seascale

Miteside

Drigg - British
Nuclear Fuels

Drigg

Muncaste
Mill

Ravenglass
for Eskdale

A

B

Ramsey

ISLE OF MAN RAILWAYS
(MANX ELECTRIC RAILWAY)
(3' 0" Derby Castle - Ramsey)
(3' 6" Laxey - Snaefell)

(Bungalow - Snaefell is temporarily
mixed gauge: 3' and 3' 6")

Bellevue

Lewaigue

Dreemskerry

Ballajora

Ballaglass

Cornaa

Glen Mona

Snaefell
(1990ft)

Dhoon Quarry

Dhoon Glen

Bungalow

ISLE
OF MAN

Depot

Laxey

Minorca

Fairy Cottage

South
Cape

Ballabeg

Garwick Glen

Baldrine

Sea Lion Rocks

GROUDLE
GLEN
RAILWAY
(2' 0")

TO BELFAST

Halfway (Baldromma)

Lhen Coan

Headland

Depots

Limekiln Halt

Groudle Glen

Howstrake

Derby Castle

DOUGLAS CORP. HORSE TRAMS
(3' 0" Pier - Derby Castle)

Douglas

Onchan Head

Loco Depot

Port
Soderick

Carr.
Depot

Douglas
Pier

TO HEYSHAM

ISLE OF MAN RAILWAYS
(STEAM OPERATED)
(3' 0")

Santon

Colby
Level

Colby

Ballabeg

Ballasalla

Ronaldsway Halt

Port Erin

Museum

Port St. Mary

Castletown

TO DUBLIN

(All Ships Isle of Man Steam Packet Company)

TO LIVERPOOL

Bootle

C

1

2

0   5   10 m.

0   5   10   15 km.

(1:350,000)

65

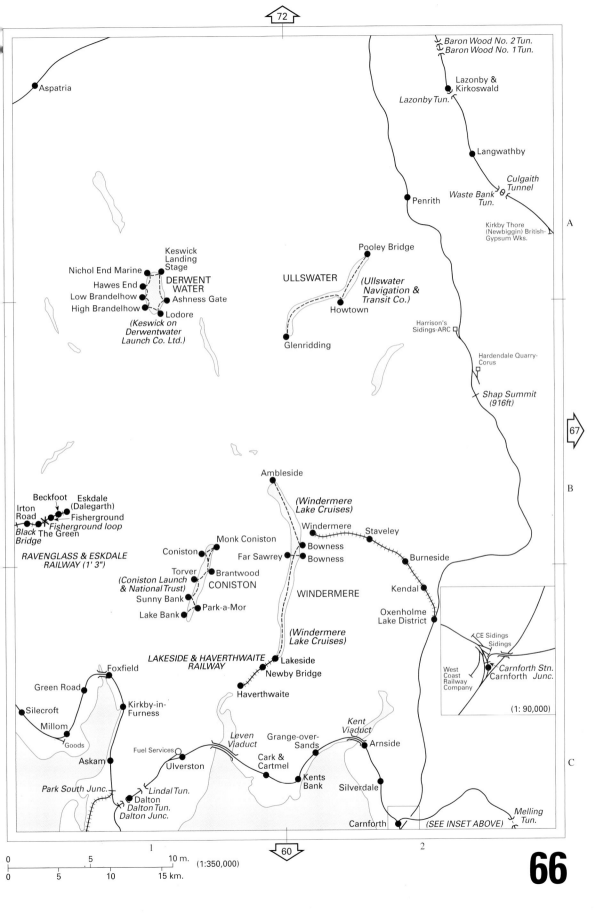

Aspatria

Baron Wood No. 2 Tun.
Baron Wood No. 1 Tun.

Lazonby &
Kirkoswald

Lazonby Tun.

Langwathby

*Culgaith
Tunnel*

*Waste Bank
Tun.*

Penrith

Kirkby Thore
(Newbiggin) British-
Gypsum Wks.

A

Keswick
Landing
Stage

Nichol End Marine

**DERWENT
WATER**

Hawes End

Low Brandelhow

Ashness Gate

High Brandelhow

Lodore

*(Keswick on
Derwentwater
Launch Co. Ltd.)*

Pooley Bridge

ULLSWATER

*(Ullswater
Navigation &
Transit Co.)*

Howtown

Harrison's
Sidings-ARC

Glenridding

Hardendale Quarry-
Corus

*Shap Summit
(916ft)*

67

B

Ambleside

*(Windermere
Lake Cruises)*

Beckfoot

Eskdale
(Dalegarth)

Irton
Road

Fisherground

Fisherground loop

Black The Green
Bridge

*RAVENGLASS & ESKDALE
RAILWAY (1' 3")*

Monk Coniston

Coniston

Far Sawrey

Windermere

Staveley

Bowness

Bowness

Burneside

Torver

Brantwood

CONISTON

*(Coniston Launch
& National Trust)*

WINDERMERE

Kendal

Sunny Bank

Park-a-Mor

Lake Bank

Oxenholme
Lake District

CE Sidings
Sidings

*(Windermere
Lake Cruises)*

*LAKESIDE & HAVERTHWAITE
RAILWAY*

Lakeside

Newby Bridge

West
Coast
Railway
Company

Carnforth Stn.
Carnforth *Junc.*

Haverthwaite

Foxfield

(1: 90,000)

Green Road

Kirkby-in-
Furness

*Leven
Viaduct*

Grange-over-
Sands

*Kent
Viaduct*

Arnside

Silecroft

Millom

Cark &
Cartmel

Fuel Services

Goods

Askam

Ulverston

Kents
Bank

Silverdale

C

Park South Junc.

Lindal Tun.

Dalton

Dalton Tun.

Dalton Junc.

*Melling
Tun.*

Carnforth

(SEE INSET ABOVE)

1

2

0   5   10 m.   (1:350,000)

0   5   10   15 km.

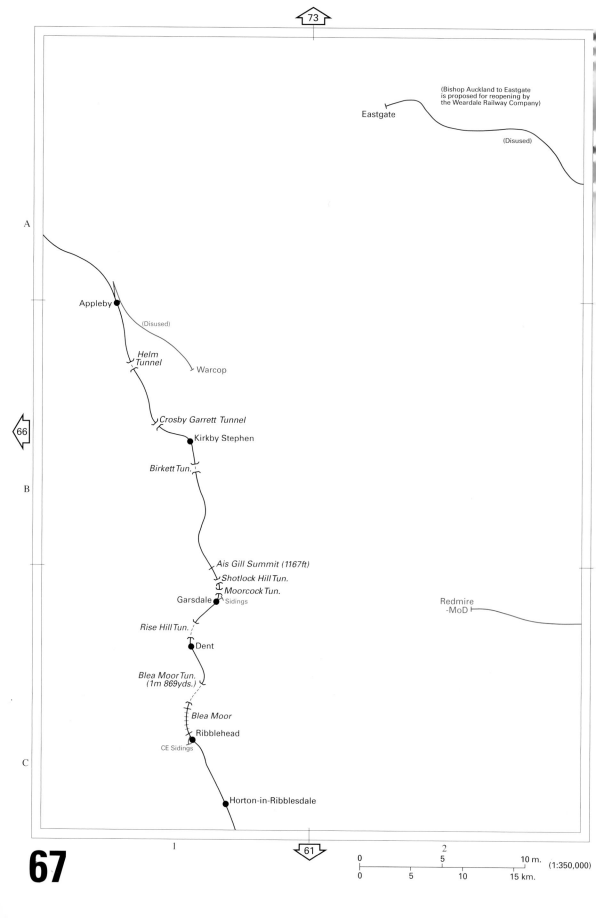

(Bishop Auckland to Eastgate
is proposed for reopening by
the Weardale Railway Company)

Eastgate

(Disused)

A

Appleby

(Disused)

Helm
Tunnel

Warcop

Crosby Garrett Tunnel

66

Kirkby Stephen

Birkett Tun.

B

Ais Gill Summit (1167ft)

Shotlock Hill Tun.

Moorcock Tun.

Garsdale   Sidings

Redmire
-MoD

Rise Hill Tun.

Dent

Blea Moor Tun.
(1m 869yds.)

Blea Moor

Ribblehead

CE Sidings

C

Horton-in-Ribblesdale

1

2

67

0   5   10 m.

0   5   10   15 km.

(1:350,000)

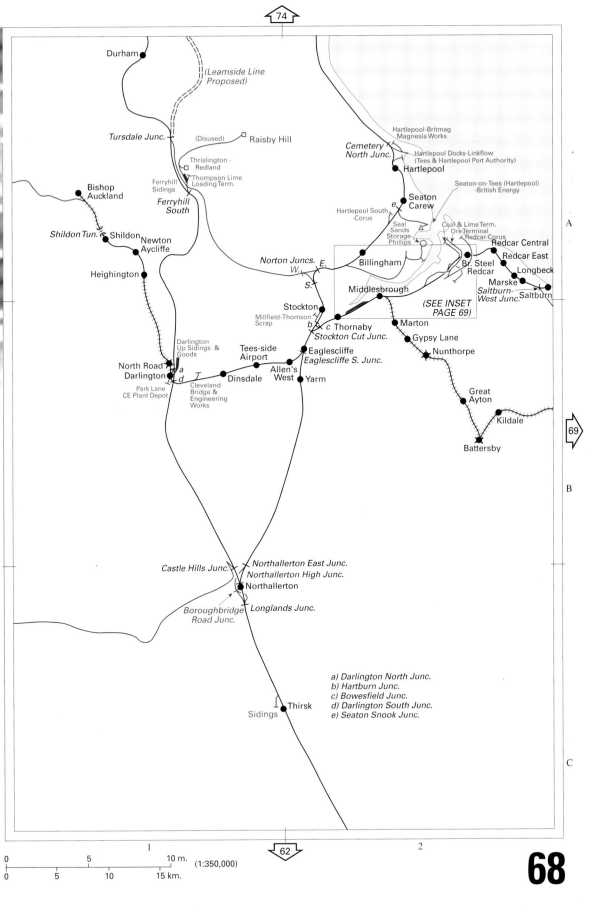

Durham

(Leamside Line Proposed)

Tursdale Junc.

(Disused) □ Raisby Hill

Thrislington - Redland

Ferryhill Sidings

Thompson Lime Loading Term.

Ferryhill South

Bishop Auckland

Shildon Tun. Shildon

Newton Aycliffe

Heighington

Darlington Up Sidings & Goods

a

North Road Darlington *d*

Park Lane CE Plant Depot

Cleveland Bridge & Engineering Works

Dinsdale

Tees-side Airport

Allen's West

Yarm

Hartlepool-Britmag Magnesia Works

Cemetery North Junc.

Hartlepool

Hartlepool Docks-Linkflow (Tees & Hartlepool Port Authority)

Seaton-on-Tees (Hartlepool) -British Energy

Seaton Carew *e*

Hartlepool South -Corus

Seal Sands Storage- Phillips

Coal & Lime Term. Ore Terminal Redcar-Corus

Redcar Central

Redcar East

Br. Steel Redcar

Longbeck

Marske

Saltburn- West Junc. Saltburn

Billingham

Norton Juncs. *E.*

W.

S.

Middlesbrough

Stockton

Millfield-Thomson Scrap

b *c* Thornaby

Stockton Cut Junc.

Eaglescliffe

Eaglescliffe S. Junc.

Marton

Gypsy Lane

Nunthorpe

(SEE INSET PAGE 69)

Great Ayton

Kildale

Battersby

Castle Hills Junc.

Northallerton East Junc.

Northallerton High Junc.

Northallerton

Boroughbridge Road Junc.

Longlands Junc.

a) *Darlington North Junc.*
b) *Hartburn Junc.*
c) *Bowesfield Junc.*
d) *Darlington South Junc.*
e) *Seaton Snook Junc.*

Thirsk

Sidings

A

B

C

1

2

0   5   10 m.

(1:350,000)

0   5   10   15 km.

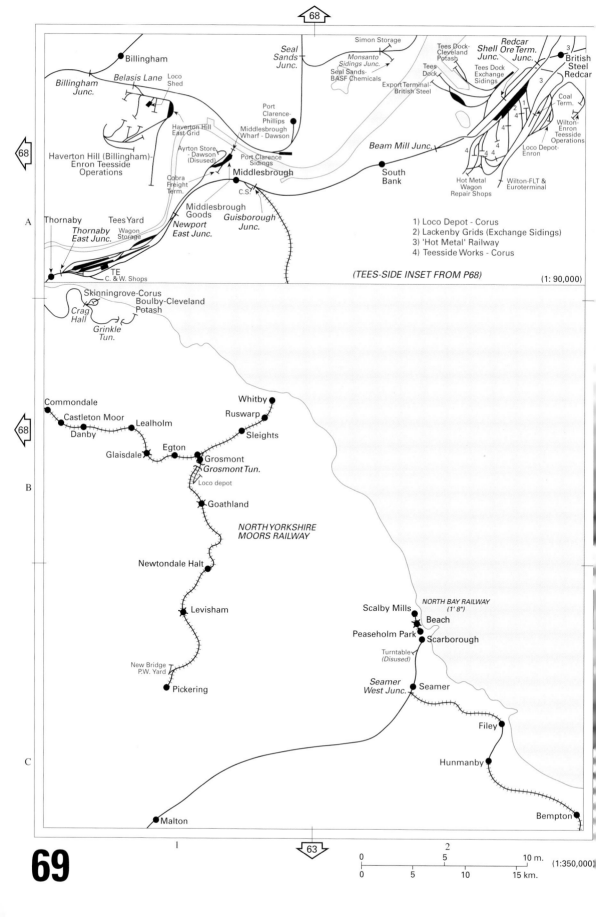

Seal Sands Junc.

Simon Storage

Tees Dock-Cleveland Potash

Monsanto Sidings Junc.

Seal Sands-BASF Chemicals

Tees Dock Exchange Sidings

Tees Dock

Shell Junc.

Redcar Ore Term. Junc.

3

3

British Steel Redcar

Billingham

Billingham Junc.

Belasis Lane

Loco Shed

Haverton Hill East Grid

Port Clarence-Phillips

Middlesbrough Wharf - Dawson

Export Terminal-British Steel

Beam Mill Junc.

Coal Term.

3

2

1

4

4

Wilton-Enron Teesside Operations

Loco Depot-Enron

Haverton Hill (Billingham)-Enron Teesside Operations

Ayrton Store - Dawson (Disused)

Port Clarence Sidings

4

4 4

Cobra Freight Term.

Middlesbrough

C.S.

South Bank

Hot Metal Wagon Repair Shops

Wilton-FLT & Euroterminal

A

Thornaby

Tees Yard

Wagon Storage

Thornaby East Junc.

Middlesbrough Goods

Newport East Junc.

Guisborough Junc.

1) Loco Depot - Corus
2) Lackenby Grids (Exchange Sidings)
3) 'Hot Metal' Railway
4) Teesside Works - Corus

TE

C. & W. Shops

(TEES-SIDE INSET FROM P68)

(1: 90,000)

Skinningrove-Corus

Crag Hall

Boulby-Cleveland Potash

Grinkle Tun.

Commondale

Castleton Moor

Danby

Lealholm

Whitby

Ruswarp

Glaisdale

Egton

Sleights

Grosmont

Grosmont Tun.

Loco depot

B

Goathland

NORTH YORKSHIRE MOORS RAILWAY

Newtondale Halt

Scalby Mills

NORTH BAY RAILWAY (1' 8")

Beach

Peaseholm Park

Levisham

Scarborough

Turntable (Disused)

New Bridge P.W. Yard

Seamer West Junc.

Seamer

Pickering

Filey

C

Hunmanby

Malton

Bempton

0   2   10 m.   (1:350,000)

0   5   15 km.

5

10

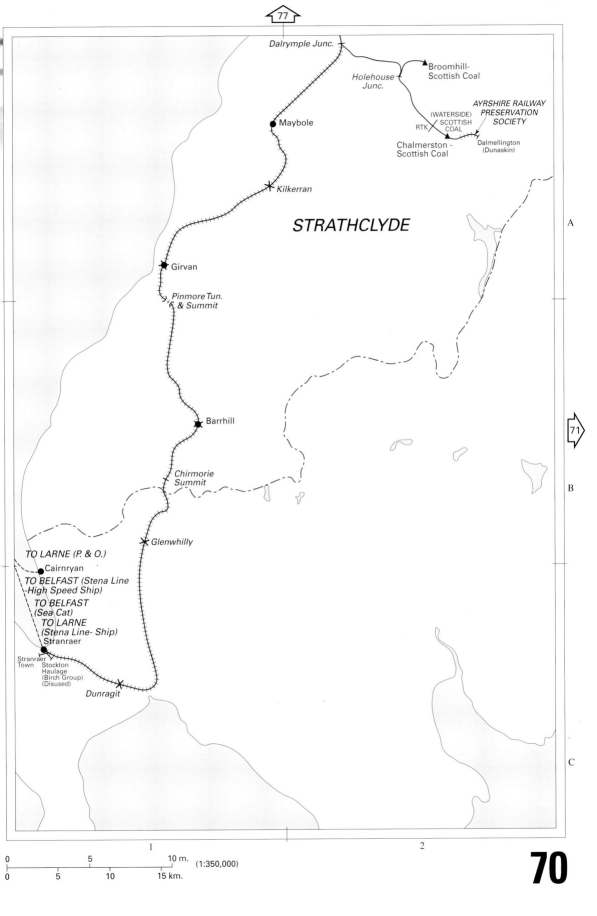

Dalrymple Junc.

Holehouse
Junc.

Broomhill-
Scottish Coal

AYRSHIRE RAILWAY
PRESERVATION
SOCIETY

(WATERSIDE)
SCOTTISH
COAL

RTK

Dalmellington
(Dunaskin)

Chalmerston -
Scottish Coal

Maybole

Kilkerran

STRATHCLYDE

Girvan

Pinmore Tun.
& Summit

Barrhill

Chirmorie
Summit

Glenwhilly

TO LARNE (P. & O.)
Cairnryan
TO BELFAST (Stena Line
High Speed Ship)
TO BELFAST
(Sea Cat)
TO LARNE
(Stena Line- Ship)
Stranraer

Stranraer
Town
Stockton
Haulage
(Birch Group)
(Disused)

Dunragit

A

B

C

1

2

| 0 | | 5 | | 10 m. | (1:350,000) |
| 0 | 5 | | 10 | | 15 km. |

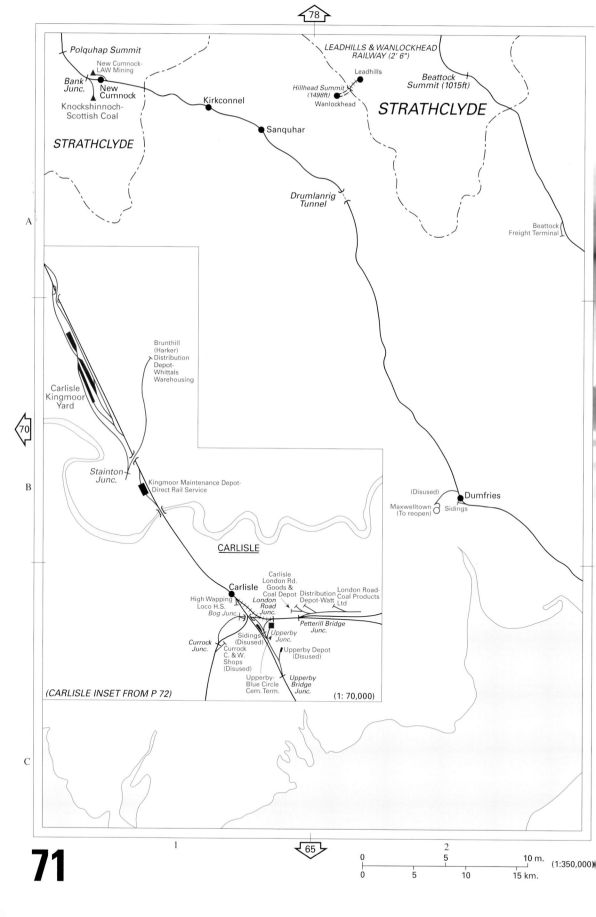

Polquhap Summit

New Cumnock-
LAW Mining

LEADHILLS & WANLOCKHEAD
RAILWAY (2' 6")

Leadhills

Bank
Junc.

New
Cumnock

Hillhead Summit
(1498ft)

Wanlockhead

Beattock
Summit (1015ft)

Knockshinnoch-
Scottish Coal

Kirkconnel

STRATHCLYDE

STRATHCLYDE

Sanquhar

Drumlanrig
Tunnel

Beattock
Freight Terminal

A

Brunthill
(Harker)
Distribution
Depot-
Whittals
Warehousing

Carlisle
Kingmoor
Yard

70

Stainton
Junc.

Kingmoor Maintenance Depot-
Direct Rail Service

B

(Disused)

Maxwelltown
(To reopen)

Sidings

Dumfries

CARLISLE

Carlisle
London Rd.
Goods &
Coal Depot

London Road-
Coal Products
Ltd

Carlisle

Distribution
Depot-Watt

High Wapping
Loco H.S.

London
Road
Junc.

Bog Junc.

Petterill Bridge
Junc.

Currock
Junc.

Sidings
(Disused)

Upperby
Junc.

Currock
C. & W.
Shops
(Disused)

Upperby Depot
(Disused)

Upperby-
Blue Circle
Cem. Term.

Upperby
Bridge
Junc.

(CARLISLE INSET FROM P 72)

(1: 70,000)

C

71

1

2

5

10 m.

(1:350,000)

0

5

10

15 km.

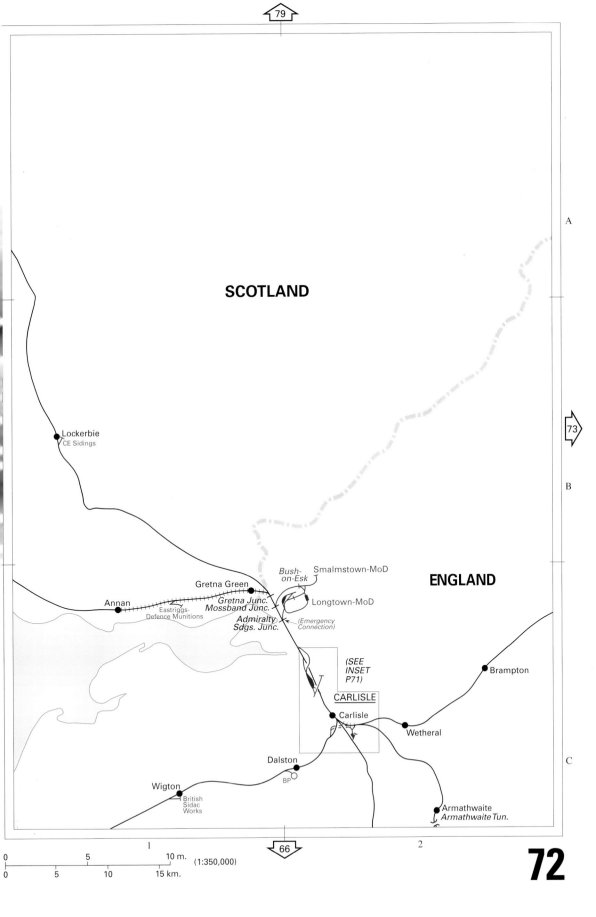

SCOTLAND

ENGLAND

Lockerbie
CE Sidings

Bush-
on-Esk Smalmstown-MoD

Gretna Green Longtown-MoD

Annan *Gretna Junc.*
Mossband Junc.
Eastriggs-
Defence Munitions *Admiralty*
Sdgs. Junc. (Emergency
Connection)

*(SEE
INSET
P71)* Brampton

CARLISLE

Carlisle

Wetheral

Dalston
BP

Wigton
British
Sidac
Works

Armathwaite
Armathwaite Tun.

73

A

B

C

1 2

0   5   10 m.   (1:350,000)
0   5   10   15 km.

72

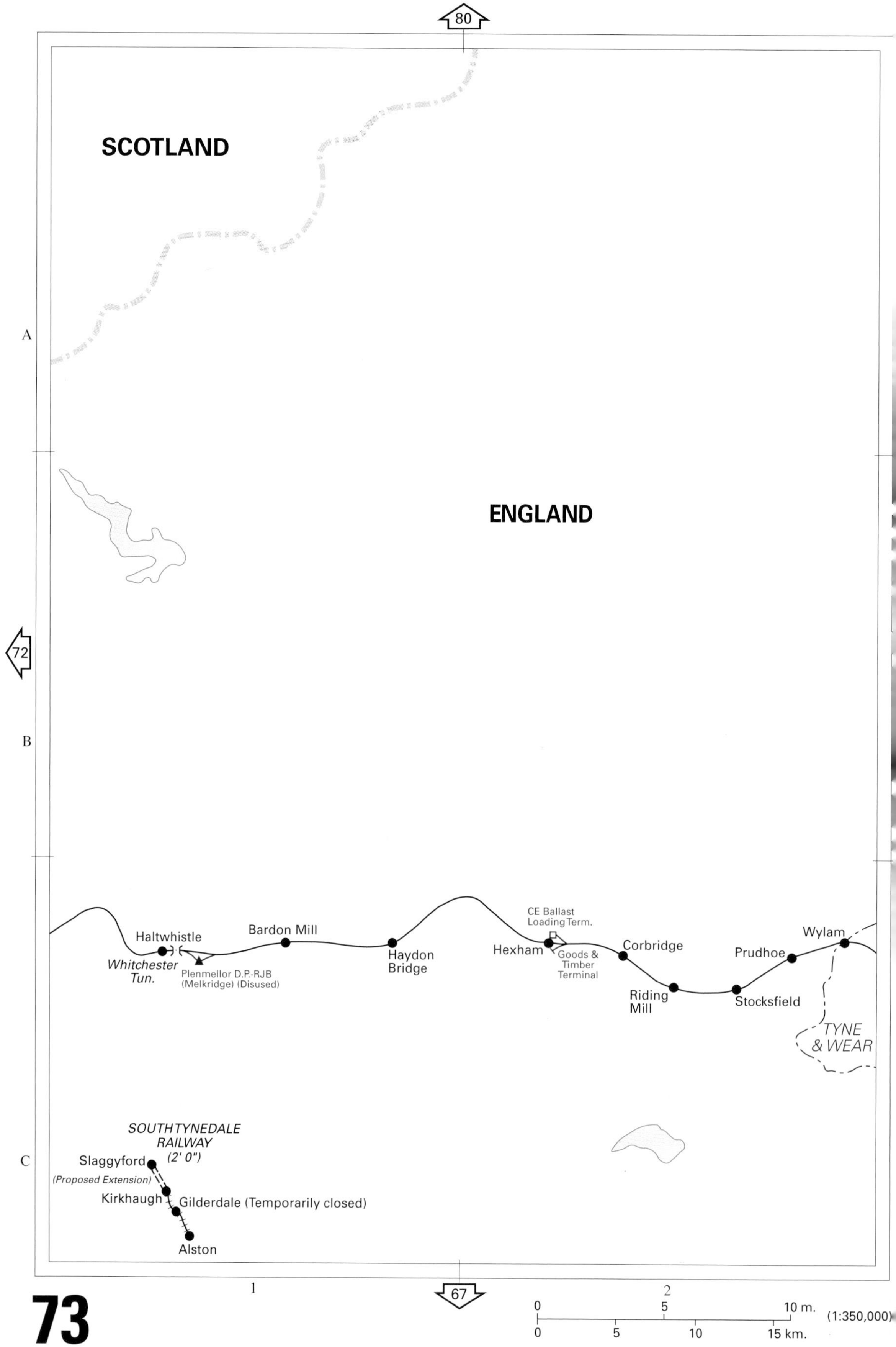

SCOTLAND

ENGLAND

A

B

Haltwhistle   Bardon Mill   Wylam

Whitchester
Tun.   Haydon   Hexham   Corbridge   Prudhoe
Plenmellor D.P.-RJB   Bridge   Goods &
(Melkridge) (Disused)   Timber
                                       Terminal

CE Ballast
Loading Term.

Riding
Mill   Stocksfield

TYNE
& WEAR

SOUTH TYNEDALE
RAILWAY
Slaggyford *(2' 0")*
(Proposed Extension)
Kirkhaugh Gilderdale (Temporarily closed)

Alston

C

0   2
                    5   10 m.
                                   (1:350,000)
0   5   10   15 km.

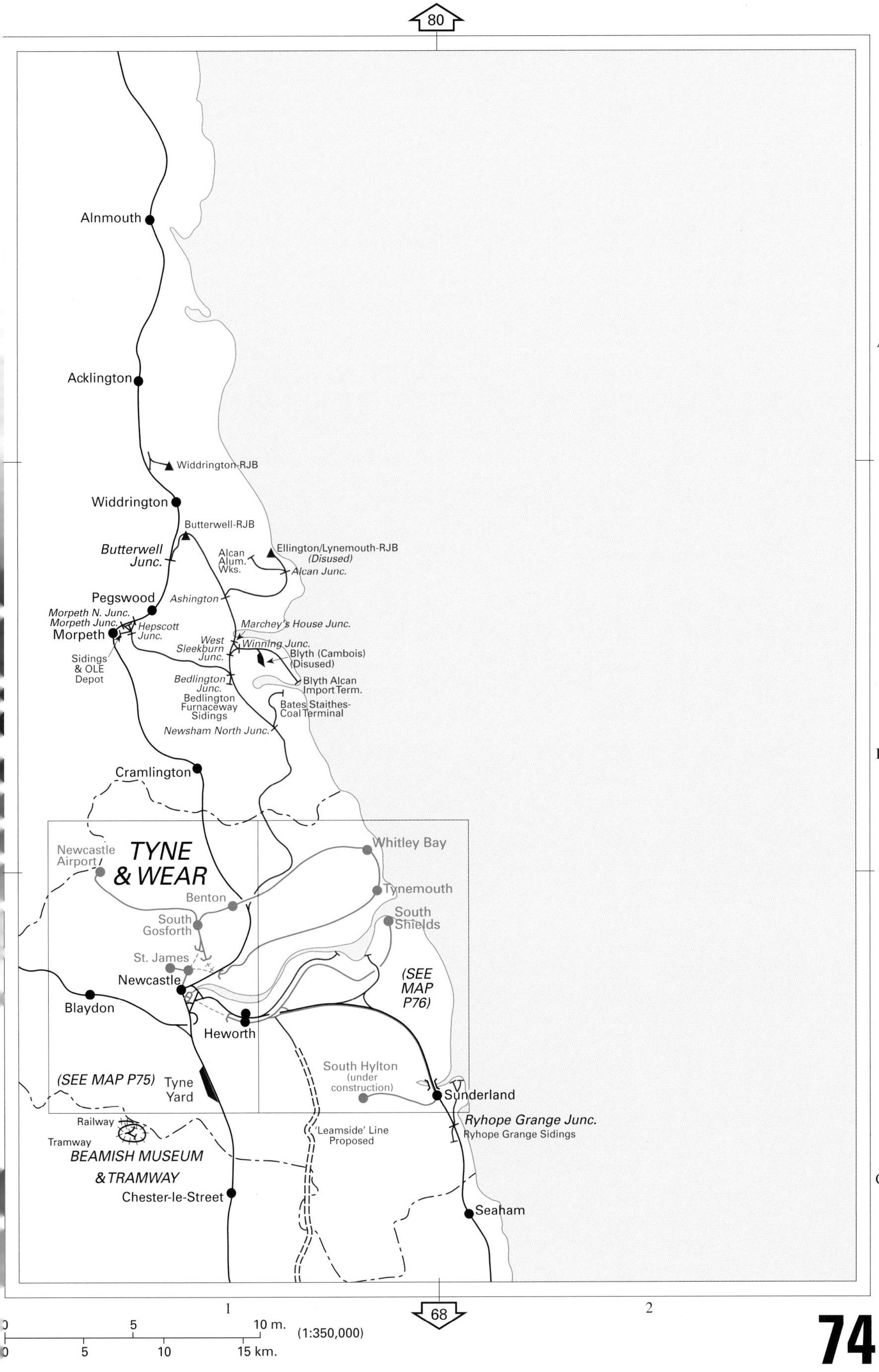

Alnmouth

Acklington

▲ Widdrington-RJB

Widdrington

Butterwell-RJB

Butterwell Junc.

Alcan Alum. Wks.

▲ Ellington/Lynemouth-RJB *(Disused)*

Alcan Junc.

Pegswood

Ashington

Morpeth N. Junc.
Morpeth Junc. Hepscott Junc.

Morpeth

Marchey's House Junc.

West Sleekburn Junc. *Winning Junc.*

▲ Blyth (Cambois) *(Disused)*

Sidings & OLE Depot

Bedlington Junc.
Bedlington Furnaceway Sidings

Blyth Alcan Import Term.

Bates Staithes-Coal Terminal

Newsham North Junc.

Cramlington

Newcastle Airport

TYNE & WEAR

Whitley Bay

Benton

Tynemouth

South Gosforth

South Shields

St. James

(SEE MAP P76)

Newcastle

Blaydon

Heworth

South Hylton *(under construction)*

Sunderland

(SEE MAP P75) Tyne Yard

Ryhope Grange Junc.
Ryhope Grange Sidings

Railway

'Leamside' Line Proposed

Tramway

BEAMISH MUSEUM & TRAMWAY

Chester-le-Street

Seaham

1   10 m. (1:350,000)   2

0   5   15 km.

74

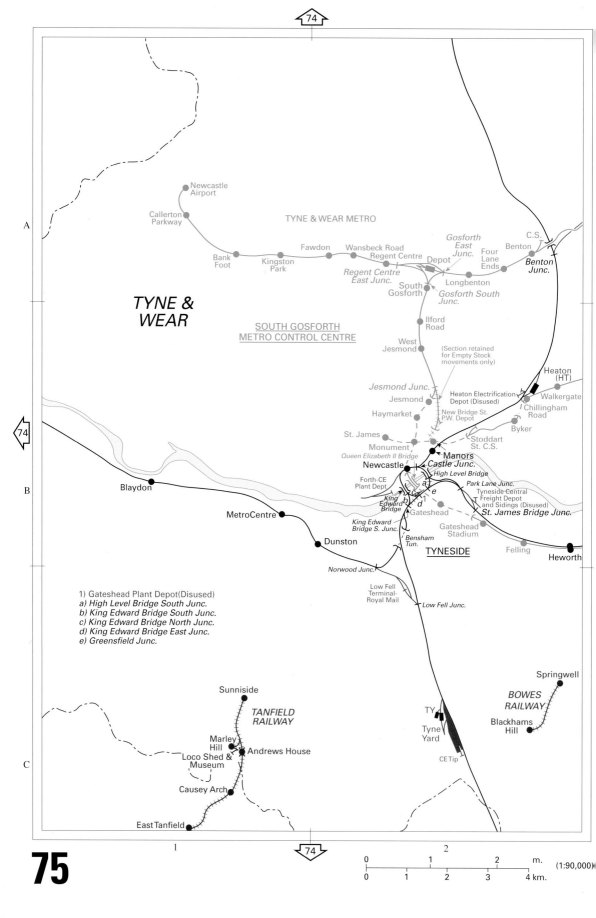

A

Newcastle Airport

Callerton Parkway

TYNE & WEAR METRO

Gosforth East Junc.

C.S.

Benton

Benton Junc.

Four Lane Ends

Longbenton

Depot

Fawdon

Wansbeck Road

Regent Centre

Bank Foot

Kingston Park

Regent Centre East Junc.

South Gosforth

Gosforth South Junc.

TYNE & WEAR

SOUTH GOSFORTH METRO CONTROL CENTRE

Ilford Road

West Jesmond

(Section retained for Empty Stock movements only)

Heaton (HT)

Jesmond Junc.

Jesmond

Heaton Electrification Depot (Disused)

Walkergate

Chillingham Road

Haymarket

New Bridge St. P.W. Depot

Byker

St. James

Stoddart St. C.S.

Monument

Queen Elizabeth II Bridge

Manors

Newcastle

Castle Junc.

74

B

Blaydon

Forth-CE Plant Dept

High Level Bridge

Park Lane Junc.

Tyneside Central Freight Depot and Sidings (Disused)

St. James Bridge Junc.

King Edward Bridge

MetroCentre

King Edward Bridge S. Junc.

Gateshead

Gateshead Stadium

Dunston

Bensham Tun.

TYNESIDE

Felling

Heworth

Norwood Junc.

Low Fell Terminal-Royal Mail

Low Fell Junc.

1) Gateshead Plant Depot(Disused)
a) High Level Bridge South Junc.
b) King Edward Bridge South Junc.
c) King Edward Bridge North Junc.
d) King Edward Bridge East Junc.
e) Greensfield Junc.

Springwell

Sunniside

BOWES RAILWAY

TY

TANFIELD RAILWAY

Tyne Yard

Blackhams Hill

Marley Hill

Andrews House

Loco Shed & Museum

C

CE Tip

Causey Arch

East Tanfield

75

0   1   2   m.

0   1   2   3   4 km.

(1:90,000)

1   2

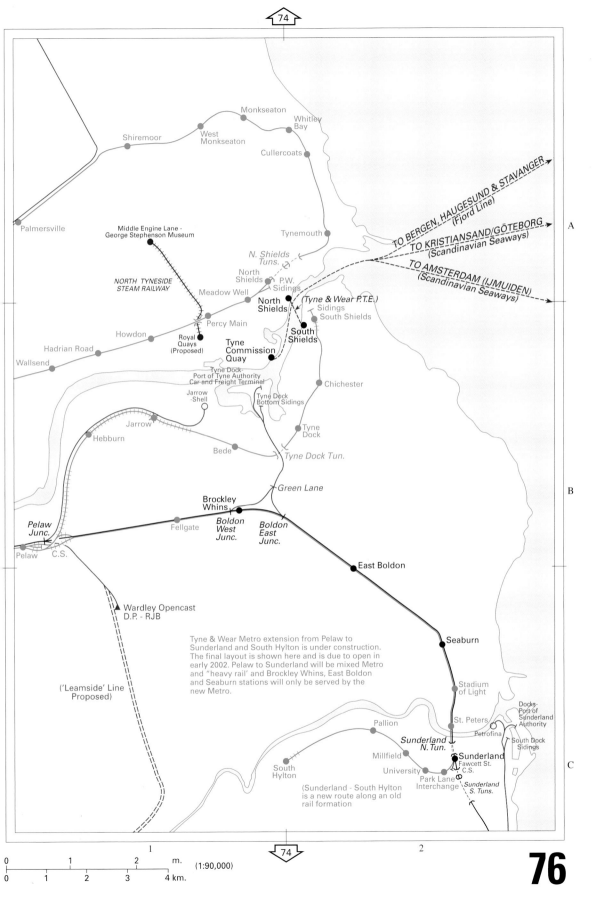

Monkseaton

Whitley
Bay

West
Monkseaton

Shiremoor

Cullercoats

Palmersville

Tynemouth

TO BERGEN, HAUGESUND & STAVANGER
(Fjord Line)

TO KRISTIANSAND/GÖTEBORG
(Scandinavian Seaways)

A

*N. Shields
Tuns.*

Middle Engine Lane -
George Stephenson Museum

TO AMSTERDAM (IJMUIDEN)
(Scandinavian Seaways)

North
Shields

P.W.
Sidings

*NORTH TYNESIDE
STEAM RAILWAY*

Meadow Well

**North
Shields**

(Tyne & Wear P.T.E.)

Sidings
South Shields

Percy Main

**South
Shields**

Howdon

Royal
Quays
(Proposed)

**Tyne
Commission
Quay**

Hadrian Road

Wallsend

Tyne Dock
Port of Tyne Authority
Car and Freight Terminal

Chichester

Jarrow
-Shell

Tyne Dock
Bottom Sidings

Jarrow

*Tyne
Dock*

Hebburn

Bede

⤏*Tyne Dock Tun.*

B

⤏*Green Lane*

**Brockley
Whins**

*Pelaw
Junc.*

Fellgate

*Boldon
West
Junc.*

*Boldon
East
Junc.*

Pelaw

C.S.

East Boldon

▲ Wardley Opencast
D.P. - RJB

Tyne & Wear Metro extension from Pelaw to
Sunderland and South Hylton is under construction.
The final layout is shown here and is due to open in
early 2002. Pelaw to Sunderland will be mixed Metro
and "heavy rail" and Brockley Whins, East Boldon
and Seaburn stations will only be served by the
new Metro.

Seaburn

Stadium
of Light

('Leamside' Line
Proposed)

Docks-
Port of
Sunderland
Authority

Pallion

St. Peters

Petrofina

South Dock
Sidings

*Sunderland
N. Tun.*

Millfield

Sunderland

South
Hylton

University

Fawcett St.
C.S.

(Sunderland - South Hylton
is a new route along an old
rail formation

Park Lane
Interchange

*Sunderland
S. Tuns.*

C

0   1   2   m.
|____|____|____| (1:90,000)
0 1 2 3 4 km.

1   ⬖ 74 ⬗   2

76

Garelochhead

Luss

(Loch Lomond Marina Co.)

LOCH LOMOND

Helensburgh Upper (Block Post)

Balloch Pier
Balloch

Helensburgh Central

Alexandria

Kilcreggan

(Clyde Marine)
(Western Ferries)

Craigendoran
Craigendoran Junc.

Cardross

Renton

(Clyde Marine)

Dalreoch
Dalreoch Tuns.

Hunter's Quay

Fort Matilda

Cardross

Gourock

Greenock West
Greenock Central
Cartsdyke

Dumbarton Cen.
Dumbarton East
Bowling

Milngavie

Dunoon

(Cal-Mac)

Branchton

James Watt Dock (Disused)
b Bogston
Woodhall

Dalmuir

No.2 Tun.

Bishopton
No.1 Tun

Singer

McInroy's Point

c
e *g*
a
Port Glasgow

Yoker

COWAL

IBM Halt

Whinhill

d

Langbank

IBM Halt
Drumfrochar

(SEE MAP P. 81)

A

Dunrod

Inverkip

British Aerospace (Disused)

Bishopton

Inverkip Tun.

Paisley Gilmour St.

Wemyss Bay

a) Ladyburn Junc.
b) Wemyss Bay Junc.
c) Newton St. Tun. (1m. 351yds)
d) Cartsburn Tun.
e) Ann St. Tun.
f) Wellpark Tun.

Johnstone
Milliken Park

Paisley Canal

Rothesay

ISLE OF BUTE

(Cal-Mac)

Howwood

Barrhead

Neilston

Lochwinnoch

(Cal-Mac) Largs

Cumbrae Slip

ISLE OF GT. CUMBRAE

MoD

Glengarnock

Lugton-Clegg
Lugton

Fairlie Tun.

Fairlie

Giffen-MoD

B

Fairlie High- Scottish Nuclear

Dunlop

(Additional loop being considered in Dunlop/Stewarton area)

Hunterston Low Level Clydeport

Hunterston Coal Import Terminal-Clydeport

Dalry- Roche Products

Swinlees

Dalry

West Kilbride

Stewarton

STRATHCLYDE

Holm Junc.

Sdgs.

Ardrossan South Beach

Kilwinning

Kilmaurs

United Distillers (Disused)

Ardrossan Harbour

C.S.

Dubbs Junc. *Byrehill Junc.*

CE Works & CE Sidings

Kilmarnock

Kay Park Junc.

(Cal-Mac)
TO BRODICK (ARRAN)

Ardrossan Town

Saltcoats

ICI Ardeer (Disused)

Riccarton -BP

Barleith-United Distillers (Disused)

Stevenston

Irvine

Locomotive Works Hunslet-Barclay (ZK)

CE Depot

CE Works

Shewalton CE Tip

Irvine- Caledonian Paper

Meadowhead

Barassie
Troon

Barassie Junc.
Troon
(Reversing Spur)

Mossgeil Tun.

Barassie CE Sidings

Mauchline Junc.

Prestwick International Airport

(SeaCat)
TO BELFAST

Prestwick - BP

Prestwick Town

Annbank Junc.

Newton- on-Ayr

C

(SEE INSET TO LEFT)

Ayr

Auchinleck

Killoch-Scottish Coal Washery

Ayr inset:

Falkland Yard
Ayr Harbour Junc.

Falkland Junc.
Down Yard
Newton- on-Ayr
Newton Junc.

Ayr Harbour & Coal Terminal

AY

Ayr

Townhead C.S.

(AYR INSET FROM RIGHT)

(1: 90,000)

77

1

0   2   5   10 m.

0   5   10   15 km.

(1:350,000)

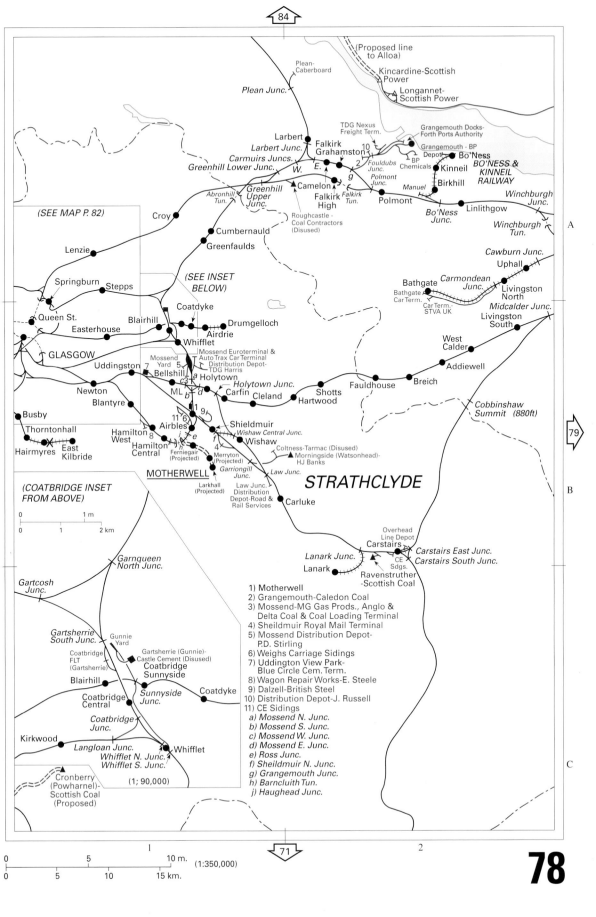

(Proposed line to Alloa)

Plean-Caberboard

Plean Junc.

Kincardine-Scottish Power

Longannet-Scottish Power

TDG Nexus Freight Term.

Grangemouth Docks-Forth Ports Authority

Larbert
Larbert Junc.
Carmuirs Juncs.
Greenhill Lower Junc.

Falkirk
Grahamston

10

Grangemouth - BP
Depot

BP Chemicals

Bo'Ness
Kinneil
Birkhill

BO'NESS & KINNEIL RAILWAY

W.
E.

Fouldubs Junc.

2

g

Polmont Junc.

Greenhill Upper Junc.

Camelon

Falkirk High

Falkirk Tun.

Polmont

Manuel

Bo'Ness Junc.

Winchburgh Junc.

Abronhill Tun.

Croy

Linlithgow

Winchburgh Tun.

A

Roughcastle - Coal Contractors (Disused)

Cawburn Junc.

(SEE MAP P. 82)

Cumbernauld
Greenfaulds

Uphall

Lenzie

Bathgate
Bathgate Car Term.

Carmondean Junc.

Livingston North

Car Term.-STVA UK

Midcalder Junc.

Springburn
Stepps

(SEE INSET BELOW)

Livingston South

Queen St.
Easterhouse

Coatdyke

Blairhill

Drumgelloch
Airdrie

West Calder

Addiewell

GLASGOW

Whifflet

Mossend Euroterminal & Auto Trax Car Terminal Distribution Depot-TDG Harris

Breich

Uddingston
Bellshill

Mossend Yard

5

a

Holytown

Fauldhouse

7

c 3

ML

b   *d*

Holytown Junc.

Newton

Carfin

Cleland

Shotts

Hartwood

Cobbinshaw Summit (880ft)

Busby
Thorntonhall

Blantyre

1 9

Shieldmuir

79

11 6

Airbles

Wishaw Central Junc.

Hairmyres
East Kilbride

Hamilton West
Hamilton Central

j   *e*

f

Wishaw

Coltness-Tarmac (Disused)
Morningside (Watsonhead)-HJ Banks

Ferniegair (Projected)

4

Merryton (Projected)

Garriongill Junc.

Law Junc.

STRATHCLYDE

(COATBRIDGE INSET FROM ABOVE)

MOTHERWELL

Larkhall (Projected)

Law Junc. Distribution Depot-Road & Rail Services

Carluke

B

0	1 m.
0	2 km.

Overhead Line Depot
Carstairs

Carstairs East Junc.
Carstairs South Junc.

Garnqueen North Junc.

Lanark Junc.

CE Sdgs.

Lanark

Ravenstruther -Scottish Coal

Gartcosh Junc.

1) Motherwell
2) Grangemouth-Caledon Coal
3) Mossend-MG Gas Prods., Anglo & Delta Coal & Coal Loading Terminal
4) Sheildmuir Royal Mail Terminal
5) Mossend Distribution Depot-P.D. Stirling
6) Weighs Carriage Sidings
7) Uddington View Park-Blue Circle Cem. Term.
8) Wagon Repair Works-E. Steele
9) Dalzell-British Steel
10) Distribution Depot-J. Russell
11) CE Sidings
a) Mossend N. Junc.
b) Mossend S. Junc.
c) Mossend W. Junc.
d) Mossend E. Junc.
e) Ross Junc.
f) Sheildmuir N. Junc.
g) Grangemouth Junc.
h) Barncluith Tun.
j) Haughead Junc.

Gartsherrie South Junc.

Gunnie Yard

Coatbridge FLT (Gartsherrie)

Gartsherrie (Gunnie)-Castle Cement (Disused)

Coatbridge Sunnyside

Blairhill

Sunnyside Junc.

Coatbridge Central

Coatdyke

Coatbridge Junc.

Kirkwood

Langloan Junc.
Whifflet N. Junc.
Whifflet S. Junc.

Whifflet

Cronberry (Powharnel)-Scottish Coal (Proposed)

(1; 90,000)

C

0	5	10 m.
0	5	10	15 km.

1

2

(1:350,000)

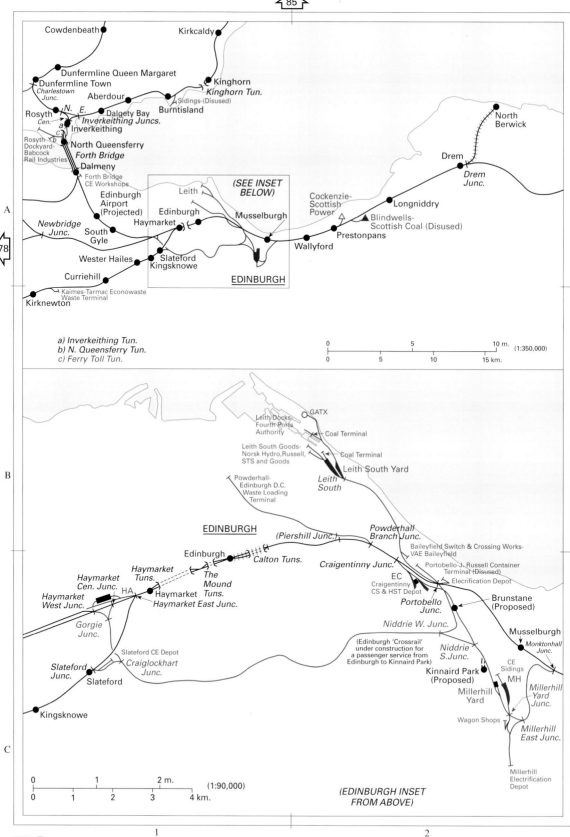

Cowdenbeath
Kirkcaldy
Dunfermline Queen Margaret
Dunfermline Town
Charlestown Junc.
Aberdour
Kinghorn
Kinghorn Tun.
Burntisland
Sidings (Disused)
Rosyth
Cen.
N. E.
Dalgety Bay
Inverkeithing Juncs.
Inverkeithing
Rosyth
Dockyard-
Babcock
Rail Industries
North Queensferry
Forth Bridge
Dalmeny
Forth Bridge
CE Workshops
Leith
(SEE INSET BELOW)
Edinburgh
Airport
(Projected)
Edinburgh
Haymarket
Musselburgh
North Berwick
Drem
Drem Junc.
Cockenzie-
Scottish
Power
Longniddry
Blindwells-
Scottish Coal (Disused)
Newbridge Junc.
South Gyle
Prestonpans
Wallyford
EDINBURGH
Wester Hailes
Slateford
Kingsknowe
Curriehill
Kaimes-Tarmac Econowaste
Waste Terminal
Kirknewton

A

78

a) *Inverkeithing Tun.*
b) *N. Queensferry Tun.*
c) *Ferry Toll Tun.*

0		5		10 m.	
0	5	10	15 km.		(1:350,000)

Leith Docks
Fourth Ports
Authority
GATX
Coal Terminal
Leith South Goods-
Norsk Hydro, Russell,
STS and Goods
Coal Terminal
Leith South Yard
Powderhall-
Edinburgh D.C.
Waste Loading
Terminal
Leith South

B

EDINBURGH
(Piershill Junc.)
Powderhall Branch Junc.
Baileyfield Switch & Crossing Works-
VAE Baileyfield
Edinburgh
Calton Tuns.
Craigentinny Junc.
Portobello-J. Russell Container
Terminal (Disused)
Electrification Depot
EC
Craigentinny
CS & HST Depot
Portobello Junc.
Brunstane
(Proposed)
Haymarket Tuns.
Haymarket Cen. Junc.
HA
The Mound Tuns.
Haymarket
Haymarket East Junc.
Haymarket West Junc.
Gorgie Junc.
Niddrie W. Junc.
Musselburgh
Monktonhall Junc.
Slateford CE Depot
Craiglockhart Junc.
(Edinburgh 'Crossrail'
under construction for
a passenger service from
Edinburgh to Kinnaird Park)
Niddrie S.Junc.
CE
Sidings
MH
Slateford Junc.
Slateford
Kinnaird Park
(Proposed)
Millerhill
Yard
Millerhill Yard Junc.
Kingsknowe
Wagon Shops
Millerhill East Junc.
Millerhill
Electrification
Depot

C

0		1		2 m.	
0	1	2	3	4 km.	(1:90,000)

(EDINBURGH INSET FROM ABOVE)

1

2

79

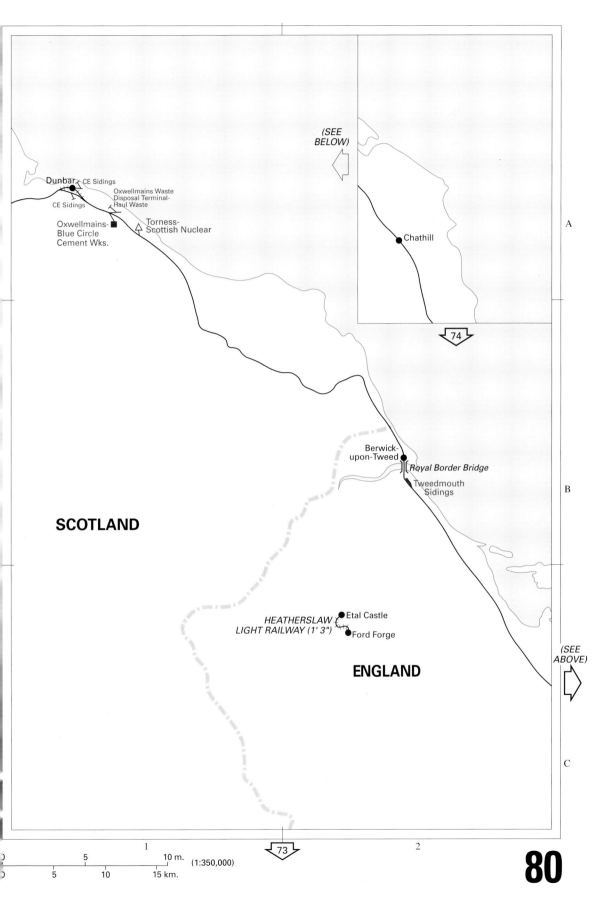

(SEE BELOW)

A

Dunbar CE Sidings

Oxwellmains Waste
Disposal Terminal-
Haul Waste

CE Sidings

Oxwellmains-
Blue Circle
Cement Wks.

Torness-
Scottish Nuclear

Chathill

74

Berwick-
upon-Tweed

Royal Border Bridge

Tweedmouth
Sidings

B

SCOTLAND

*HEATHERSLAW
LIGHT RAILWAY (1' 3")*

Etal Castle

Ford Forge

ENGLAND

(SEE
ABOVE)

C

1

5

10 m.   (1:350,000)

5

10

15 km.

73

2

80

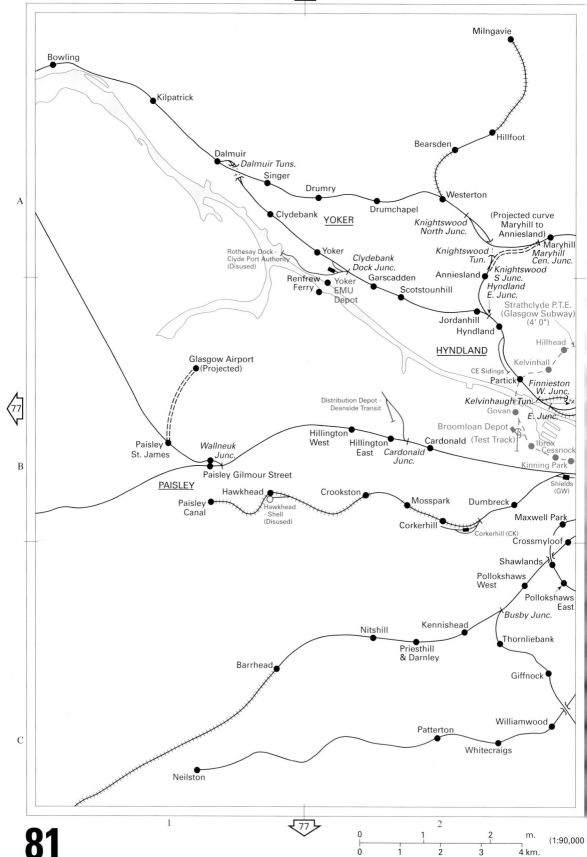

Milngavie

Bowling

Kilpatrick

Hillfoot

Bearsden

Dalmuir

Dalmuir Tuns.

Singer

Drumry

Westerton

Drumchapel

Clydebank

YOKER

(Projected curve
Maryhill to
Anniesland)

*Knightswood
North Junc.*

Yoker

*Knightswood
Tun.*

Maryhill

*Maryhill
Cen. Junc.*

Rothesay Dock -
Clyde Port Authority
(Disused)

*Clydebank
Dock Junc.*

Garscadden

Anniesland

*Knightswood
S Junc.*

*Hyndland
E. Junc.*

Renfrew
Ferry

Yoker
EMU
Depot

Scotstounhill

Strathclyde P.T.E.
(Glasgow Subway)
(4' 0")

Jordanhill

Hyndland

Hillhead

HYNDLAND

Kelvinhall

Glasgow Airport
(Projected)

CE Sidings

Partick

*Finnieston
W. Junc.*

Distribution Depot -
Deanside Transit

Kelvinhaugh Tun.

Govan

E. Junc.

Paisley
St. James

*Wallneuk
Junc.*

Hillington
West

Hillington
East

Cardonald

Broomloan Depot
(Test Track)

Ibrox

Cessnock

*Cardonald
Junc.*

Kinning Park

Paisley Gilmour Street

PAISLEY

Shields
(GW)

Hawkhead

Crookston

Mosspark

Dumbreck

Maxwell Park

Paisley
Canal

Hawkhead -
Shell
(Disused)

Corkerhill

Corkerhill (CK)

Crossmyloof

Shawlands

Pollokshaws
West

Pollokshaws
East

Busby Junc.

Nitshill

Kennishead

Thornliebank

Priesthill
& Darnley

Barrhead

Giffnock

Williamwood

Patterton

Whitecraigs

Neilston

81

1

2

0	1	2	m.
0	1	2	3	4 km.

(1:90,000)

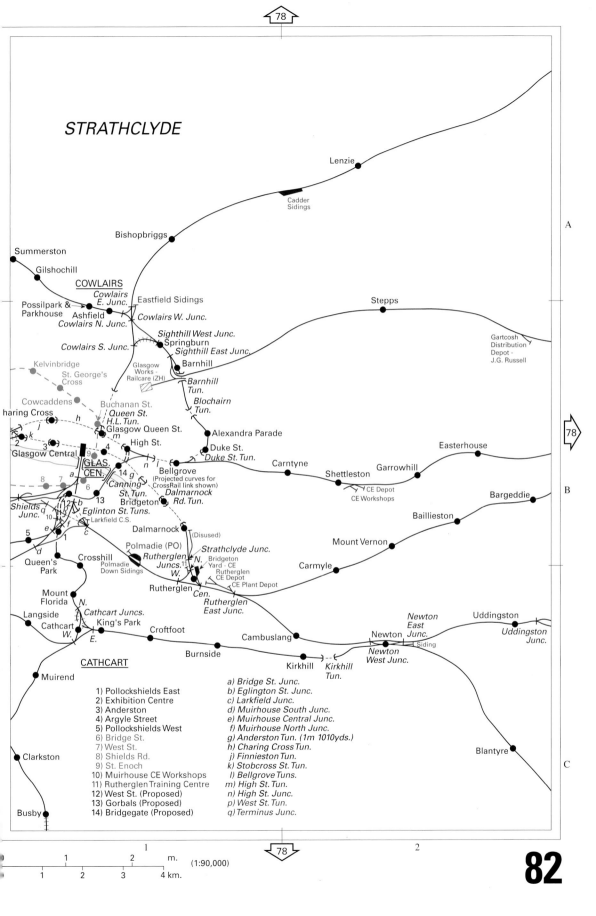

ISLE OF SKYE

Kylerhea   Glenelg

CANNA

Armadale

Inverie

(Bruce Watt Cruises)

RHUM

Mallaig

(Cal-Mac)

Morar

LOCH NEVIS

Tarbet

A

(Cal-Mac)

EIGG

Arisaig

Beasdale

Beasdale Tuns.

Borrodale Tun.

(M.Grant)

Lochailort Tun.

Lochailort

Glenfinnan

Locheilside

Glenfinnan

MUCK   *(Cal-Mac)*

(Loch Shiel Cruises)

ARDNAMURCHAN

Acharacle

LOCH SHIEL

TO LOCHBOISDALE (SOUTH UIST)

TO CASTLEBAY (BARRA)

Kilchoan

Ardgour

(Cal-Mac)   *(Cal-Mac)*

COLL

Tobermory

MORVERN

TIREE

ISLAND OF MULL

(Cal-Mac)

Lismore

Port Appin

Lochaline

(Cal-Mac)

B

ULVA

Fishnish

Lismore

STAFFA

STRATHCLYDE

Craignure
Tarmstedt

(Cal-Mac)

Shell (Disused)

Connel Ferry (Block Post)

Taynuilt Pier

Torosay Castle

Taynuilt

MULL & WEST HIGHLAND RAILWAY (10¼")

Oban

Timber Loading Term.

IONA

Fionnphort

Goods & Timber Loading Term.

(Cal-Mac)

Isle of Seil

Isle of Luing

(Cal-Mac)

COLONSAY

C

JURA

TO PORT ASKAIG (ISLAY)

83

1   2

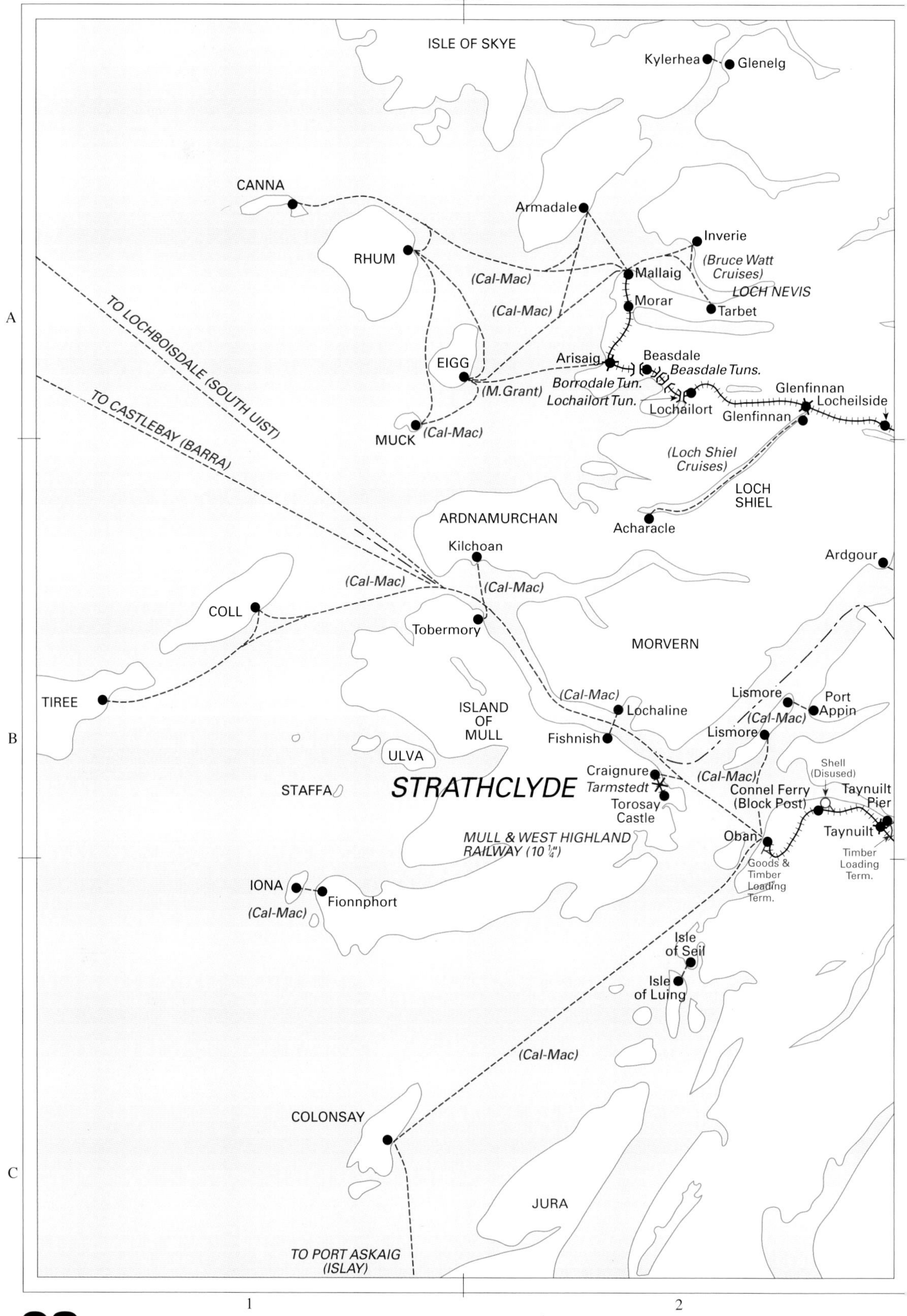

0   5   10 m.

0   5   10   15 km.

(1:350,000

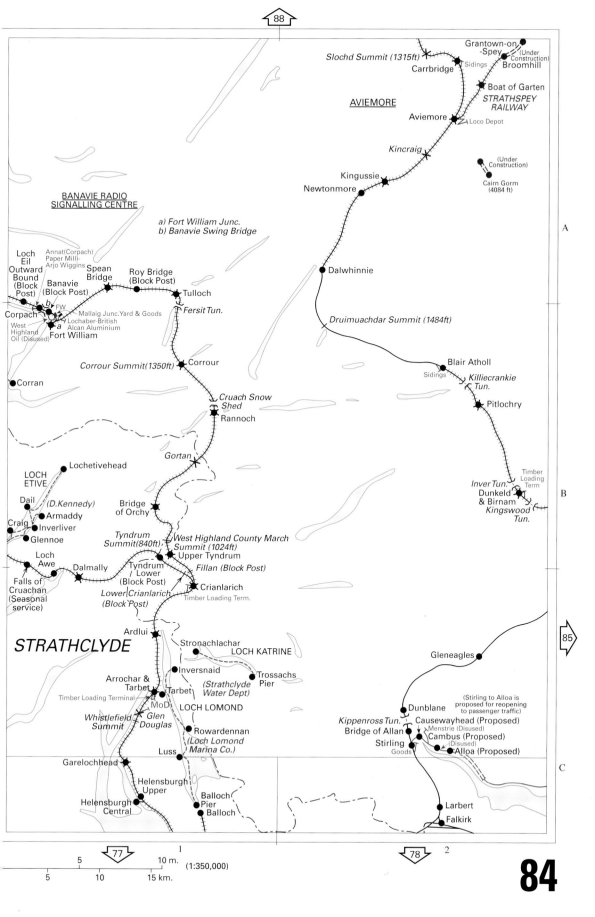

Grantown-on-Spey
(Under Construction)
Broomhill
Slochd Summit (1315ft)
Sidings
Carrbridge
Boat of Garten
STRATHSPEY RAILWAY
AVIEMORE
Aviemore
Loco Depot
Kincraig
(Under Construction)
Kingussie
Cairn Gorm (4084 ft)
Newtonmore

A

BANAVIE RADIO SIGNALLING CENTRE

a) Fort William Junc.
b) Banavie Swing Bridge

Dalwhinnie

Loch Eil Outward Bound (Block Post)
Annat(Corpach) Paper Mill)- Arjo Wiggins
Spean Bridge
Roy Bridge (Block Post)
Banavie (Block Post)
b FW
Tulloch
Fersit Tun.

Druimuachdar Summit (1484ft)

Corpach
a
West Highland Oil (Disused)
Fort William
Mallaig Junc.Yard & Goods
Lochaber-British Alcan Aluminium

Blair Atholl
Sidings
Killiecrankie Tun.

Corrour Summit(1350ft)
Corrour

Corran

Pitlochry

Cruach Snow Shed
Rannoch

Lochetivehead
LOCH ETIVE
Gortan

Timber Loading Term.
Inver Tun.
Dunkeld & Birnam
Kingswood Tun.

B

Dail
(D.Kennedy)
Armaddy
Craig
Inverliver
Glennoe

Bridge of Orchy

West Highland County March Summit (1024ft)
Tyndrum Summit(840ft)
Upper Tyndrum
Tyndrum / Lower (Block Post)
Fillan (Block Post)

Loch Awe
Dalmally
Crianlarich
Timber Loading Term.

Falls of Cruachan (Seasonal service)
Lower Crianlarich (Block Post)

Gleneagles

STRATHCLYDE

Ardlui

Stronachlachar
LOCH KATRINE
Inversnaid
Trossachs Pier
(Strathclyde Water Dept)

(Stirling to Alloa is proposed for reopening to passenger traffic)

Arrochar & Tarbet
Tarbet
Dunblane
Kippenross Tun.
Causewayhead (Proposed)
Menstrie (Disused)
Cambus (Proposed)
(Disused)
Alloa (Proposed)
Timber Loading Terminal
MoD
LOCH LOMOND
Whistlefield Summit
Glen Douglas
Bridge of Allan
Stirling
Goods
Rowardennan
(Loch Lomond Marina Co.)
Luss

Garelochhead
Helensburgh Upper

C

Balloch Pier
Balloch

Larbert
Falkirk

Helensburgh Central

I
2

5   10 m.
5   10   15 km.
(1:350,000)

85

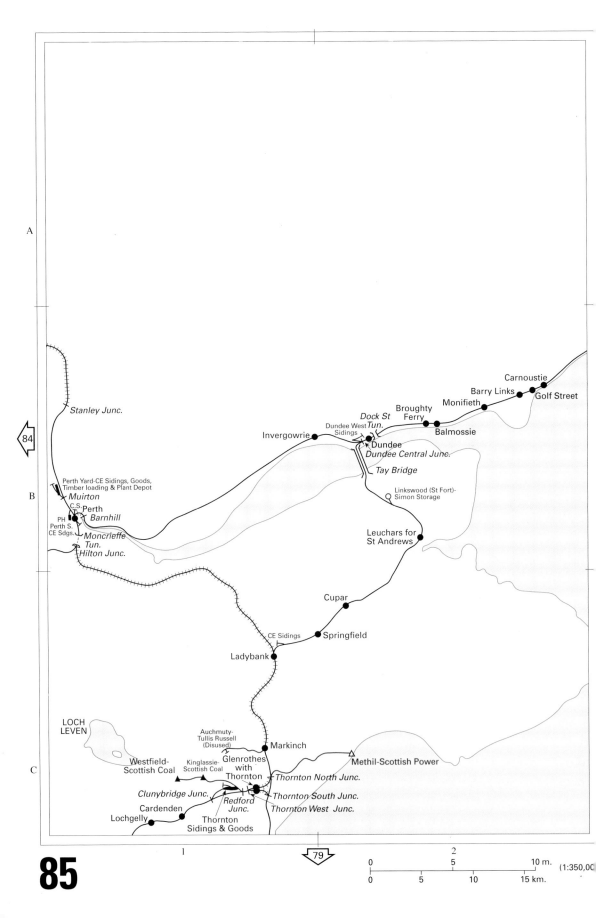

Stanley Junc.

Carnoustie

Barry Links

Golf Street

Monifieth

Dock St
Tun.

Broughty
Ferry

Dundee West
Sidings

Balmossie

Invergowrie

Dundee

Dundee Central Junc.

Tay Bridge

Perth Yard-CE Sidings, Goods,
Timber loading & Plant Depot

Muirton

C.S.

Perth

Barnhill

PH
Perth S.
CE Sdgs.

Moncrleffe
Tun.

Hilton Junc.

Linkswood (St Fort)-
Simon Storage

Leuchars for
St Andrews

Cupar

CE Sidings

Springfield

Ladybank

LOCH
LEVEN

Auchmuty-
Tullis Russell
(Disused)

Markinch

Methil-Scottish Power

Westfield-
Scottish Coal

Kinglassie-
Scottish Coal

Glenrothes
with
Thornton

Thornton North Junc.

Clunybridge Junc.

Redford
Junc.

Thornton South Junc.

Thornton West Junc.

Cardenden

Lochgelly

Thornton
Sidings & Goods

85

1

2

| 0 | 5 | 10 m. |
| 0 | 5 | 10 | 15 km. |

(1:350,00

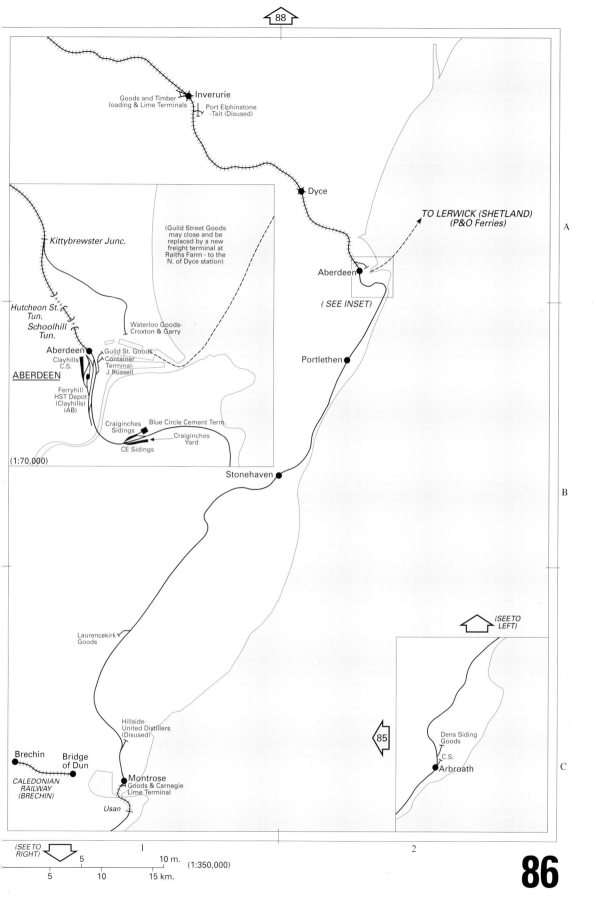

Inverurie
Goods and Timber
loading & Lime Terminals
Port Elphinstone
-Tait (Disused)

Dyce

TO LERWICK (SHETLAND)
(P&O Ferries)

Aberdeen

(SEE INSET)

A

Kittybrewster Junc.

(Guild Street Goods
may close and be
replaced by a new
freight terminal at
Raiths Farm - to the
N. of Dyce station)

Hutcheon St.
Tun.
Schoolhill
Tun.

Waterloo Goods-
Croxton & Garry

Aberdeen
Clayhills
C.S.

ABERDEEN

Guild St. Goods
Container
Terminal-
J. Russell

Ferryhill
HST Depot
(Clayhills)
(AB)

Craiginches
Sidings

Blue Circle Cement Term.

Craiginches
Yard

CE Sidings

(1:70,000)

Portlethen

Stonehaven

B

Laurencekirk
Goods

(SEE TO
LEFT)

85

Hillside-
United Distillers
(Disused)

Dens Siding
Goods

C.S.

Arbroath

C

Brechin

Bridge
of Dun

Montrose
Goods & Carnegie
Lime Terminal

CALEDONIAN
RAILWAY
(BRECHIN)

Usan

(SEE TO
RIGHT)

5

1

2

10 m.

(1:350,000)

5   10   15 km.

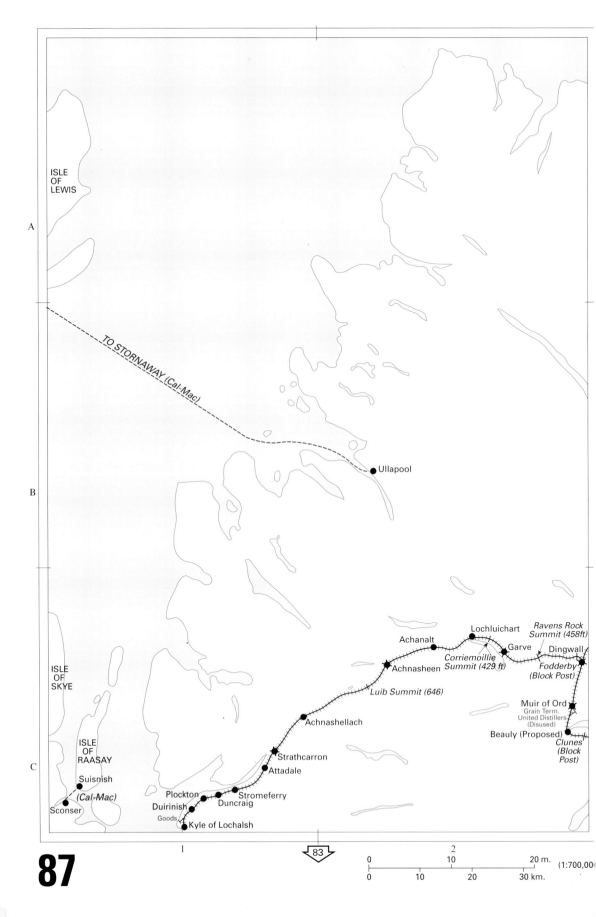

ISLE
OF
LEWIS

A

TO STORNAWAY (Cal-Mac)

B

Ullapool

ISLE
OF
SKYE

Lochluichart

Ravens Rock
Summit (458ft)

Achanalt

Garve

Dingwall

Corriemoillie
Summit (429 ft)

Fodderby
(Block Post)

Achnasheen

Luib Summit (646)

Muir of Ord
Grain Term.
United Distillers
(Disused)

Achnashellach

Beauly (Proposed)

Clunes
(Block
Post)

ISLE
OF
RAASAY

C

Suisnish

Strathcarron

Attadale

(Cal-Mac)

Sconser

Plockton

Stromeferry

Duncraig

Duirinish

Goods

Kyle of Lochalsh

1

83

2

0   10   20 m.

0   10   20   30 km.

(1:700,00

87

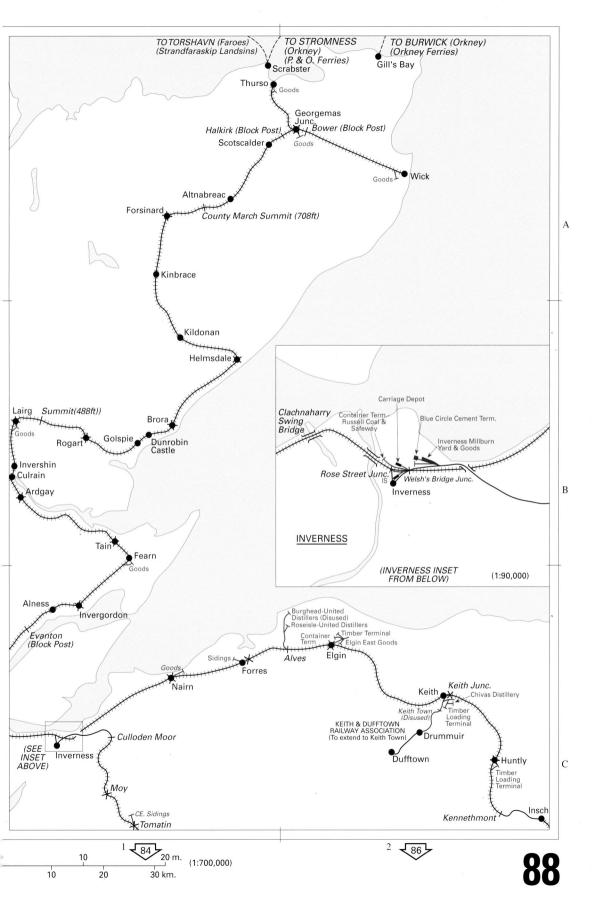

TO TORSHAVN (Faroes)
(Strandfaraskip Landsins)

TO STROMNESS
(Orkney)
(P. & O. Ferries)

TO BURWICK (Orkney)
(Orkney Ferries)

Gill's Bay

Scrabster
Thurso
Goods

Georgemas
Junc.
Halkirk (Block Post)   Bower (Block Post)
Scotscalder
Goods

Goods   Wick

Altnabreac
Forsinard
County March Summit (708ft)

Kinbrace

Kildonan
Helmsdale

Lairg   Summit(488ft)
Goods
Rogart   Golspie   Brora
Invershin   Dunrobin
Culrain   Castle
Ardgay

Tain
Fearn
Goods

Alness
Invergordon
Evanton
(Block Post)

Clachnaharry
Swing
Bridge

Carriage Depot

Container Term.
Russell Coal &
Safeway

Blue Circle Cement Term.

Inverness Millburn
Yard & Goods

Rose Street Junc.
IS
Welsh's Bridge Junc.
Inverness

INVERNESS

(INVERNESS INSET
FROM BELOW)   (1:90,000)

Burghead-United
Distillers (Disused)
Roseisle-United Distillers

Container   Timber Terminal
Term   Elgin East Goods
Sidings   Alves   Elgin
Goods
Forres

Nairn   Keith   Keith Junc.
Chivas Distillery

(SEE
INSET
ABOVE)   Inverness   Culloden Moor

Keith Town
(Disused)   Timber
Loading
Terminal

KEITH & DUFFTOWN
RAILWAY ASSOCIATION
(To extend to Keith Town)   Drummuir

Moy   Dufftown   Huntly

CE. Sidings
Tomatin   Timber
Loading
Terminal

Kennethmont   Insch

1   84   20 m.   (1:700,000)
10
10   20   30 km.

2   86

88

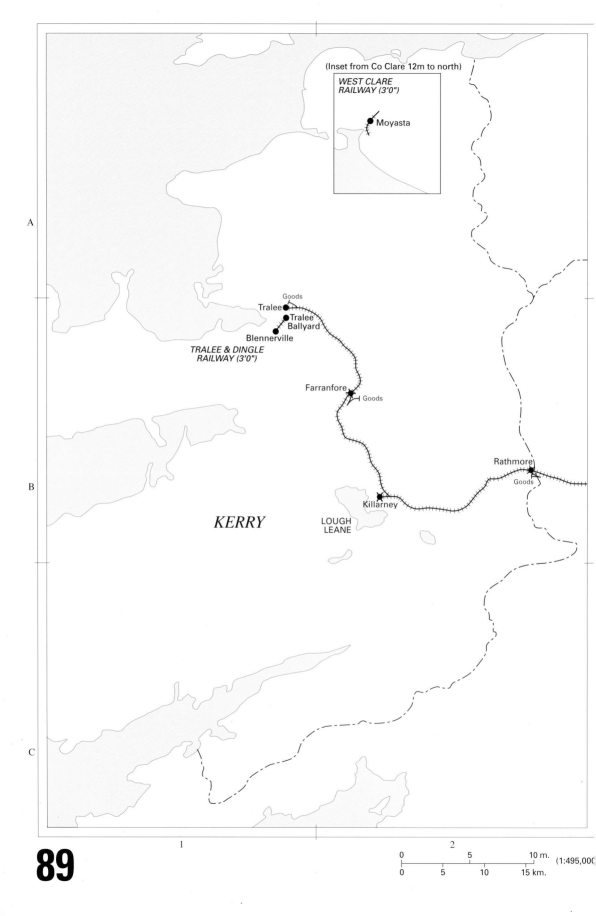

(Inset from Co Clare 12m to north)

WEST CLARE RAILWAY (3'0")

● Moyasta

A

Goods
Tralee ●
● Tralee Ballyard
Blennerville ●
TRALEE & DINGLE RAILWAY (3'0")

Farranfore
Goods

Rathmore
Goods

B

KERRY

Killarney

LOUGH LEANE

C

89

1

2

0   5   10 m.
0   5   10   15 km.

(1:495,000)

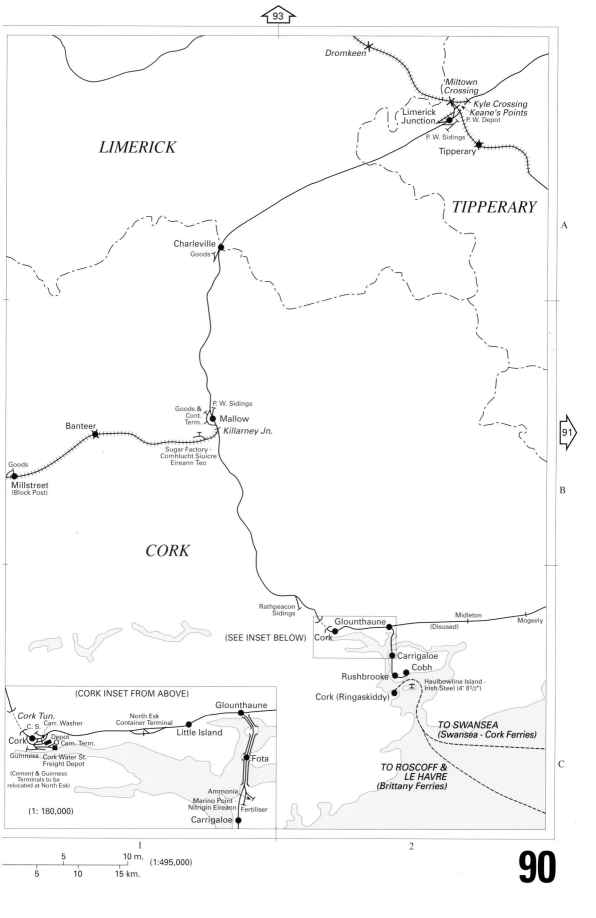

Dromkeen

Miltown Crossing

Kyle Crossing
Keane's Points
P. W. Depot

Limerick
Junction

P. W. Sidings

LIMERICK

Tipperary

TIPPERARY

A

Charleville
Goods

91

P. W. Sidings

Goods &
Cont.
Term.

Mallow
Killarney Jn.

Banteer

Sugar Factory -
Comhlucht Siuicre
Eireann Teo

B

Goods

Millstreet
(Block Post)

CORK

Rathpeacon
Sidings

Glounthaune

Midleton

Mogeely

(Disused)

(SEE INSET BELOW)

Cork

Carrigaloe

Cobh

Rushbrooke

Haulbowline Island -
Irish Steel (4' 8½")

Cork (Ringaskiddy)

TO SWANSEA
(Swansea - Cork Ferries)

(CORK INSET FROM ABOVE)

Cork Tun.
C. S. Carr. Washer

North Esk
Container Terminal

Glounthaune

Cork

Depot
Cem. Term.

Little Island

Guinness   Cork Water St.
Freight Depot

Fota

(Cement & Guinness
Terminals to be
relocated at North Esk)

Ammonia -
Marino Point -
Nitrigin Eireann   Fertiliser

(1: 180,000)

Carrigaloe

*TO ROSCOFF &
LE HAVRE*
(Brittany Ferries)

C

1

5

10 m.   (1:495,000)

5   10   15 km.

2

90

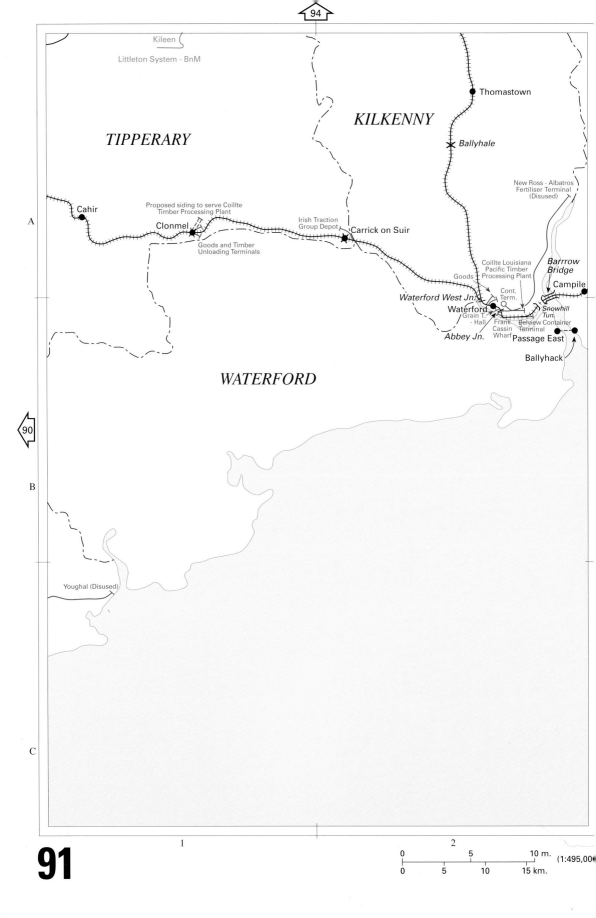

Kileen

Littleton System - BnM

KILKENNY

Thomastown

TIPPERARY

Ballyhale

New Ross - Albatros
Fertiliser Terminal
(Disused)

Cahir

Proposed siding to serve Coillte
Timber Processing Plant

A

Clonmel

Irish Traction
Group Depot

Carrick on Suir

Goods and Timber
Unloading Terminals

Coillte Louisiana
Pacific Timber
Processing Plant

Barrrow
Bridge

Goods

Campile

Waterford West Jn.

Cont.
Term.

Snowhill
Tun.

Waterford

Grain T.
- Hall

Frank
Cassin
Wharf

Belview Container
Terminal

Abbey Jn.

Passage East

Ballyhack

WATERFORD

90

B

Youghal (Disused)

C

1

2

0 5 10 m.
0 5 10 15 km.

(1:495,00

91

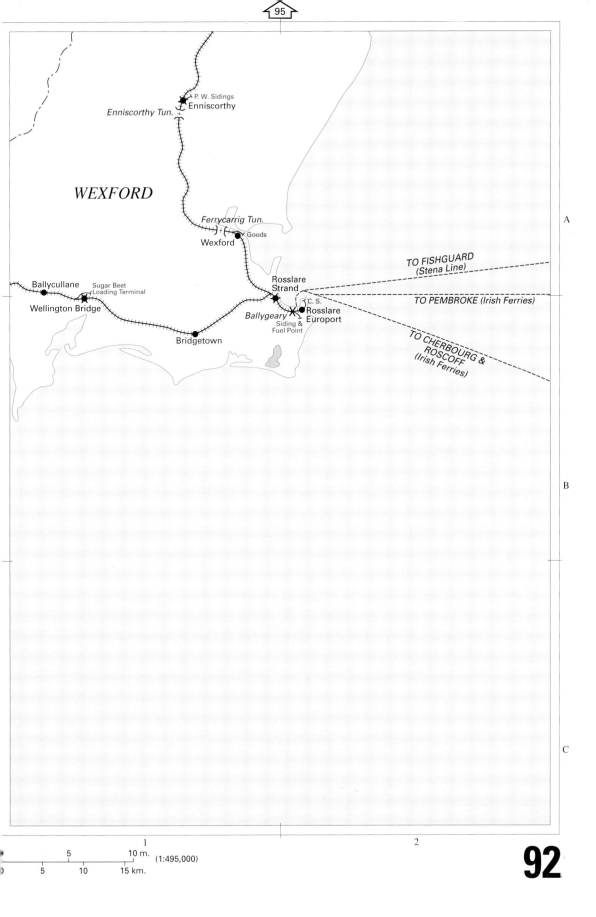

P. W. Sidings
Enniscorthy
Enniscorthy Tun.

WEXFORD

Ferrycarrig Tun.
Wexford • Goods

Ballycullane • Sugar Beet
Loading Terminal
Wellington Bridge

Rosslare
Strand
C. S.
Ballygeary Rosslare
Siding & Europort
Fuel Point

Bridgetown

TO FISHGUARD
(Stena Line)

TO PEMBROKE (Irish Ferries)

TO CHERBOURG &
ROSCOFF
(Irish Ferries)

A

B

C

1
10 m.
(1:495,000)
5
5   10   15 km.

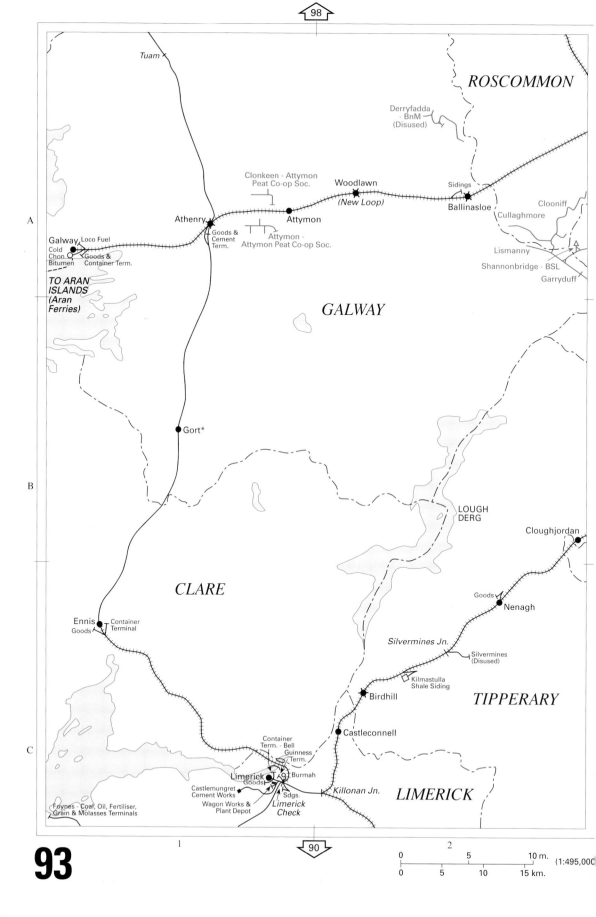

Tuam

ROSCOMMON

Derryfadda
- BnM —
(Disused)

Clonkeen - Attymon
Peat Co-op Soc.

Woodlawn
(New Loop)

Sidings

Ballinasloe

Clooniff

Cullaghmore

Athenry

Attymon

Goods &
Cement
Term.

Attymon -
Attymon Peat Co-op Soc.

Lismanny

Shannonbridge - BSL

Garryduff

A

Galway / Loco Fuel

Cold
Chon
Bitumen

Goods &
Container Term.

GALWAY

**TO ARAN
ISLANDS**
(Aran
Ferries)

Gort*

B

**LOUGH
DERG**

Cloughjordan

CLARE

Goods

Nenagh

Ennis

Goods

Container
Terminal

Silvermines Jn.

Silvermines
(Disused)

Kilmastulla
Shale Siding

Birdhill

TIPPERARY

C

Castleconnell

Container
Term. - Bell

Guinness
Term.

Burmah

Limerick

Goods

Castlemungret
Cement Works

Wagon Works &
Plant Depot

Sdgs.

*Limerick
Check*

Killonan Jn.

LIMERICK

Foynes - Coal, Oil, Fertiliser,
Grain & Molasses Terminals

93

1

2

0   5   10 m.   (1:495,000

0   5   10   15 km.

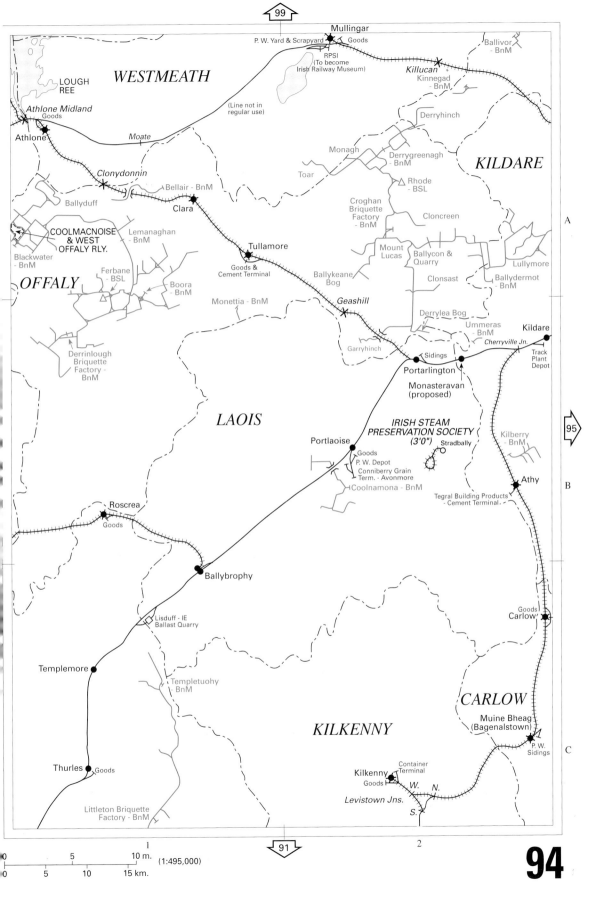

WESTMEATH

LOUGH REE

Mullingar
P. W. Yard & Scrapyard — Goods
RPSI
(To become
Irish Railway Museum)
(Line not in
regular use)

Ballivor
- BnM

Killucan

Kinnegad
- BnM

Derryhinch

Athlone Midland
Goods

Athlone

Moate

Clonydonnin

Bellair - BnM

Ballyduff

Clara

Monagh

Toar

Derrygreenagh
- BnM

Rhode
- BSL

Croghan
Briquette
Factory
- BnM

Cloncreen

KILDARE

A

COOLMACNOISE
& WEST
OFFALY RLY.

Blackwater
- BnM

Lemanaghan
- BnM

Tullamore
Goods &
Cement Terminal

Mount
Lucas

Ballycon &
Quarry

Clonsast

Lullymore

Ballydermot
- BnM

OFFALY

Ferbane
- BSL

Boora
- BnM

Ballykeane
Bog

Monettia - BnM

Geashill

Derrylea Bog

Ummeras
- BnM

Kildare

Derrinlough
Briquette
Factory -
BnM

Garryhinch

Sidings
Portarlington

Cherryville Jn.

Track
Plant
Depot

Monasteravan
(proposed)

LAOIS

IRISH STEAM
PRESERVATION SOCIETY
(3'0")

Stradbally

Kilberry
- BnM

95

Portlaoise
Goods
P. W. Depot
Conniberry Grain
Term. - Avonmore
Coolnamona - BnM

Tegral Building Products
- Cement Terminal -

Athy

B

Roscrea
Goods

Ballybrophy

Lisduff - IE
Ballast Quarry

Goods
Carlow

Templemore

Templetuohy
- BnM

CARLOW

Muine Bheag
(Bagenalstown)
P. W.
Sidings

C

KILKENNY

Container
Terminal

Thurles Goods

Kilkenny
Goods
W.   N.

Littleton Briquette
Factory - BnM

Levistown Jns.
S.

1   10 m.
(1:495,000)

0   5
0   5   10   15 km.

2

94

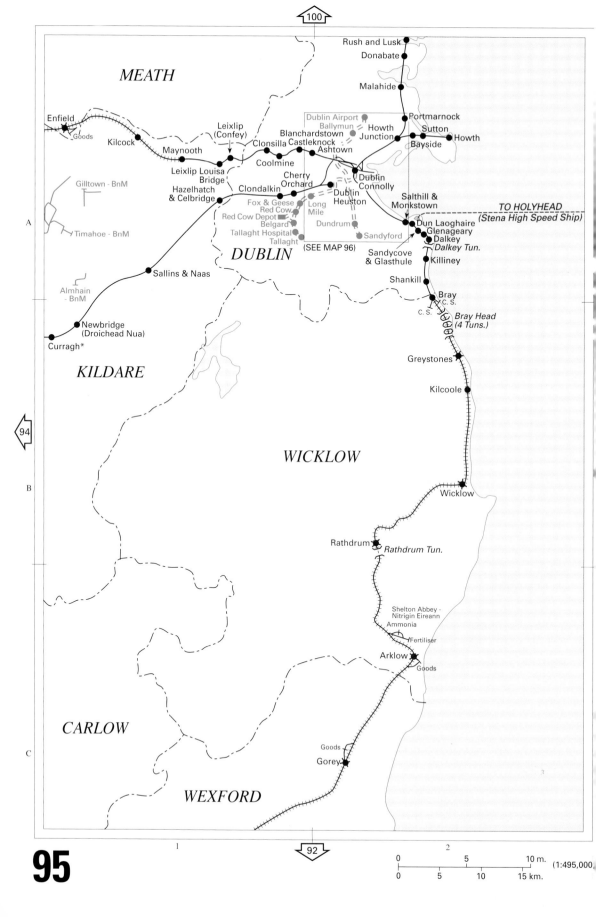

MEATH

Enfield
Goods
Kilcock
Maynooth
Leixlip Louisa
Bridge
Hazelhatch
& Celbridge
Leixlip (Confey)
Clonsilla
Coolmine
Castleknock
Blanchardstown
Ashtown
Cherry
Orchard
Clondalkin

Rush and Lusk
Donabate
Malahide
Portmarnock
Sutton
Howth
Dublin Airport
Ballymun
Howth
Junction
Bayside

Gilltown - BnM

Timahoe - BnM

A

Almhain
- BnM

Sallins & Naas

Newbridge
(Droichead Nua)
Curragh*

KILDARE

Fox & Geese
Red Cow
Red Cow Depot
Belgard
Tallaght Hospital
Tallaght

DUBLIN

Dublin
Heuston
Long
Mile

Dundrum

(SEE MAP 96)

Sandyford

Dublin
Connolly

Salthill &
Monkstown

Dun Laoghaire
Glenageary
Dalkey
Dalkey Tun.
Killiney

Sandycove
& Glasthule

Sandycove

TO HOLYHEAD
(Stena High Speed Ship)

94

Shankill

Bray
C. S.
C. S.
Bray Head
(4 Tuns.)

Greystones

Kilcoole

B

WICKLOW

Wicklow

Rathdrum
Rathdrum Tun.

Shelton Abbey -
Nitrigin Eireann
Ammonia
Fertiliser
Arklow
Goods

CARLOW

C

Goods
Gorey

WEXFORD

1

2

0   5   10 m.
0   5   10   15 km.   (1:495,000)

95

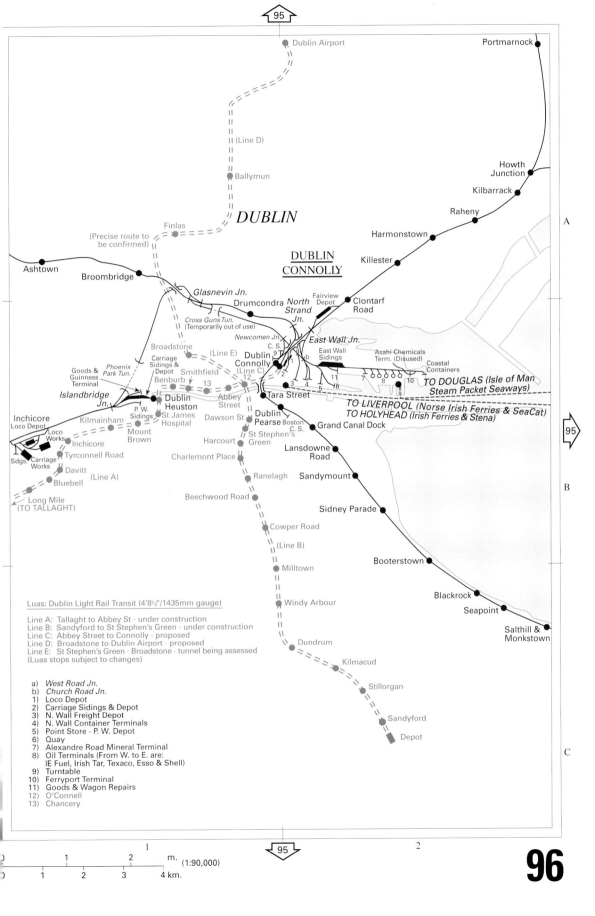

Portmarnock

Dublin Airport

DUBLIN

Howth
Junction

(Line D)

Kilbarrack

Ballymun

Raheny

Harmonstown

**DUBLIN
CONNOLLY**

Finlas

Killester

(Precise route to
be confirmed)

Ashtown

Broombridge

Glasnevin Jn.

Drumcondra *North
Strand*

Clontarf
Road

*Fairview
Depot*

Cross Guns Tun.
(Temporarily out of use)

Newcomen Jn.
C. S.

East Wall Jn.

Broadstone

Carriage
Sidings &
Depot

(Line E)

**Dublin
Connolly**
(Line C)

9
b

*East Wall
Sidings*

Asahi Chemicals
Term. (Disused)

Coastal
Containers

Goods &
Guinness
Terminal

*Phoenix
Park Tun.*

Smithfield

Benburb

13

*Islandbridge
Jn.*

P. W.
Sidings

**Dublin
Heuston**

12

Abbey
Street

Tara Street

1

2

3 4
5

11

7

8

16

10

TO DOUGLAS (Isle of Man
Steam Packet Seaways)

Inchicore
Loco Depot

Kilmainham

St James
Hospital

Dawson St

Boston
C. S.

**Dublin
Pearse**

TO LIVERPOOL (Norse Irish Ferries & SeaCat)
TO HOLYHEAD (Irish Ferries & Stena)

Loco
Works

Mount
Brown

Inchicore

Harcourt

St Stephen's
Green

Grand Canal Dock

Sdgs.

Carriage
Works

Tyrconnell Road

Davitt

(Line A)

Charlemont Place

**Lansdowne
Road**

Bluebell

Ranelagh

Sandymount

Long Mile
(TO TALLAGHT)

Beechwood Road

Sidney Parade

Cowper Road

(Line B)

Milltown

Booterstown

Windy Arbour

Blackrock

Seapoint

Luas: Dublin Light Rail Transit (4'8½"/1435mm gauge)

Line A: Tallaght to Abbey St - under construction
Line B: Sandyford to St Stephen's Green - under construction
Line C: Abbey Street to Connolly - proposed
Line D: Broadstone to Dublin Airport - proposed
Line E: St Stephen's Green - Broadstone - tunnel being assessed
(Luas stops subject to changes)

Dundrum

**Salthill &
Monkstown**

Kilmacud

Stillorgan

a) *West Road Jn.*
b) *Church Road Jn.*
1) Loco Depot
2) Carriage Sidings & Depot
3) N. Wall Freight Depot
4) N. Wall Container Terminals
5) Point Store - P. W. Depot
6) Quay
7) Alexandre Road Mineral Terminal
8) Oil Terminals (From W. to E. are:
    IE Fuel, Irish Tar, Texaco, Esso & Shell)
9) Turntable
10) Ferryport Terminal
11) Goods & Wagon Repairs
12) O'Connell
13) Chancery

Sandyford

Depot

1   m.   (1:90,000)   2

0   1   2   4 km.

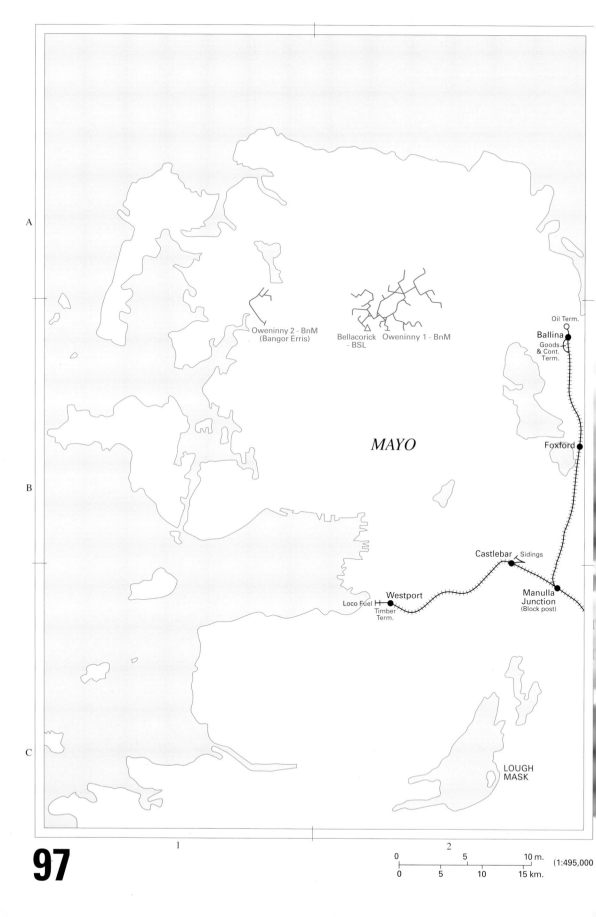

A

Oil Term.

Ballina

Goods
& Cont.
Term.

Oweninny 2 - BnM
(Bangor Erris)

Bellacorick   Oweninny 1 - BnM
- BSL

MAYO

Foxford

B

Castlebar   Sidings

Manulla
Junction
(Block post)

Westport

Loco Fuel

Timber
Term.

C

LOUGH
MASK

97

1   2

0   5   10 m.

(1:495,000

0   5   10   15 km.

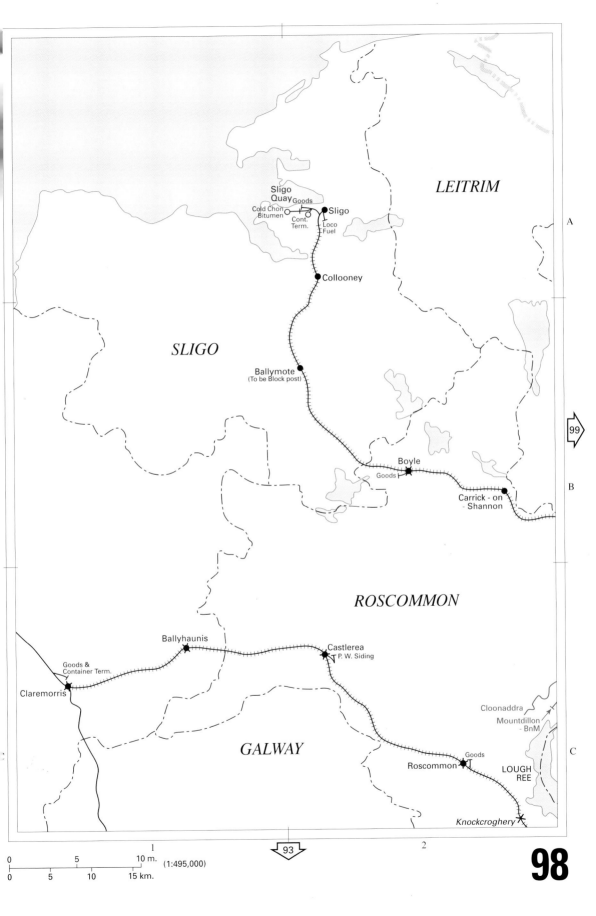

LEITRIM

Sligo
Quay
Goods
Cold Chon
Bitumen
Cont.
Term.
Sligo
Loco
Fuel

Colooney

SLIGO

Ballymote
(To be Block post)

Boyle
Goods

Carrick - on
- Shannon

99

A

B

ROSCOMMON

Ballyhaunis
Castlerea
P. W. Siding

Goods &
Container Term.

Claremorris

Cloonaddra
Mountdillon
- BnM

GALWAY

Roscommon
Goods

LOUGH
REE

C

Knockcroghery

0   5   10 m.
|———|———|———| 1
0   5   10   15 km.
(1:495,000)

93

2

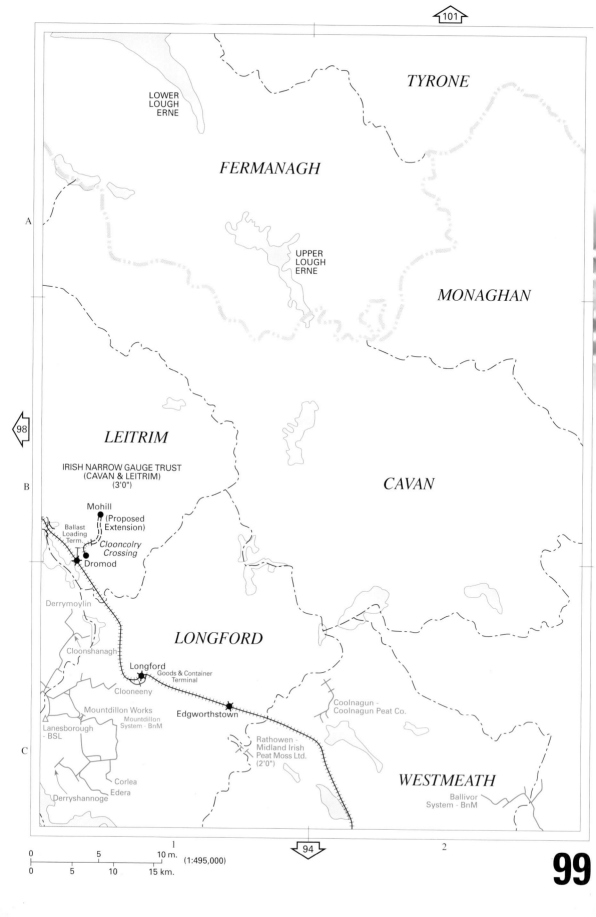

Portadown

PORTADOWN

Sidings

ARMAGH

Scarva

P. W. Siding   Poyntzpass

DOWN

*DOWNPATRICK &
ARDGLASS RAILWAY
(5'3")*

Inch Abbey
Downpatrick
Ballydugan
King Magnus's
Halt

Newry

TRANSLINK
(5'3")

IARNROD
EIREANN
(5'3")

MONAGHAN

Ardee Road
Goods &
Container
Terminal   Dundalk

Kingscourt
(Gypsum
Loading)

LOUTH

Dunleer*

*Boyne
Bridge*

Wagon Repair Depot
π DMU Depot (proposed)
Goods
Platin Cement
Works   Drogheda
Gypsum
Oil   Laytown

Cement

Mosney

Tara Mines   Tara
(Lead &   Mines
Zinc Ores)   Jn.   P. W.
Sidings   Gormanston
Navan*

MEATH   Balbriggan

Skerries

DUBLIN

0 ———— 5 ———— 10 m.
0 ——— 5 ——— 10 ——— 15 km.   (1:495,000)

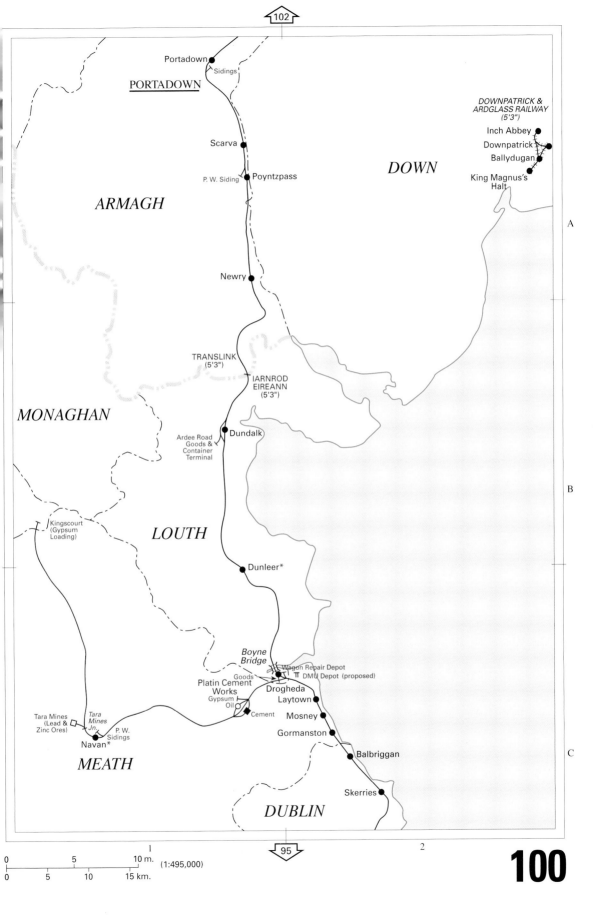

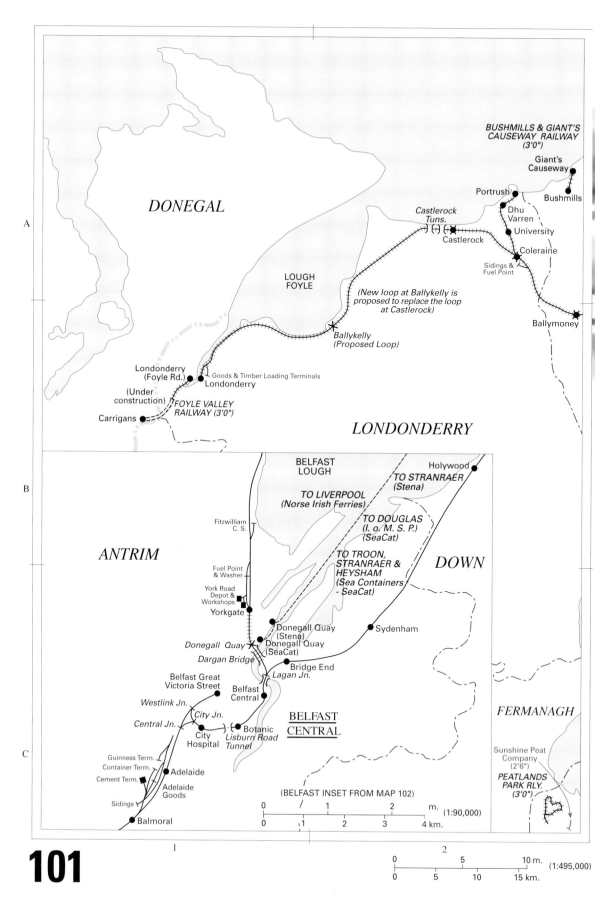

DONEGAL

LOUGH
FOYLE

BUSHMILLS & GIANT'S
CAUSEWAY RAILWAY
(3'0")

Giant's
Causeway

Portrush
Dhu
Varren
University
Coleraine
Bushmills

Castlerock
Tuns.

Castlerock

Sidings &
Fuel Point

(New loop at Ballykelly is
proposed to replace the loop
at Castlerock)

Ballymoney

Ballykelly
(Proposed Loop)

Londonderry
(Foyle Rd.)
Goods & Timber Loading Terminals
Londonderry

(Under
construction)
FOYLE VALLEY
RAILWAY (3'0")

Carrigans

LONDONDERRY

BELFAST
LOUGH
Holywood

TO STRANRAER
(Stena)

TO LIVERPOOL
(Norse Irish Ferries)

ANTRIM

Fitzwilliam
C.S.

Fuel Point
& Washer

York Road
Depot &
Workshops
Yorkgate

Donegall Quay

Dargan Bridge

Belfast Great
Victoria Street
Westlink Jn.
Central Jn.
City Jn.
City
Hospital
Botanic
Lisburn Road
Tunnel

Guinness Term.
Container Term.
Cement Term.
Sidings
Balmoral
Adelaide
Adelaide
Goods

TO DOUGLAS
(I. o. M. S. P.)
(SeaCat)

TO TROON,
STRANRAER &
HEYSHAM
(Sea Containers
- SeaCat)

DOWN

Donegall Quay
(Stena)
Donegall Quay
(SeaCat)

Sydenham

Bridge End
Lagan Jn.

Belfast
Central

BELFAST
CENTRAL

FERMANAGH

Sunshine Peat
Company
(2'6")

PEATLANDS
PARK RLY.
(3'0")

(BELFAST INSET FROM MAP 102)

0   /   1   2   m.   (1:90,000)
0   1   2   3   4 km.

B

C

A

1

2

101

0   5   10 m.
0   5   10   15 km.   (1:495,000)

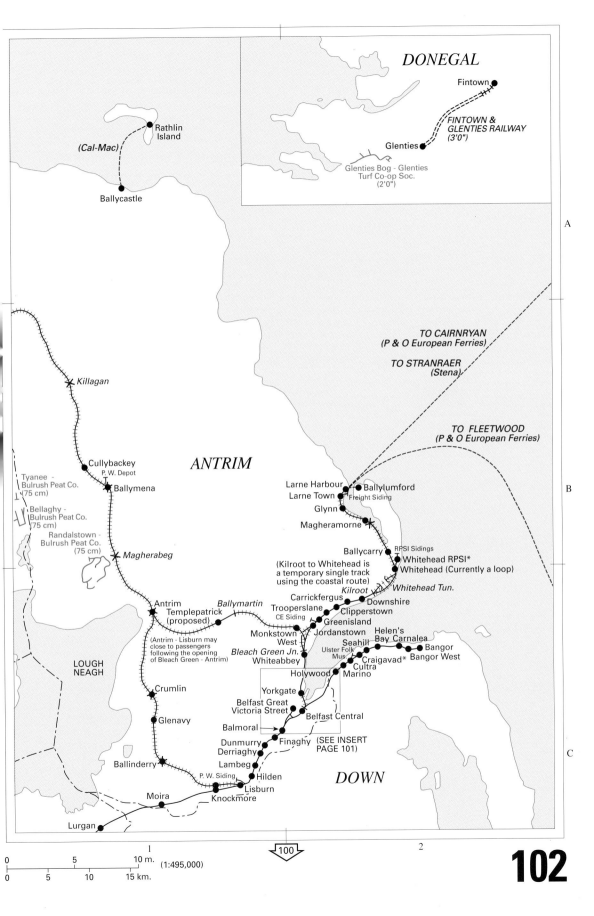

DONEGAL

Fintown

FINTOWN &
GLENTIES RAILWAY
(3'0")

Glenties

Glenties Bog - Glenties
Turf Co-op Soc.
(2'0")

Rathlin
Island

(Cal-Mac)

Ballycastle

A

TO CAIRNRYAN
(P & O European Ferries)

TO STRANRAER
(Stena)

TO FLEETWOOD
(P & O European Ferries)

Killagan

ANTRIM

Cullybackey
P. W. Depot

Ballymena

Larne Harbour   Ballylumford
Larne Town   Freight Siding
Glynn

Magheramorne

B

Tyanee -
Bulrush Peat Co.
(75 cm)

Bellaghy -
Bulrush Peat Co.
(75 cm)

Randalstown -
Bulrush Peat Co.
(75 cm)

Magherabeg

Ballycarry   RPSI Sidings
Whitehead RPSI*
Whitehead (Currently a loop)

(Kilroot to Whitehead is
a temporary single track
using the coastal route)

Kilroot   *Whitehead Tun.*

Antrim
Templepatrick
(proposed)

Ballymartin

Trooperslane   Carrickfergus   Downshire
CE Siding   Clipperstown
Greenisland

Monkstown   Jordanstown   Helen's
West   Bay Carnalea

Seahill   Bangor
Ulster Folk   Bangor West
Mus.   Craigavad*

Bleach Green Jn.
Whiteabbey   Cultra
Holywood   Marino

(Antrim - Lisburn may
close to passengers
following the opening
of Bleach Green - Antrim)

LOUGH
NEAGH

Crumlin

Yorkgate

Belfast Great
Victoria Street

Glenavy

Balmoral   Belfast Central

Dunmurry   Finaghy   (SEE INSERT
Derriaghy   PAGE 101)

DOWN

Ballinderry   Lambeg

P. W. Siding   Hilden

Moira   Lisburn

Knockmore

Lurgan

1   10 m.   (1:495,000)

0   5 |
0   5   10   15 km.

100   2

102

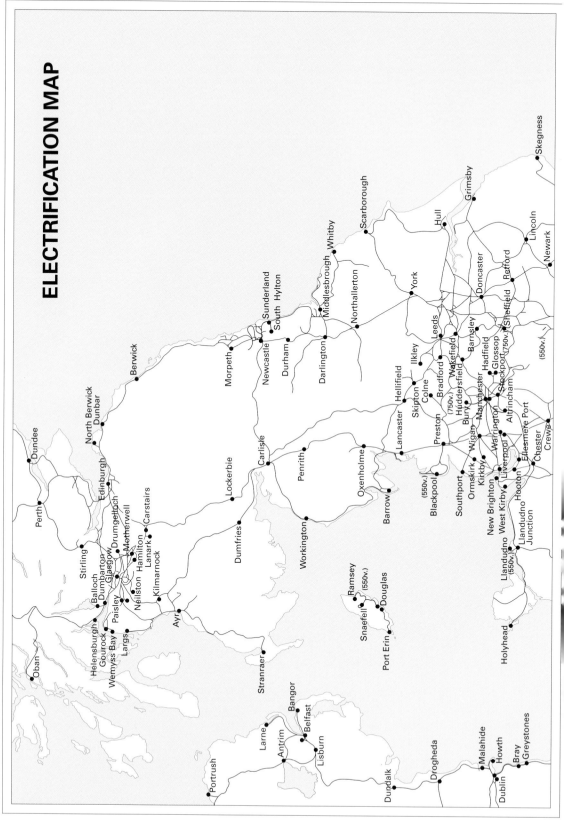

ELECTRIFICATION MAP

103

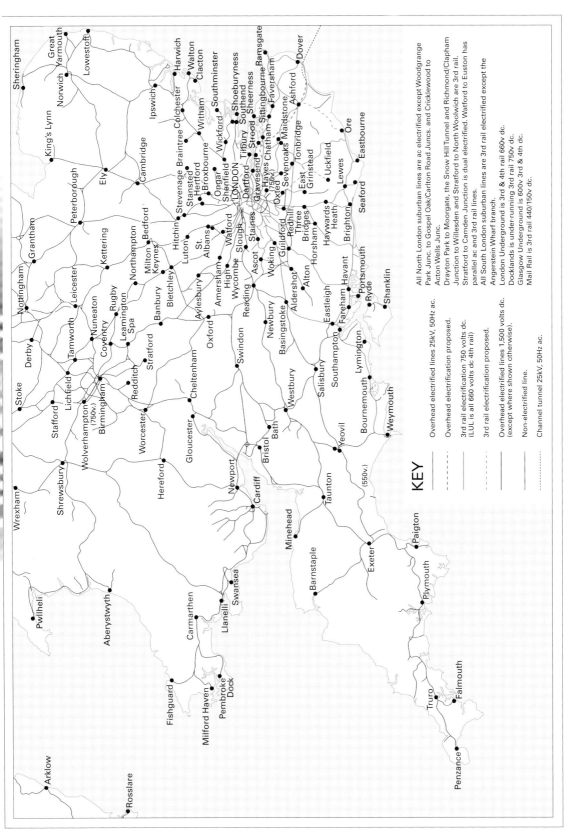

KEY

——— Overhead electrified lines 25kV, 50Hz. ac.

‒ ‒ ‒ Overhead electrification proposed.

——— 3rd rail electrification 750 volts dc.
(LUL is all 660 volts dc 4th rail)

- - - - 3rd rail electrification proposed.

——— Overhead electrified lines 1,500 volts dc.
(except where shown otherwise).

——— Non-electrified line.

········· Channel tunnel 25kV, 50Hz. ac.

All North London suburban lines are ac electrified except Woodgrange
Park Junc. to Gospel Oak/Carlton Road Juncs, and Cricklewood to
Acton Wells Junc.

Drayton Park to Moorgate, the Snow Hill Tunnel and Richmond/Clapham
Junction to Willesden and Stratford to North Woolwich are 3rd rail.
Stratford to Camden Junction is dual electrified. Watford to Euston has
parallel ac and 3rd rail lines.

All South London suburban lines are 3rd rail electrified except the
Angerstein Wharf branch.

London Underground is 3rd & 4th rail 660v dc.
Docklands is under-running 3rd rail 750v dc.
Glasgow Underground is 600v 3rd & 4th dc.
Mail Rail is 3rd rail 440/150v dc.

104

INDEX

All passenger stations are included in this index. Freight terminals, junction names, tunnels and other significant locations are indexed where their names or map references differ from a passenger station.

* denotes an unadvertised or excursion station. (eg Curragh*)

106

119

INDEX TO LOCOMOTIVE STABLING POINTS, CARRIAGE DEPOTS AND RAILWAY WORKS